ON TO GLORY!

CARDIFF CITY FOOTBALL CLUB
2012-2013

MARK DENHAM
Foreword by Barrie McAuliffe

First Edition Published 2013

Cardiff City Football Club
Cardiff City Stadium
Leckwith Road
Cardiff
CF11 8AZ
www.cardiffcityfc.co.uk
club@cardiffcityfc.co.uk

Written & Compiled by Mark Denham (@MarkDen_CCFC)
Cover and design by Neil Williams and Barrie McAuliffe

ISBN: 978-0-9576819-0-3

Printed in Wales by
Provincial Printing & Publishing Co. Ltd.
Sanatorium Road, Cardiff CF11 8DG

CONTENTS

CARDIFF CITY FOOTBALL CLUB

Cardiff City Stadium, Leckwith Road, Cardiff CF11 8AW
Telephone: 0845 365 1115
E-Mail: club@cardiffcityfc.co.uk
Website: www.cardiffcityfc.co.uk

Acting Chairman/Chief Executive: Simon Lim

Non-Executive Directors: Steve Borley, Derek Chee Seng Chin, Mehmet Dalman, Michael Isaac, Len Win Kong, Meng Kwong Lim, Danni Rais, Datuk Vincent Lye Ek Seang

Club Management: Jamie DeCruz, Steve Ellis, Tom Gorringe, Nic Heslop, Helen Jackson, Julian Jenkins, Barrie McAuliffe, Wayne Nash, Katyann Owens, Mona Sabbuba, Richard Thompson, Scott Young

Club Secretary: Nick Alford

Team Manager: Malky Mackay

Assistant Manager: David Kerslake

Academy Manager: Dick Bate

Senior Coaches: Joe McBride, James Hollman, Kevin Cooper

Head of Performance: Richard Collinge MCSP SRP

Club Doctor: Dr Len Nokes

Head of Recruitment: Iain Moody

CLUB HONOURS

FA CUP WINNERS 1927

FA CUP FINALISTS 1925, 2008

LEAGUE CUP FINALISTS 2012

FA CUP SEMI FINALISTS 1921

FA CHARITY SHIELD WINNERS 1927

DIVISION 1 RUNNERS UP 1924

CHAMPIONSHIP WINNERS 2013

DIVISION 2 RUNNERS UP 1921, 1952, 1960

CHAMPIONSHIP PLAY-OFF RUNNERS-UP 2010

DIVISION 3 (S) CHAMPIONS 1947

DIVISION 3 CHAMPIONS 1993

DIVISION 3 RUNNERS UP 1976, 1983, 2001

DIVISION 3 THIRD PLACE 1999

DIVISION 4 RUNNERS UP 1988

DIVISION 2 PLAY-OFF WINNERS 2003

WELSH CUP WINNERS
1912, 1920, 1922, 1923, 1927, 1928, 1930, 1956, 1959,1964, 1965, 1967, 1968, 1969, 1970, 1971, 1973, 1974,1976, 1988, 1992, 1993

ALGARVE CHALLENGE CUP WINNERS 2008

EUROPEAN CUP-WINNERS CUP SEMI-FINALISTS 1968

FAW PREMIER CUP WINNERS 2002

FOOTBALL LEAGUE CUP SEMI-FINALISTS 1965/66

F.A. YOUTH CUP FINALISTS 1970/71

FOREWORD

Barrie McAuliffe

Since joining the club full time in 2004, one of my goals has been to continually improve Cardiff City's written media and photographic output, enhancing the match-day experience in some part via the official programme. For want of a better expression, it became my baby... though at times, certainly in the first few years, working on my own into the early hours behind the Canton Stand at Ninian Park, it felt like I'd created a monster.

As the years have progressed I'm proud to say that we have pushed the boundaries and developed innovative ideas, for example adding personality to the writing or being among the first to champion interactive supporter led content within our pages. It's now made much easier through social media of course. Everyone, or at least a large majority of us it seems are 'plugged in' and continually connected these days, so why not take advantage and share the spotlight?

Design has also been a big factor in what we do here. I'll be honest, before taking on the 'gig' I didn't really enjoy football programmes, especially the design. They all felt very samey, safe and one dimensional, so from the humble beginnings to where we are today, we've pushed forward, trying to adopt the styling of high end publications rather than that of the standard stock many of our contemporaries embrace.

What we do here is not always taken as well as we'd like, certainly from those judging awards, but the feedback from City supporters has always been extremely well received, appreciated and is at the core of what we do, year on year.

Most importantly, the main reason behind our print and web based development has been the list of talented contributors I've had the pleasure, at least most of the time, to work with. The mainstay, here long before my time has been club historian and stats Jedi Richard Shepherd, while my closest collaborator and writing partner for a good while now has been Mark Denham, the name on the front of this book. Mark has professionally developed from remote contributor, part time staffer to full time media editor here, next season fully taking the mantle by dropping the 'sub' from his editor title, continuing the sterling work of writing and compiling Cardiff City content, while coordinating contributors. On that note, all of my contributors, from the early days to last season have been hugely appreciated, a good number going on to full time careers in sports media.

Again, adding design magic next season, continuing from his first eighteen months, will be tea drinking aficionado and Photoshop God Neil Williams, who without blowing my own trumpet was the first person I interviewed who could put me firmly in my place when trying to make pages look the part. Photography is also an integral part of how the pages look, so on that note, we wouldn't be where we are without the help of club snapper Pete Thomas, along with the relationships we enjoy with our photo agency partners.

The final note has to go to the squad, in particular the lads who gave us our long craved top flight promotion after going so close in recent years. I've had my fair share of dealing with difficult players during my time, but the last two years, led by the example of the ever approachable and professional Malky Mackay, putting content together for your pleasure has been as enjoyable as I can remember. Each of the players have been excellent to work with, putting up with our continual harassment, of which we are grateful.

Thanks again to all who contributed to our pages and well done to Mark on a top class book. It's certainly going to take pride of place on the McAuliffe bookshelf. And now, on to the Premier League... it sounds good, doesn't it?

by MARK DENHAM

There were two thoughts behind the production of this book. Primarily there was the Club's desire to commemorate a season that will no doubt be remembered as one that defined a generation. Secondly, we wanted to replicate and compile the game by game analysis printed over the course of the season in the Club's official match-day programme, CF11.

In the summer of 2012, having undertaken a comprehensive fan survey, Head of Communications Barrie McAuliffe, Designer Neil Williams, Club Historian Richard Shepherd and I discussed what we believed supporters wanted from their programme for the season ahead. In the build up to each of our twenty-three home games we worked towards the finished product; but we couldn't have met the high standards we'd set for CF11 was it not for the assistance of a dedicated team of contributors and support staff. As such, I wanted to use this page as a way of tipping my hat to those people.

LAYOUTS & PRODUCTION

Since December 1958, Cardiff-based printers **Provincial Printing & Publishing** have worked with Cardiff City Football Club. **Ian Fitzgerald, Isabel Butcher** and their staff have been responsible for the prompt, quality production and delivery of the programme since (and before) I joined the Club in 2008. Their patience and understanding, whilst helping us mould our product, has been invaluable. Again, we thank them for the production of this book.

FEATURE CONTRIBUTORS

Contributor, part-time commentator, media assistant, film critic, food expert, fashion guru and fine beard owner **Ashley James** has written for the Club programme and website since 2007. A popular and ever-enthusiastic chap, Ash's knowledge of the game is immense and his enthusiasm infectious. My pal – and one of the unsung heroes.

Sam Roberts, Liam Jones, Will Pallot, Tom Phillips and **Oliver Roderick** began the 2012/13 season as our new contributing core. I'm sure each of them will agree that they sent their email applications to me at the opportune time! Decent first season, eh lads?!

Sam's primary focus over the course of the campaign was on our Academy and Development content. To say we've been impressed by his passion and commitment would be a huge understatement and I'm sure I speak on behalf of our age-level teams and coaches when I say he's been a priceless asset. Young players are enthused and encouraged when they see their pictures in programmes and on websites and they have Sam to thank for the level of coverage we've been able to deliver.

Each edition of CF11 featured an eight page opposition section, primarily taken care of by Liam and Oliver. Will and Tom's focus over the course of the campaign was on divisional analysis and match reporting (much of which has been used in the central section of this book), allowing us to provide the best possible coverage for City supporters and visiting fans alike. Again, the application of these four lads has been first-class, as has their assistance on match-days. I couldn't have asked for more from them.

(L-R): Neil Williams, Barrie McAuliffe, Richard Shepherd and Mark Denham.

Amy McNiven and **Michael Lamont** completed our team of regular contributors in 2012/13. Amy's cross-platform contribution that sees her present Cardiff City Player's weekly magazine show in addition to her editorial work has been extremely well received, while her knowledge of the British game and that of football on the continent is vast. Michael meanwhile paid us a visit from Ayr, Scotland just after Christmas and made such a strong impression that we were thrilled to incorporate him into our team.

PHOTOGRAPHY

Senior Club Photographer **Peter Thomas** is the man responsible for visually documenting everything we do. A passionate City supporter who works tirelessly for the Club, Pete is responsible for the majority of photographs used in this book, on the Club website and in the pages of CF11. Another City supporter and talented snapper working with Pete on match-days is **Mike Griffiths,** while we've been extremely grateful to **Paul Keevil** for his contribution, especially on the road. Special thanks also go to **Huw Evans Agency, PA Sport** and **Andrew Orchard** for their online resources.

I sincerely hope you enjoy this book and that it finds a comfortable slot on your bookshelves from which to spend the coming years. 2012/13 was a terrific season for us all and perhaps this publication can serve as something of a keepsake. As I've tried to convey, huge credit must go to our contributors and staff that made the production of CF11 and **On To Glory!** possible.

On a personal note, this has been a privilege to write and compile. Finally I'd like to congratulate Malky and his squad on their magnificent achievement and thank them for helping us, as a City, realise our dream.

9

INTRODUCING...
THE CHAMPIONSHIP WINNING MANAGER
AND HIS STAFF

MANAGER: MALKY MACKAY

Born in Bellshill, Scotland, **Malky Mackay** was appointed Cardiff City Manager on 17th June 2011. A Scottish international who played for Queen's Park, Celtic, Norwich City, West Ham United and then Watford, Malky began his managerial career with the Hornets (having initially been first team coach) in 2009. During his first season at Cardiff City Stadium he guided the Club to the Championship Play-Offs and League Cup Final, before achieving the ultimate success of automatic promotion in 2012/13.

FIRST TEAM COACHES

Malky's senior coaching staff joined him at Cardiff City Stadium during the summer of 2011 and brought with them a wealth of top level experience. Assistant Manager **David Kerslake** (formerly of Tottenham Hotspur and Leeds United) and **Joe McBride** (of Everton) followed Malky from similar positions at Watford, while Goalkeeping Coach **James Hollman** linked up having previously held the same post with Ipswich Town under Roy Keane and Norwich City with Nigel Worthington.

ACADEMY & DEVELOPMENT

The vastly experienced and respected **Dick Bate** left his role as Elite Coaching Director of the English Football Association to become Cardiff City's Academy Manager in October 2012. Previous roles saw Dick manage England's U17, 18, 19 and 20 squads. **Kevin Cooper** oversaw our Development Squad's achievements in 2012/13. Kevin, a Cardiff City first team regular between 2005-08, helped establish a crucial link between our youngsters and the first team. Both men are assisted by a dedicated support team of Academy coaches and administration staff.

KIT MANAGEMENT

Kit Manager **Ian Lanning** joined the Club back in 2001, working for three previous Cardiff City managers prior to Malky. Assisted in his role by **Vinny**

Leach, Ian is supported around the clock on a daily basis by the Club's laundry department at Cardiff City Stadium, the Vale Pavilion and on match days.

MEDICAL

Richard Collinge MCSP SRP as Head of Performance is the man that oversees the Medical, Physiotherapy and Sport Science departments at Cardiff City. He works on a daily basis with senior physiotherapists **Sean Connelly MCSP SRP** and **Adam Rattenberry MCSP SRP,** who as a trio are in regular close consultation with Club Doctor **Len Nokes. Nilton Terroso** is our resident Sport Scientist, supported by a diligent team of interns including **Alun Andrews, Mike Beere, James Evans, Daryl Parry** and **Callum Walsh.**

RECRUITMENT

Head of Recruitment **Iain Moody** plays an essential role in locating and recruiting the best players for the Football Club, working closely on a day to day basis with Club Secretary, **Nick Alford.** Chief Scout **Mark Stow** heads up the Club's scouting network and helps provide a priceless link between the Academy, Development and Senior set-ups. A team of dedicated analysts are also attached to this department, comprising of former top flight goalkeeper **Martin Hodge, Enda Barron** and **Graham Younger.**

SPECIAL MENTIONS

Osteopath **Garry Trainer,** running coach **Darren Campbell MBE,** soft-tissue specialist **Paul Harris** and yoga expert **Ray Hassan** offer their therapies and skills by way of complementing the more traditional approaches towards player care and rehabilitation. These four individuals are on hand as needed by our Medical and Sport Science departments and provide helpful support and insight. **Victoria McCracken** is a valued member of the team in her administrative role at the Vale Pavilion, while the lads wouldn't get too far without the fuel that food provides, given to them by caterers **Julie Moore** and **Julia Williams.**

(L-R) Back Row: Nilton Terroso, Callum Walsh, Dick Bate, Vinny Leach, Iain Moody, Graham Younger, Enda Barron, Ian Lanning.

(L-R) Front Row: Kevin Cooper, Adam Rottenberry, Richard Collinge, David Kerslake, Malky Mackay, Joe McBride, James Hollman, Len Nokes, Sean Connelly.

INTRODUCING...

First team squad members that took Cardiff City to the Championship title

25 Malaysia LEON BARNETT

Born: Stevenage, 30/11/85
'12/13 Stats: Games 8, Goals 0
On loan from Norwich City during March and April, centre-half Leon instantly became a popular dressing room figure and significant presence at the back in the absence of Mark Hudson. City conceded in only three of the eight games Leon figured in.

39 Malaysia CRAIG BELLAMY

Born: Cardiff, 31/07/79
'12/13 Stats: Games 33, Goals 5
Back with his hometown club for 2012/13 from Liverpool after a loan spell from Manchester City in 2010/11, the Wales International and Great Britain Olympic forward or winger was a major factor in the team's emphatic success.

27 Malaysia FRAIZER CAMPBELL

Born: Huddersfield, 13/09/87
'12/13 Stats: Games 12, Goals 7
England International forward Fraizer signed from Sunderland in mid-January, scoring on his City debut as substitute in the 1-0 win at Leeds on February 2nd. He soon made the starting line-up and scored seven crucial goals in the run-in.

12 Malaysia MATTHEW CONNOLLY

Born: Barnet, 24/09/87
'12/13 Stats: Games 36, Goals 5
Signed from Queen's Park Rangers on August 21st 2012, former Arsenal defender Matthew proved a vital member of the side, playing either in central defence or at right-back. He also proved useful in front of goal, scoring five times.

11 Malaysia CRAIG CONWAY

Born: Irvine, 02/05/85
'12/13 Stats: Games 27, Goals 2
Scottish international Craig became Malky Mackay's first signing when he joined City from Dundee United in June 2011. Injury curbed early season progress, though Craig was immense from December to May.

8 Malaysia DON COWIE

Born: Inverness, 15/02/83
'12/13 Stats: Games 25, Goals 2
Don followed Malky Mackay from Watford at the start of July 2011. The versatile midfielder played a crucial part in the majority of City's fixtures, offering a calm and stabilising presence in the centre of the park.

25 *Malaysia* **KERIM FREI**

Born: **Feldkirch, 19/11/93**
'12/13 Stats: **Games 3, Goals 0**

On loan from Fulham during October and November, Kerim contributed to our home win over Burnley and featured at Bolton and Charlton. His anticipated impact in the Premier League could be matched at international level for Turkey in the coming years.

15 *Malaysia* **RUDY GESTEDE**

Born: **Essey-lès-Nancy, 10/10/88**
'12/13 Stats: **Games 27, Goals 5**

Signed in July 2011 after having been at FC Metz, the powerful striker contributed five goals during 2012/13. His brace against Nottingham Forest in April helped all but secure the Championship title.

17 *Malaysia* **ARON GUNNARSSON**

Born: **Akureyri, 22/04/89**
'12/13 Stats: **Games 45, Goals 8**

Gunnarsson's contribution during the season was invaluable. Captain of Iceland and a born leader on the pitch for City, the central midfielder scored eight times as he established himself as a genuine 'Player of the Season' contender.

22 *Malaysia* **HEIDAR HELGUSON**

Born: **Dalvik, 22/08/77**
'12/13 Stats: **Games 38, Goals 8**

Heidar signed from QPR in early August 2012 and proved a precious addition to the promotion winning squad. His physical presence saw him not only score eight goals himself, but provide six assists. Endearing and influential.

5 *Malaysia* **MARK HUDSON**

Born: **Guildford, 30/03/82**
'12/13 Stats: **Games 33, Goals 4**

Awarded the Supporters Trust's 'Player of the Season' trophy, skipper Mark was one of the outstanding figures in our title-winning side. Injury curtailed his season in March, though his presence and influence remained unwavering.

4 *Malaysia* **FILIP KISS**

Born: **Dunajská Streda, 13/10/90**
'12/13 Stats: **Games 2, Goals 0**

The Slovakian Under-21 International captain came from Slovan Bratislava on a season-long loan in July 2011 and was signed on a full contract at the end of that season. He made two Championship appearances during '12/13.

13 *Malaysia* **KIM BO-KYUNG**

Born: Gurye County, 06/10/89
'12/13 Stats: Games 28, Goals 2

The South Korean International and Olympic representative signed from Japanese club Cerezo Osaka in July 2012. As his confidence grew, Kim went on to wow supporters with his undoubted Premier League talent.

24 *Malaysia* **SIMON LAPPIN**

Born: Glasgow, 25/01/83
'12/13 Stats: Games 2, Goals 0

Full-back Simon joined City on loan from Norwich City on November 21st and made two appearances in the Championship during that spell. He returned to Cardiff City on a permanent contract in late January.

32 **JOE LEWIS**

Born: Bury St. Edmunds, 06/10/87
'12/13 Stats: Games 0, Goals 0

The likeable Joe provided bench cover for David Marshall in all forty-six of City's Championship fixtures. A very able goalkeeper who proved a vital member of the first team squad.

1 **DAVID MARSHALL**

Born: Glasgow, 05/03/85
'12/13 Stats: Games 46, Goals 0

Colossal from start to finish. Marshy played every minute of City's title-winning campaign and broke back into the Scottish international starting eleven in March. Kept a phenomenal eighteen clean sheets.

20 *Malaysia* **JOE MASON**

Born: Plymouth, 13/05/91
'12/13 Stats: Games 28, Goals 6

The former Plymouth forward signed in July 2011 and had a very promising first season, that included a goal against Liverpool in the Carling Cup Final. Scored six goals during '12/13 and is expected to shine again at the higher level.

23 *Malaysia* **NICKY MAYNARD**

Born: Winsford, 11/12/86
'12/13 Stats: Games 4, Goals 1

Nicky's 2012/13 had seemingly been brought to a halt by an ACL rupture in October's game at Millwall. However, returning as a substitute against Hull on final day, the striker tucked home an injury time penalty to the delight of his team-mates.

2 | Malaysia | **KEVIN McNAUGHTON**

Born: Dundee, 28/08/82
'12/13 Stats: Games 27, Goals 0
Already established as a Club legend, Kevin marked the completion of his seventh season at Cardiff City with promotion to the top flight. His pitch celebration images post Charlton will remain iconic.

37 | Malaysia | **STEPHEN McPHAIL**

Born: Westminster, 09/12/79
'12/13 Stats: Games 0, Goals 0
Macca may not have made a League appearance during '12/13 but his influence and experience remained as crucial to the squad's success as ever. Like team-mate McNaughton, McPhail's seen it all at Cardiff City.

18 | Malaysia | **JORDON MUTCH**

Born: Alvaston, 02/12/91
'12/13 Stats: Games 22, Goals 0
Having begun the season as a first team regular, injury curtailed the autumn and winter months for the highly rated Jordon. A return at the start of April brought out some terrific displays from the heart of midfield.

16 | Malaysia | **CRAIG NOONE**

Born: Kirkby, 17/11/87
'12/13 Stats: Games 32, Goals 7
A late August 2012 signing from Brighton, Craig firmly established himself as a fan-favourite at City with some scintillating wing-play. Contributed seven goals and eight assists.

31 | Malaysia | **BEN NUGENT**

Born: Welwyn Garden City, 28/11/93
'12/13 Stats: Games 12, Goals 1
Signed as a professional in the summer of 2012, Hertfordshire-born defender Ben made twelve first team appearances, scored against Barnsley and picked up the Trust's Young Player of the Year award. The season's break-through star.

21 | Malaysia | **JOE RALLS**

Born: Aldershot, 13/10/93
'12/13 Stats: Games 4, Goals 0
Having burst on to the first team scene during 2011/12, Academy Graduate Joe continued to mature and develop during 2012/13. He made four first team appearances in the promotion campaign, demonstrating positional versatility.

14 *Malaysia* ## TOMMY SMITH

Born: **Hemel Hempstead, 22/05/80**
'12/13 Stats: **Games 24, Goals 1**
One of the hardest working players in the side, injury put Tommy out of action in mid-October 2012 which kept him on the sidelines until the New Year. Returned with a fantastic strike at Blackpool and proved an assuring, mature presence.

3 *Malaysia* ## ANDREW TAYLOR

Born: **Hartlepool, 01/08/86**
'12/13 Stats: **Games 43, Goals 0**
Made more outfield appearances during 2012/13 than any other player and an undoubted candidate for 'Player of the Season.' Captained City three times and led by example at left-back.

6 *Malaysia* ## BEN TURNER

Born: **Birmingham, 21/01/88**
'12/13 Stats: **Games 31, Goals 1**
2012/13 saw Ben establish himself further as one of the finest young centre-halves in the country. Comfortable with partners Hudson, Connolly or Nugent, Turner is set to flourish at the top level.

9 *Malaysia* ## ETIEN VELIKONJA

Born: **Sempeter pri Gorici, 26/12/88**
'12/13 Stats: **Games 3, Goals 0**
A likeable and ambitious young squad member, Eti top-scored for the Development Squad in 2012/13 with thirteen League goals. A Slovenian international with talent and a sweet strike.

7 *Malaysia* ## PETER WHITTINGHAM

Born: **Nuneaton, 08/09/84**
'12/13 Stats: **Games 40, Goals 8**
It was another influential year for former England U21 midfielder Whittingham, named in the P.F.A. Championship Team of the Season and scoring eight league goals. Whitts has been a Premier League player in waiting for some time.

SPECIAL MENTIONS:

(NO LONGER WITH CLUB)

Rob Earnshaw	0 apps
Dekel Keinan	0 goals

(DEVELOPMENT PLAYERS INVOLVED IN CUP COMPETITIONS)

Luke Coulson	1 app, 0 goals
Kadeem Harris	1 app, 0 goals
Nat Jarvis	2 apps, 1 goal
Declan John	2 apps, 0 goals
Adedeji Oshilaja	2 apps, 0 goals
Tommy O'Sullivan	2 apps, 0 goals
Theo Wharton	2 apps, 0 goals

Front Row: Fraizer Campbell, Tommy Smith, Nicky Maynard, Mark Hudson, Kevin McNaughton, Aron Gunnarsson, David Kerslake, Malky Mackay, Joe McBride, James Hollman, Peter Whittingham, Craig Bellamy, Craig Noone, Etien Velikonja, Craig Conway.

(L-R) Back Row: Simon Lappin, Joe Mason, Kim Bo-Kyung, Kadeem Harris, Rudy Gestede, Joe Ralls, Jordon Mutch, Don Cowie, Andrew Taylor, Joe Lewis, David Marshall, Filip Kiss, Ben Turner, Ben Nugent, Matt Connolly, Stephen McPhail.

CF ELEVEN

THE OFFICIAL CARDIFF CITY FC MATCH PROGRAMME

CARDIFF CITY

VERSUS

HUDDERSFIELD TOWN

FRI 17TH AUG 7:45PM

npower CHAMPIONSHIP   MATCH 01 £3

MATCH SPONSOR: CIRCLE IT

MATCH BALL SPONSOR: ARUP

Malaysia **PUMA** Player

01

LET'S GET IT

Good evening and welcome to Cardiff City Stadium for our opening game of the season.

I'll start tonight by extending a warm welcome to Simon Grayson, along with his staff and players from Huddersfield Town who have made the long trip down to Wales from Yorkshire this evening. No doubt they will come here with a sense of excitement after having won promotion in such a thrilling penalty shoot-out against Sheffield United back in May. Simon is an experienced Championship manager and has made some astute purchases so far this summer, so I expect a tough game, one in which we will have to be at our best to get the season off to a positive start.

On that subject, it has felt like a strange beginning to the new campaign, what with the Capital One Cup tie last Tuesday, coming before this first league fixture, then the international friendly on Wednesday. Because of that fixture clash and the fact that we start on a Friday night, I was left with little choice but to use an inexperienced line up for the tie at Northampton in the week.

Despite the best of possible starts with a debut goal from Heidar Helguson in the first five minutes, we found it tough going against a physically strong, direct team that I expect to feature amongst the leaders in League Two in this season. We had three teenagers in the back four and nine players aged 21 or under on the pitch, so we knew it was going to be a difficult tie. That said, I was still disappointed to go out of the Cup at the first hurdle, particularly when you consider how much fun we had in the same competition last season. I would hope the youngsters who played will have learned some valuable lessons on Tuesday and they will now go on to take that education and use it to spur their footballing development as their careers take shape.

On a more positive note, we produced a top class performance to beat Newcastle United 4-1 here last Saturday in the last friendly of our pre-season programme. I thought we looked like a very good side, particularly during the first half when we raced into a 3-0 lead. I feel sure there's a lot to come from this team and we're still hoping to add two or three more new faces if the right players are available at the right price for us.

Talk of new faces obviously brings us to our latest signing, Craig Bellamy. Thanks to the support from Tan Sri Vincent Tan and Dato' Chan Tien Ghee I was delighted to be able to capture a player of Craig's class and pedigree. I'd also like to take this chance to thank Brendan Rodgers and Ian Ayre at Liverpool, without whose co-operation and goodwill the transfer would never have been possible. I have known Craig since we were together at Norwich City – him as an opinionated teenager and myself a more established pro at Carrow Road! I can't wait to work with him again because I believe the passion he brings to the whole club will be as important as his undoubted technical qualities that will be obvious on the pitch. He's also a Cardiff boy, born and bred, so his homecoming brings the club and fans closer together – I know there's nothing more inspiring than seeing one of 'your own' producing the goods on the pitch for your team, so I'm sure the whole place will get a lift from his arrival.

I can't wait for the season to start, so please get behind the lads tonight. By sticking together, there's no limit to what we can achieve. Enjoy the game, enjoy the season ahead.

STARTED

"THERE'S A LOT TO COME FROM THIS TEAM"

NORTHAMPTON 2
Artell (37), Nicholls (48)

CARDIFF CITY 1
Helguson (Pen 4)

TUESDAY ▶ 14TH AUGUST ▶ 7.45PM | Full Attendance **2,819**

🏠 **2,431**
🚌 **388**

A youthful Cardiff City side bowed out in the first tound of the Capital One Cup after encountering a resolute Northampton inside a fierce Sixfields Stadium.

It took the Bluebirds less than five minutes to open the scoring. Heidar Helguson marked his debut by winning and converting an early penalty, the ice-man keeping his cool from the spot to beat young Northampton keeper Snedker. Stephen McPhail left the field with injury after twenty minutes, to be replaced by trainee Tommy O'Sullivan, before Northampton's new signing David Artell got a headed equaliser for the League Two side ten minutes before the end of the first half.

The second half started in controversy: Northampton took the lead through another header, this time by Alex Nicholls, but the goal was scored when Cardiff were down to ten men, Jordon Mutch having been refused permission to enter the field of play to replace Joe Mason for what appeared to be a problem with his footwear. It was a sickener for the young City side who had defended so well in the first half.

City were unable to get an equaliser, though the match will have provided vital experience for the many debutants, all of who produced fine contributions.

FANS SAY
"I thought we started off well with a penalty in the first four minutes. The back four held their shape well and I was especially chuffed to see how Mason and Helguson played together." – *Brad Baston*

MALKY
"We were without a lo of players for various reasons, but the players out there gave everything they had and I was very proud o the youngsters. Now our entire focus is on Huddersfield on Friday night."

LEWIS
"It was a busy night and a very direct game, with a lot of high balls put in to the area. I think I did alright, but I probably had to come for balls in the air more than I normally would. The tactic was effective fo them as they scored from two set plays."

BOOTHROYD
"I don't want to get too carried away, but I'm really excited about the players we've got and what we might be able to do this season. It's important we celebrate tonight but then focus on the next league game and not get too carried away."

THE BREAKDOWN

REFEREE: Mr D. Phillips

10 04

51% 49%

POSSESSION

0 3

SHOTS

7 ON

5 OFF

Post-match reaction from Malky Mackay, Joe Lewis and Aidy Boothroyd on Cardiff City **Player**

Northampton Town: Snedker, Johnson, Langmead (c), Artell, Widdowson, Hackett (Mukendi), Harding, Guttridge, Tozer, Platt (Akinfenwa), Nicholls.
Subs not used: Wilson, Robinson, Demontagnac, Charles, Heath.

Cardiff City:
Lewis, Oshilaja,
Keinan, Nugent, John,
Conway, McPhail (c)
(O'Sullivan), Ralls, Sainte-Luce,
Mason (Mutch), Helguson (Jarvis).
Subs not used: Parish (GK), Darko,
Hill, Wharton.

23

Blooding them. Craig Conway couldn't help steer a youthful City side to Cup satisfaction at Sixfields.

THE CHAMPIONSHIP

It's back! The 2012/13 npower Championship kicks off tonight with City and the Terriers squaring up against each other, though the twenty-two other teams have to wait until tomorrow afternoon to try and get their first points on the board. Thomas Phillips looks at the opening weekend and picks out a few key new boys to keep an eye over the coming season.

DING DING – ROUND ONE!

It's fair to say that some intriguing ties have been conjured up for this opening weekend of Championship football!

The three Premier League fallers have all been handed tricky opening weekend away ties, with **Wolverhampton Wanderers** arguably facing up to the trickiest. They take on **Leeds United** in tomorrow's lunchtime kick-off at Elland Road as one of the favourites to go up this season, though Leeds will have promotion ambitions themselves. Expectations are always high at Leeds – don't expect anything different this time around.

Blackburn Rovers look to start their recovery with a trip to **Ipswich Town.** The pressure will instantly be on Steve Kean's Rovers – especially following Club adviser Sebby Singh's public promise to sack the manager should he lose three games on the bounce. Ipswich will certainly be a tough first test, although few may regard them as genuine promotion candidates this term after a difficult few years. **Bolton Wanderers** meanwhile have been drawn a Lancashire derby to welcome them to the Championship. Owen Coyle will take his side to face former club **Burnley** at Turf Moor, Bolton having been in the top flight for the past eleven seasons.

The three other Championship new boys are newly promoted **Huddersfield Town, Charlton Athletic** and **Sheffield Wednesday.** League One

Champions Charlton have an away game against last year's Play-Off semi finalists Birmingham City to contend with tomorrow – undoubtedly a tough test despite Blues' off-field difficulties. The Addicks will be hoping to emulate Norwich and Southampton by sailing through the Championship to the top flight in just the one season – as will Dave Jones' Sheffield Wednesday whose campaign starts with a trip to perennial underachievers of recent years, **Derby County.**

Other promotion hopefuls face difficult looking away ties on this opening weekend of games. Defeated Play-Off finalists **Blackpool** open their season at **Millwall,** while **Brighton & Hove Albion** face fellow candidates **Hull City** at KC stadium and **Middlesbrough** travel to **Barnsley.** There are home ties for well fancied **Leicester City** and **Nottingham Forest** against **Peterborough United** and **Bristol City** respectively, as well as an all London affair at Selhurst Park with **Watford** visiting **Crystal Palace.**

26

INCOMING!

The summer transfer window is far from shut, but there has been plenty of activity already. There have been some notable exits from championship clubs, with the likes of Jay Rodriguez leaving Burnley, Nathaniel Clyne leaving Crystal Palace and Robert Snodgrass leaving Leeds for Premier League football.

But there have already been some standout Championship signings this summer too. Out of the three relegated teams, Blackburn Rovers have been the busiest with the chequebook. **Danny Murphy** *(pictured)* has years of top flight experience, while the acquisitions of **Leon Best** and Portuguese veteran **Nuno Gomes** will add intimidating striking presence to the Ewood ranks. Wolves have also strengthened with the signing of **Björn Sigurdarson**, though their success could well come down to whether they can hold on to the talented trio of Steven Fletcher, Matt Jarvis and Kevin Doyle.

Other well-established Premier League players have made the drop down to the highly competitive second flight too. Brighton have picked up former England international **Wayne Bridge** and goalkeeper **Tomasz Kuszczak,** while the signings of **Zak Whitbread, Márkó Futács** and **Jamie Vardy** seem astute by ambitious Leicester City. Following his release by Stoke City, **Jonathan Woodgate** could prove to be a valuable returning asset for Middlesbrough.

But there have been a couple of deals done this summer that have raised eyebrows rather than expectations. Barnsley's new signing **Mido** has arguably reached the twilight of his career, while new Leeds addition **El Hadji Diouf** certainly has a colourful past. Can Gaffers Hill and Warnock get the best out of them? Time will tell!

TOMORROW'S FIXTURES
(All games kick-off at 3pm unless otherwise stated)

Saturday 18th August
Barnsley v Middlesbrough
Birmingham City v Charlton Athletic
Burnley v Bolton Wanderers
Crystal Palace v Watford
Derby County v Sheffield Wednesday
Hull City v Brighton & Hove Albion
Ipswich Town v Blackburn Rovers
Leeds Utd v Wolves (12.45pm)
Leicester City v Peterborough United
Millwall v Blackpool
Nottingham Forest v Bristol City

2011/12 NPOWER CHAMPIONSHIP LEAGUE TABLE

Pos	Team	P	W	D	L	GD	Pts
1	Reading	46	27	8	11	28	89
2	Southampton	46	26	10	10	39	88
3	West Ham Utd	46	24	14	8	33	86
4	Birmingham	46	20	16	10	27	76
5	Blackpool	46	20	15	11	20	75
6	**Cardiff City**	**46**	**19**	**18**	**9**	**13**	**75**
7	Middlesbrough	46	18	16	12	1	70
8	Hull City	46	19	11	16	3	68
9	Leicester City	46	18	12	16	11	66
10	Brighton	46	17	15	14	0	66
11	Watford	46	16	16	14	-8	64
12	Derby County	46	18	10	18	-8	64
13	Burnley	46	17	11	18	3	62
14	Leeds United	46	17	10	19	-3	61
15	Ipswich Town	46	17	10	19	-8	61
16	Millwall	46	15	12	19	-2	57
17	Crystal Palace	46	13	17	16	-5	56
18	Peterborough	46	13	11	22	-10	50
19	Nottm Forest	46	14	8	24	-15	50
20	Bristol City	46	12	13	21	-24	49
21	Barnsley	46	13	9	24	-25	48
22	Portsmouth	46	13	11	22	-9	40
23	Coventry City	46	9	13	24	-24	40
24	Doncaster	46	8	12	26	-37	36

CF ELEVEN

THE OFFICIAL CARDIFF CITY FC MATCH PROGRAMME

CARDIFF CITY

● VERSUS ●

WOLVERHAMPTON WANDERERS

SUN 2ND SEP 2:00PM

npower CHAMPIONSHIP   MATCH 04 £3

ASSOCIATE MATCH SPONSOR
HEINEKEN UK LIMITED

Malaysia **PUMA** Player

02

MALKY MACKAY

NEW FACES

Good afternoon and welcome back to the CCS for today's match with Wolves.

I look forward to pitting my wits against a bright Norwegian manager who will no doubt bring some fresh thinking and approaches to Championship football, so I welcome Ståle Solbakken and all of his staff and players who have made the trip down from the Midlands today.

As you will have seen, we have been very busy over the last couple of weeks of the transfer window, so I'd like to start by thanking **Tan Sri Vincent Tan** and **Dato' Chan Tien Ghee** for their continued support for what we are building here.

Matthew Connolly is a player I have long admired who has built up an impressive career after starting out as a youngster at Arsenal. He earned his stripes in the less glamorous surroundings of a loan spell at Colchester United before developing into a high-quality defender during his spell with QPR. He brings a comfort on the ball and a versatility to our squad which make him a great asset for us.

As well as Matthew, **Tommy Smith** made the same trip from West London to Wales and he was another player I have pursued for some time. Obviously I know Tommy very well as both a player and a man since our time together at Watford and I believe you will struggle to find a better player than Tommy operating in the Championship this season.

Craig Noone is a different kind of attacking player to Tommy – an old fashioned winger if you like – and it has been well publicised that we have been trying to sign him for some time. Craig is exactly the kind of exciting young talent who is entering a phase of his

career which makes him ideal for Cardiff City. Already an accomplished Championship performer, I also believe there is a lot more development to come from him and I look forward to watching his progress in a City shirt over the next few seasons.

Our numbers have been further bolstered this week by the arrival of **Kim Bo-Kyung** who has joined the squad after having had to return to South Korea at the end of the Olympics. All of the administrative hurdles have now been cleared so Bo-Kyung has trained fully with us this week and is available for selection from now on. He has already impressed the coaching staff with what he has shown in training so we look forward to seeing him bring that ability to a wider audience on the pitch.

On the departure front, **Darcy Blake** decided to join Crystal Palace ten days ago and we wish Darcy all the best in his time in London. I think the timing of the move was right for all parties and it was a sound business decision, allowing us to pick up a decent fee for a player who had entered the last ten months of his contract.

Obviously these notes have been written just before the window closed so there may have been further developments that I am unable to comment on here. Needless to say, last week's game against Bristol City was a big disappointment. We had suffered a few injuries in the build-up to the match so had two debutants on the pitch but that is no excuse for an uncharacteristically below-par performance. Lessons have already been learnt from that match and I'm sure you'll see the benefits of that today. Enjoy the match.

"WE HAVE BEEN VERY BUSY OVER THE LAST COUPLE OF WEEKS"

CARDIFF CITY 1
Hudson (90+1)
HUDDERSFIELD TOWN 0

FRIDAY ▶ 17TH AUGUST ▶ 7.45PM | Full Attendance **21,127**

🏠 **20,573**
🚌 **554**

MALKY

"It was a performance full of character. We had to stay patient because Huddersfield worked to frustrate us, and we did that. Our fans were fantastic again; they see players out in Cardiff City shirts who care about this football club and I'm thrilled we got the win for them."

GRAYSON

"It was very cruel but I think the players can look back on their performances with a lot of pride. We are all disappointed at the moment, but if we perform like that for the rest of the season we will do well. We managed to frustrate them and counter attacked well."

HUDSON

"We're happy with the three points. They sat – tried to make it difficult, but that's the way it is. We tried a game plan and stuck to it. I'm just happy to be in the right position to get the goal, but Marshall was brilliant tonight to keep the clean sheet."

An even first half saw both sides create a handful of chances without managing to sustain a continued period of pressure on the opposition's goal. Midfielders Scott Arfield and the excellent Oliver Norwood came closest for the Terriers, while at the other end, Heidar Helguson smashed a powerful header against the bar from an in-swinging Bellamy corner.

The second half was a scrappier affair, but nevertheless, chances continued to fall to both sides. Novak and Scannell looked lively for the visitors, while Norwood and Arfield continued to try their luck from distance. The now established back five for Cardiff were solid throughout – particularly David Marshall, who pulled off several more good saves to keep the scores level. However, as a stalemate seemed inevitable, the announcement of five minutes of injury time clearly galvanised both the home team and fans. With time running out, Mark Hudson, who had remained up field following a late corner, fired home Joe Mason's knock down in the box to kick start the season with a bang.

FANS SAY

"This game was an eye opener showing that in this league, anyone can beat anyone. Cardiff showed great courage to snatch the three points though with a goal from our Captain!" – *Kieron Jenkins*

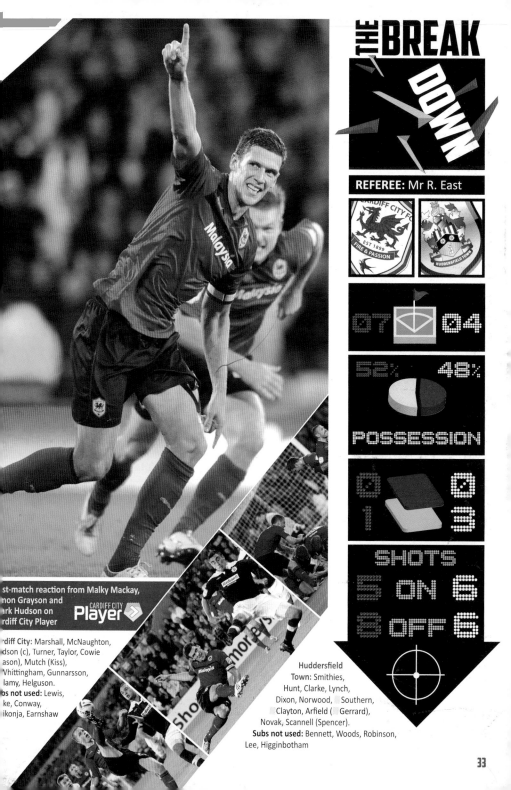

THE BREAKDOWN

REFEREE: Mr R. East

07 ⚑ 04

52% 48%

POSSESSION

0   0
1   3

SHOTS
5 ON 6
0 OFF 6

...st-match reaction from Malky Mackay,
...non Grayson and
...rk Hudson on
...rdiff City Player

CARDIFF CITY Player »

...diff City: Marshall, McNaughton,
...dson (c), Turner, Taylor, Cowie
...ason), Mutch (Kiss),
...Vhittingham, Gunnarsson,
...lamy, Helguson.
...bs not used: Lewis,
...ke, Conway,
...ikonja, Earnshaw

**Huddersfield
Town:** Smithies,
Hunt, Clarke, Lynch,
Dixon, Norwood, Southern,
Clayton, Arfield (Gerrard),
Novak, Scannell (Spencer).
Subs not used: Bennett, Woods, Robinson,
Lee, Higginbotham

33

Leaving it late. The Skipper finds the golden touch to see off Huddersfield on opening night.

BRIGHTON 0
CARDIFF CITY 0

TUESDAY ▶ 21ST AUGUST ▶ 7.45PM | Full Attendance 25,518 ▶

🏠 **24,693**
🚌 **825**

MALKY

"I was delighted with the discipline out there from my team, and with the way my squad played against a very good Brighton side. I thought our possession was fantastic – both teams ended with five shots on target, so it was a pretty even game."

POYET

"It was a game full of chances and great saves, but it's incredible that we needed to finish the game thinking that Tomasz had earned us a point. There were plenty of shots, plenty of chances and some very good saves, but we cannot score at the moment."

McNAUGHTON

"I thought we started the game very well, especially in the opening twenty minutes. Huds came close again for us as did Eti, while Marshy made another couple of excellent saves. If we can go to Bristol City on Saturday and win, we'll have had a good start."

It was clear from the offset that this was going to be a much more open game than City's previous encounter with Huddersfield. The two sides attacked freely, with high tempo, and a series of chances falling both ways on the night.

Mark Hudson came within inches of scoring as his goal-bound header was cleared off the line, while Kuszczak was on hand to keep out Whittingham's spectacular free kick later on. The best chance of the half fell to Heidar Helguson, though the Icelandic international couldn't break the deadlock from close range.

Ashley Barnes and Craig Noone, who had both caused problems for City in the first half, looked just as lively in the second. Former Valencia defender Bruno also saw his low drive kept out by Marshall, who was having another excellent game. But the Bluebirds could have won it late on, only for Kuszczak to deny substitute Etien Velikonja as the striker followed up a Joe Mason volley.

FANS SAY | "Four points out of six and clean sheets for the first two games – nobody can complain. Cardiff played much better against Brighton with some good passes and link ups" – *Rhys Lee*

REFEREE: Mr M. Halsey

BRIGHTON & HOVE ALBION

CARDIFF CITY
EST 1899
FIRE & PASSION

14 ⬛ 05

55 45

POSSESSION

0 0

0 1

SHOTS

9 ON 6

7 OFF 4

ee post-match reaction of this game from
Malky Mackay, and
Gus Poyet on
Cardiff City Player

CARDIFF CITY Player

Brighton & Hove Albion:
Kuszczak, El-Abd, Bruno,
Greer (c), Bridge, Noone
(Vicente), Bridcutt, Crofts,
Dicker (Harley), Mackail-
smith, Barnes (LuaLua).
Subs not used:
Ankergren, Dunk,
Calderon,
Agdestein.

Cardiff City:
Marshall,
McNaughton, Hudson
(c), Turner, Taylor, Cowie,
Gunnarsson, Whittingham,
Mutch (Mason), Helguson
(Velikonja), Bellamy (Conway).
Subs not used: Lewis, Blake, Kiss, Earnshaw.

37

Swapping shirts. Soon to be Bluebird Craig Noone faces City for one last time at the Amex.

BRISTOL CITY 4

Pearson (32), Woolford (45+1 & 70), Baldock (87)

CARDIFF CITY 2

Mason (57), Helguson (82)

SATURDAY ▶ 25TH AUGUST ▶ 1.00PM | Full Attendance **14,368**

🏠 **12,506**
🚌 **1,862**

MALKY

"Defensive mistakes cost us today. We gave away possession cheaply in dangerous areas, and too many of my usually dependable players were below par. It's not something that's been a regular occurrence with m team, but you can have days like that. When you do, you get punished."

McINNES

"We have a lot of different strikers, who pose threats in various ways. All the clubs I hav been at, who were successful, had good strength in depth when it came to strikers. It is very early days, but aft last season I'm delighte to be challenging at the right end of the table."

New signings Matthew Connolly and Tommy Smith made their débuts at Ashton Gate, the pair impressing despite the result. The home side were first to score, when on thirty-two minutes, Albert Adomah pounced on Aron Gunnarsson's loose pass, cutting back to Stephen Pearson who slotted home. Bristol struck again just before the break, with the consistent Jon Stead laying off Martyn Woolford for a simple finish.

A change of formation at half-time seemed to revitalise Cardiff, with Joe Mason being brought on for Gunnarsson. The striker's introduction had an immediate effect, Mason heading home Helguson's flick on from a Peter Whittingham corner. However, hope of a comeback was short lived. Woolford added his second of the game when he capitalised on a shot that hit the post from substitute Baldock. A late, cool finish from Helguson after a wayward McNaughton shot gave Cardiff hope on eighty-two minutes, but Baldock put the game to bed when he put the ball beyond Marshall's reach after latching onto a Greg Cunningham through ball.

SMITH

"Today was disappointing, but I'm sure this is just a blip. It was really disappointing today to lose in the manner we did, but I'm sure we are going to bounce back in the wee and we have a big game to look forward to on Sunday against Wolves.'

FANS SAY "There were a lot of defensive errors at Bristol, while Tommy Smith was definitely our best player. He tried his best to impress going forward, whereas the long ball tactic into Helguson wasn't always working." – *Jordan Jones*

THE BREAK DOWN

REFEREE: Mike Jones

05 | **05**

55 | **45**

POSSESSION

SHOTS
6 ON **3**
7 OFF

Post-match reaction from Malky Mackay, Derek McInnes and Tommy Smith on Cardiff City Player

CARDIFF CITY Player

Bristol City: Heaton, Wilson, Fontaine, Carey, Cunningham, Woolford, Skuse, Pearson, Adomah (Davies), Stead, Baldock), Taylor (Elliott).
Subs not used: Carey, Foster, Wilson, Morris.

Cardiff City:
Marshall,
McNaughton, Taylor,
Hudson, Connolly,
Whittingham, Cowie,
Gunnarsson (Mason), Mutch (Ralls),
Smith (Velikonja), Helguson.
Subs not used: Lewis, Nugent, Kiss, Earnshaw.

41

'Alright lad?' Joe Mason shares a joke with former City favourite Tom Heaton at Ashton Gate.

THE CHAMPIONSHIP

Any Championship manager would testify that while a good start can set the tone for the rest of the season, it rarely provides little bearing on the final standings come May. However, CF11 has decided to put this theory to the test – taking a quick look at last year's table after the opening three games to see if it offered any early indications of how the rest of the season would pan out.

The story was rather different for last season's champions though. **Reading** found themselves down in tenth place after three games, and spent nearly all of the season in mid-table until their sensational run in February saw them rise to first. It just goes to show that the final outcome of the Championship continues to be as unpredictable as ever and that no silverware is ever decided upon in August.

THE POWER OF THREE

It was just over a calendar year ago that Malky Mackay's new-look Cardiff City side had narrowly beaten Oxford United in the first round of the Carling Cup, en route to the final. But comparisons can be drawn between City's League start this year and last. Having been unbeaten in the first two games of both campaigns, defeat was finally tasted in the third, with losses at home to Brighton & Hove Albion and Bristol City respectively.

So, what significance does City's fifteenth place position after three games hold – if any? Well, it's eight places (just two points) below our corresponding position last season, although the team in fifteenth place at this point last year was **Birmingham City** who went on to have an excellent campaign – finishing in fourth spot.

The most interesting discovery, however, is that **Coventry City** and **Doncaster Rovers** were the only two teams to still be on 'nil points' after three games last year, taking up positions twenty-three and twenty-four as a result. Their fans will know only too well that they occupied the very same positions on the last day of the season. Could this be a worrying omen for **Crystal Palace** and **Peterborough United** supporters in 2012/13?

A similar pattern was seen at the other end of the table, at least in the case of **Southampton.** Top of the league and one of three teams with unblemished records after the first three matches (alongside **Brighton** and **Derby County** who both ended up in mid-table), the Saints never dropped out of the top two from that point onwards, finishing the season in second position. Time will tell whether this season's only team on a full nine points, **Blackpool,** can emulate them in that respect.

TRANSFER UPDATE

The summer transfer window, unlike the weather, certainly began heating up in the run up towards Friday's deadline. City made sure they were in the thick of the action once more, with players moving in both directions since our last outing at the CCS. **Darcy Blake** called an end to his fourteen year stay at City to join Crystal Palace, making his Eagles debut in their 2-1 defeat at Middlesbrough last weekend.

time was wasted in making up for summer departures, however, as Malky brought in two more experienced Championship competitors towards the end of the month. Tommy Smith and Matthew Connolly were part of the QPR squad that finished first in the 2010-11 season – both having also been promoted to the top flight with other clubs.

Today's visitors, Wolves, have been fairly busy in the market themselves. The main beneficiary of such dealings has been their bank manager though, as the sale of Matt Jarvis and Steven Fletcher to West Ham United and Sunderland respectively brought in a total of close to £25 million for the West Midlands club. How much of this Ståle Solbakken is given to put back into his team remains to be seen, although Austrian defender Georg Margreitter did cost the club £2 million towards the end of last week while Razak Boukari from Rennes came in on a four year deal for an undisclosed fee.

Plenty of Championship teams have been eager to make full use of this summer's loan market as well. None more so than Watford, who have made former Italian international

Marco Cassetti their seventh loan signing from Udinese and Granada – the two other clubs of new owner Giampaolo Pozzo. Middlesbrough have also secured the services of Chelsea youngster Josh McEachran for the season, while City's opening day opponents Huddersfield Town have added to their list of recruits by bringing in James Vaughan from Norwich City.

Tommy Smith battles with Jay Bothroyd before the pair became teammates

NEXT WEEKEND'S FIXTURES
(All games kick-off at 3pm unless otherwise stated)

Friday 14th September
Brighton v Sheffield Wednesday (7:45pm)
Charlton Athletic v Crystal Palace (7:45pm)

Saturday 15th September
Barnsley v Blackpool
Bolton Wanderers v Watford
Bristol City v Blackburn Rovers
Burnley v Peterborough United
Cardiff City v Leeds United
Huddersfield Town v Derby County
Hull City v Millwall
Middlesbrough v Ipswich Town
Nottingham Forest v Birmingham City

Sunday 16th September
Wolves v Leicester City (1:15pm)

2012/13 NPOWER CHAMPIONSHIP LEAGUE TABLE

Pos	Team	P	W	D	L	GD	Pts
1	Blackpool	3	3	0	0	9	9
2	Sheffield Wed	3	2	1	0	2	7
3	Blackburn	3	2	1	0	2	7
4	Bristol City	3	2	0	1	4	6
5	Watford	3	2	0	1	2	6
6	Middlesbrough	3	2	0	1	1	6
7	Leeds United	3	2	0	1	1	6
8	Nottm Forest	3	1	2	0	1	5
9	Charlton	3	1	2	0	1	5
10	Brighton	3	1	1	1	3	4
11	Wolves	3	1	1	1	1	4
12	Huddersfield	3	1	1	1	1	4
13	Bolton	3	1	1	1	0	4
14	Hull City	3	1	1	1	0	4
15	Cardiff City	3	1	1	1	-1	4
16	Ipswich Town	3	1	1	1	-5	4
17	Leicester City	3	1	0	2	0	3
18	Burnley	3	1	0	2	-1	3
19	Millwall	3	1	0	2	-2	3
20	Barnsley	3	1	0	2	-5	3
21	Derby County	3	0	2	1	-2	2
22	Birmingham	3	0	1	2	-3	1
23	Peterborough	3	0	0	3	-4	0
24	Crystal Palace	3	0	0	3	-5	0

DETAILS PRIOR TO THIS WEEKEND'S GAMES

CF ELEVEN

THE OFFICIAL CARDIFF CITY FC MATCH PROGRAMME

CARDIFF CITY

VERSUS

LEEDS UNITED

SAT 15TH SEP 3:00PM

npower CHAMPIONSHIP MATCH 05 £3

MATCH SPONSOR: ABN AMRO

MATCH BALL SPONSOR: KELTBRAY RAIL

Malaysia PUMA Player

03

TAKING SHAPE

Good afternoon and welcome back for today's match with Leeds United. We've been looking forward to this game ever since the referee blew the final whistle in our win over Wolves two weeks ago. It was an excellent result for us and a very encouraging performance, so it was a bit of a shame that we have had to wait to get back into action.

Having said that, we could not ask for a better fixture to resume action as we welcome Neil Warnock, his staff, players and everyone from Leeds down to South Wales today. It's also our first Saturday game at 3pm this season, so it's fitting that it brings together two such good teams.

I love pitting my wits against Neil every time I have come up against one of his teams. He is a man for whom I have enormous respect because he brings a knowledge and wisdom to his work that comes with having performed at the highest levels for such a long time. We talk a lot about fostering a learning environment for the staff and players here in Cardiff and it is important to take as many lessons as we can, so I have no doubt that there will be plenty of things I can pick up from Neil today. I always enjoy meeting up with Neil after the game – win or lose, we've always managed to have a good natter and catch up.

Going back to our last game, I was delighted to see some of our new signings make such a positive early impression. All three of the attacking players – Tommy Smith, Craig Noone and Nicky Maynard played significant roles in helping us to beat what I expect to be a very good Wolves team – still packed with players who have been plying their trade in the Premier

League in recent seasons – and Matthew Connolly helped keep us looking secure at the back.

My last set of programme notes were obviously written before we had managed to finalise the transfer of Nicky Maynard from West Ham, so I'd like to take this opportunity to welcome him to the club. I believe we are the perfect stage for him to move his career on to the next stage in just the same way that he is the ideal man to help us achieve what we have set out to do.

I am really pleased with the shape of the squad as we come out of the summer window and we would not have been able to achieve that without the fantastic support we have had from the owner, chairman and so many members of staff who have worked so hard to make sure things ran as smoothly as they did.

We were very honoured to see so many of our players travel to represent their countries in World Cup qualifiers over the last two weeks – in total, ten Cardiff City players were called up and that is a reflection of both the quality of players that we have here and the hard work that all of them have put in. I was immensely proud when I was called up to represent Scotland during my playing days so I will never underplay the importance of pulling on the shirt. Equally pleasing was the fact that they have all come back fit and well!

I'm sure there will be a packed house here today and we are counting on your support – by sticking together, I believe we can achieve so much.

Enjoy the match.

" I WAS
DELIGHTED
TO SEE SOME OF
OUR NEW SIGNINGS
MAKE SUCH A
POSITIVE EARLY
IMPRESSION "

CARDIFF CITY 3
Whittingham (Pen 11, 14, 65)

WOLVES 1
Sako (10)

SUNDAY ▶ 2ND SEPTEMBER ▶ 2.00PM | Full Attendance 22,020

🏠 **20,541**
🚌 **1,479**

MALKY

"We signed ten new players in the transfer window and it takes time for them all to integrate. Some of them only met a few days before the match against Wolves. I am delighted with the players we have brought in and the way things are progressing."

SOLBAKKEN

"I think the key point for me was that we talked long and hard about not conceding stupid free kicks and penalties. We were 1-0 up and we didn't really get the chance to protect that lead. Then we gave Whittingham another chance to use his left foot – and it was all over."

WHITTINGHAM

"To go a goal down today and show the character we did was brilliant. To get a goal back when we did was pretty important and I thought we went on from there. The hat trick was nice, but it's always about the points."

Looking for a second consecutive home victory, the Bluebirds started solidly before an excellent free kick from Wolves debutant Bakary Sako beat David Marshall at his near post in the ninth minute. The response was immediate though, Craig Noone beating Ronald Zubar with some sublime footwork inside the box to win a penalty. Peter Whittingham, cool as ever, slotted home, before giving City the lead four minutes later after firing home from twenty yards following some superb build-up by Nicky Maynard.

The second half started ominously for Wolves, with Whittingham hitting a fantastic free kick that Ikeme did well to save, before some Noone trickery earned Cardiff another free kick to the left of the goal, twenty-five yards out. There was only ever going to be one person stood over the ball; Whittingham bagged his hat trick with an audacious whipped shot into the far right corner of the goal. Wolves offered nothing offensively after the third, with the Bluebirds finishing a routine half hour strongly. Whittingham claimed the man of the match with a fantastic hat trick, but the plaudits had to be shared with Noone who enjoyed an exceptional debut.

FANS SAY "A great result and performance from the team. Noone looks impressive and what a hat trick from Whittingham! I also liked Smith's work and, of course, the defensive work of Kevin McNaughton." – *Frank Shipton*

REFEREE: Mr A. D'Urso

11 ⚑ 06

51% 49%
POSSESSION

🟨 1   🟨 1

SHOTS
ON 4
OFF 7

st-match reaction from Malky Mackay,
ale Solbakken and
ter Whittingham
a Cardiff City Player

CARDIFF CITY Player

rdiff City: Marshall,
cNaughton, Taylor, Hudson
, Connolly, Whittingham,
one (Cowie), Mutch
unnarsson), Smith,
elguson, Maynard
lason).
bs not used:
wis, Nugent,
n, Velikonja.

Wolves:
Ikeme, Ward,
Johnson, Berra, Zubar
(Stearman), Edwards (Nouble),
Peszko (Forde), Bakary Sako,
Doumbia, Ebanks-Blake, Doyle.
Subs not used: De Vries, Elokobi, Batth, Davis.

51

The perfect debut. New signing Noone helps tear Wolves apart with the aid of the mercurial Peter Whittingham.

THE CHAMPIONSHIP

The table is certainly starting to shape up as we continue with the fifth round of Championship fixtures this afternoon, meaning all teams will be eager to get some points on the board and build up momentum heading into autumn.

Early pace-setters **Blackpool** had got off to a great start, winning their first three games of the campaign. But, having suffered their first defeat last time out, they'll be looking to bounce back as they travel to **Barnsley**. Another team that has hit the ground running this season is newly relegated **Blackburn Rovers**, and they'll also be buoyed by their recent capture of former Huddersfield striker Jordon Rhodes. He'll be looking to get off the mark for his new club against **Bristol City** today.

Continuing the 'B' theme (there are eight teams beginning with that letter in the Championship this season!), **Birmingham City** have had a surprisingly poor start to this term, finding themselves down in twenty-first position. They'll need to improve if they are to get anything out of this weekend's encounter with **Nottingham Forest,** who have been guided to third place with former Doncaster boss Sean O'Driscoll at the helm.

Another team making up the play-off positions are **Hull City,** who host our Tuesday night opponents **Millwall** this weekend. The Lions will be hoping former City man Andy Keogh can keep up his scoring form, having bagged a brace against Middlesbrough last time out.

Other than Blackburn, the sides relegated from the Premier League haven't made the best of starts to their Championship campaigns. **Wolverhampton Wanderers** have suffered from the loss of several big-name players this summer, and they face a tough task at home to **Leicester City** on Sunday. **Bolton Wanderers,** on the other hand, have managed to retain the services of players such as Zat Knight, Lee Chung-Yong and Kevin Davies – but this hasn't aided their early form. Their start has seen them join Wolves on just four points – but a home win against **Watford** today will see them spring up the table.

Huddersfield Town meanwhile, who have recently secured the services of both Adam Hammill and James Vaughan on loan deals, face fellow mid-table side **Derby County** in West Yorkshire. While **Burnley** another side who have had a disappointing start, will hope to improve on their tally of just three points against **Peterborough United**. Finally, **Ipswich Town** have the longest journey of the weekend as they make a five hundred mile round trip to face **Middlesbrough** at the Riverside.

FAIR PLAY

The Championship is often portrayed as one of the most competitive leagues in the world. Due to this, some outsiders seem to assume that the football played in the second tier is not always of the highest quality – with teams full of uncompromising centre halves, fifty-fifty loving midfielders and big forwards that take no prisoners.

However, this is far from the truth – and the figures prove that. Many of the teams promoted from the Championship in the past few seasons, such as Norwich and Blackpool, have received plaudits in the media for the

ay that they play the game. And it doesn't stop there.
oncaster competed in the Championship for several
easons playing attractive, free flowing football under Sean
'Driscoll, and the majority of sides, be they promotion
hallengers or clubs on a shoe-string budget, have strived to
o the same.

his has been reflected in the most remarkable statistic of
e season so far. In the 48 matches played in the npower
hampionship, there has been **just one red card,** with **Bobby
assell** of Barnsley the sole offender! To put this into context
there have been 5 red cards in just 29 Premiership matches
is campaign, while League 1 has seen a massive 16
ismissals in 58 games.

City have had an excellent disciplinary record
themselves in recent years. In fact, you have
to go back to a match against Barnsley on
2nd October 2010 for our last sending off,
when Darcy Blake was shown red for two
bookable offences – almost two
calendar years ago!

Back to this season and the
Bluebirds have an admirable
record once more – sitting in
joint second place in the fair
play league with just 4
yellow cards in our 4
games. **Hull, Ipswich,
Derby** and **Wolves** are
the good boys of the
division, with just 3
cautions each, while at
the bottom, both
Nottingham Forest and
Sheffield Wednesday have
amassed ten bookings apiece. On an
individual level, Luke Varney, of
today's opponents **Leeds United** is
the only player in the whole division
to have received more than 2 yellow
cards so far.

Let's pay tribute to this
demonstration of fair play and
sportsmanship in football – and long
may it continue!

THIS WEEKEND'S FIXTURES
*(All games kick-off at
3pm unless otherwise stated)*

Friday 14th September
Brighton v Sheffield Wednesday (7:45pm)
Charlton Athletic v Crystal Palace (7:45pm)

Saturday 15th September
Barnsley v Blackpool
Bolton Wanderers v Watford
Bristol City v Blackburn Rovers
Burnley v Peterborough United
Cardiff City v Leeds United
Huddersfield Town v Derby County
Hull City v Millwall
Middlesbrough v Ipswich Town
Nottingham Forest v Birmingham City

Sunday 16th September
Wolves v Leicester City (1:15pm)

2012/13 NPOWER CHAMPIONSHIP LEAGUE TABLE

Pos	Team	P	W	D	L	GD	Pts
1	Blackpool	4	3	0	1	8	9
2	Blackburn	4	2	2	0	2	8
3	Nottm Forest	4	2	2	0	2	8
4	Brighton	4	2	1	1	5	7
5	Hull City	4	2	1	1	2	7
6	Sheffield Wed	4	2	1	1	1	7
7	**Leeds United**	4	2	1	1	1	7
8	**Cardiff City**	4	2	1	1	1	7
9	Bristol City	4	2	0	2	3	6
10	Leicester City	4	2	0	2	1	6
11	Millwall	4	2	0	2	0	6
12	Middlesbrough	4	2	0	2	-1	6
13	Watford	4	2	0	2	-2	6
14	Barnsley	4	2	0	2	-4	6
15	Derby County	4	1	2	1	2	5
16	Huddersfield	4	1	2	1	1	5
17	Charlton	4	1	2	1	0	5
18	Ipswich Town	4	1	2	1	-5	5
19	Wolves	4	1	1	2	-1	4
20	Bolton	4	1	1	2	-2	4
21	Birmingham	4	1	1	2	-2	4
22	Burnley	4	1	0	3	-3	3
23	Crystal Palace	4	1	0	3	-4	3
24	Peterborough	4	0	0	4	-5	0

DETAILS PRIOR TO THIS WEEKEND'S GAMES

CF ELEVEN

THE OFFICIAL CARDIFF CITY FC MATCH PROGRAMME

CARDIFF CITY

• VERSUS •

BLACKPOOL

SAT 29TH SEP 3:00PM

npower CHAMPIONSHIP   MATCH 08 £3

MATCH SPONSOR: eCOSWAY UK

**MATCH BALL SPONSOR:
PAGE INDUSTRIAL COATINGS LTD**

TEAM SPONSOR: BIG YELLOW STORAGE

04

MALKY MACKAY

SEIZE IT BACK

Good afternoon and welcome back for today's match with Blackpool. I'll start by also welcoming Ian Holloway and his staff and players who have made the long trip down from the North West.

Last week's game at Crystal Palace obviously ended up disappointingly for us, particularly having made such a good start. It's an old cliché about 2-0 being a dangerous lead, but Palace getting a penalty immediately after half-time changed the momentum of the match and we didn't manage to seize it back. What made it even more disappointing was the form we had been in coming into the match – we went to Selhurst looking for our fourth consecutive victory and had played so well in beating Millwall, Leeds United and Wolves in the three matches before.

We had shown excellent tenacity allied with considerable talent and skill to overcome Neil Warnock's Leeds side here two weeks ago. It had turned into a typical match against one of Neil's teams where competing for every ball is so important, so you can then build a solid platform to allow yourself the right to start adding style to the hard graft and I felt we did that well. The only small frustration was giving away a silly goal from a set piece with ten minutes left which gave us a few nervous moments in the closing stages when it really should have been a much more comfortable win.

We then followed that up by going to Millwall, never an east proposition, and coming away with a convincing 2-0 victory thanks to excellently taken goals from Peter Whittingham and Craig Noone, his first for the club. Obviously that win was slightly overshadowed by the serious injury which Nicky Maynard sustained during the match. Nicky had performed excellently in his first three matches in a Cardiff shirt, so it's frustrating to lose him so early in his City career. However, he is now in the care of our first class medical team who will be working really hard with Nicky to make sure he comes back in tip top condition.

I'd like to wish Nicky all the best for his recovery because personal experience of being in the same position has taught me that there will be some tough days ahead for him. However, the support he receives, both from the medical staff and from the camaraderie of his team mates will get him through and back to action as soon as possible.

His injury also opens the door for other members of our squad to stake a claim for more first team football, so the challenge is there now for them to step up and make sure that we get back to winning ways quickly. If that winning run is to start today, we know we will have to be at our absolute best, because Blackpool have already shown this season that they are one of the very strongest teams in the division, currently sitting fourth in the table, level on points with ourselves. We will have to match their commitment and skill if we are to emerge victorious from this afternoon's encounter and we will need the usual fantastic levels of support from you in the stands to help us achieve that.

It was good to see the under-21 development team chalk up a 2-0 win over Charlton here at the stadium on a rainy Tuesday night this week. The new league in which they compete is all part of the much-heralded Elite Player Performance Plan (EPPP) which has come into force this season. It was good to see match which was played in the right competitive spirit and a win for which the lads had to work hard. Two great goals, from Craig Conway and Declan Joh was enough to beat a decent Charlton side and allo Kevin Cooper to pick up his second win in charge of the development group. They also appreciate the support they received from the stands and look forward to seeing more of you here for their forthcoming home matches.

Enjoy today's match.

" THE CHALLENGE
IS THERE NOW
FOR THEM TO
STEP UP "

CARDIFF CITY 2
Bellamy (67), Whittingham (Pen 73)

LEEDS UNITED 1
Austin (77)

SATURDAY ▶ 15TH SEPTEMBER ▶ 3.00PM Full Attendance **23,836**

🏠 **21,609**
🚌 **1,777**

MALKY

"I thought Paddy Kenny was magnificent for them today, pulling off some great saves, especially at the end. Or another day we could have scored three or four. We now have three solid home wins to our credit, which is great, and now we go on the road to London twice in the space of a week."

WARNOCK

"It's nice to bring Craig Bellamy on when we brought a first-year pro on! For (Bellamy's) free kick we should have had the wall better. It's a fantastic goal, but from our point of view it's disappointing. I thought overall that we deserved a point."

MUTCH

"Leeds were a bit more direct than Wolves and we had to learn from mistakes in the first half. We came out in the second half and changed the game and I think that's what got us the three points. The players will be looking to go to Millwall and Palace and take maximum points."

Fixtures between these two sides are regularly competitive affairs and this was no exception. The first half saw numerous crunching tackles with both sides keen to put their stamp on the game. A player from each side entered the book as the first half remained goalless, despite some half-hearted penalty appeals for both sides. Former City striker Ross McCormack was forced to leave the field with injury with just five minutes gone.

Cardiff took the lead in the second half thanks to the returning Craig Bellamy, whose thunderous left-sided, right-footed free kick flew into the top corner of Paddy Kenny's net. The Bluebirds' lead was doubled less than five minutes later, and again it was a set piece that beat Kenny; Peter Whittingham stepped up to score from the penalty spot after Nicky Maynard had been felled inside the area. The final minutes of the game were nervy for the home fans after Rodolph Austin's free kick pulled one back, but thankfully for the Bluebirds it proved to be nothing more than a consolation, with Cardiff taking all three points. It proved a fitting display and result for the late Simon Insole.

FANS SAY "It was never going be easy with a team that's got Warnock in charge, but they had no answer to us. Stubborn defence from Leeds in the first half, but fitness and class in the second-half paid off." – *Liam Davies*

THE BREAKDOWN

REFEREE: Mr P. Tierney

61% 39%

POSSESSION

SHOTS

st-match reaction from Malky Mackay,
eil Warnock, Jordon
utch and Craig Noone
n Cardiff City Player

CARDIFF CITY Player

rdiff City: Marshall,
cNaughton, Taylor, Hudson (c),
nnolly, Whittingham,
utch (Gunnarsson),
Smith, Noone (Bellamy),
elguson, Maynard
owie).

bs not used:
wis, Kim,
ason,
ugent.

Leeds United:
Kenny, Peltier (c),
Drury (Diouf), Lees,
Pearce, Austin, White,
 Tonge, Byram, Becchio,
McCormack (Varney, Poleon).
Subs not used: Ashdown, Kisnorbo,
Brown, Gray.

61

A moving tribute. Cardiff City Stadium pays its respects to Club friend, the late Simon Insole, ahead of victory over Leeds.

MILLWALL 0
CARDIFF CITY 2

Whittingham (53), Noone (55)

TUESDAY ▶ 18TH SEPTEMBER ▶ 7.45PM Full Attendance 9,295

🏠 8,826
🚌 469

MALKY

"The players are beginning to get to know each other now, and the more they get to know each other the better. T come away to the Den i never easy, but to keep clean sheet and score twice is pleasing. It's all about putting little runs together and we have to do that."

JACKETT

"Fine margins win and lose games. We weren't a million miles away but ultimately we've lost a game and that's a frustration. Two quick goals at the start of the second half gave us a mountain to climb. We need clean sheets – that will make us competitive enough to pick up points."

TAYLOR

"We showed character, defended great and deserved the goals. I think we've been very good as a back four against Leeds and Millwall. To get the clea sheet tonight gave us th opportunity to build on base and win the game. We go to Palace now with confidence."

Victory was tasted in Bermondsey for the first time in thirty years as two superb quick-fire goals in the second half secured the three points for the Bluebirds.

The first half had been a well fought and even affair, and a third successive goalless draw with the Lions seemed to be on the cards. James Henry went closest for Millwall in the first half, seeing his twenty-five yard free kick well saved by David Marshall. At the other end, City were extremely unlucky not to take the lead as Whittingham's terrific free kick from the right flank was ruled out for an alleged tug in the box.

But it was in the second half that the difference between the two sides was shown. First Craig Noone cut in from the left and set up Whittingham to fire a trademark shot into the top corner from twenty-five yards, giving the Bluebirds the lead. And just two minutes later provider turned scorer as the lively winger, who has had an excellent start to his Cardiff City career, stepped up to curl the ball into the far corner with his right foot after good work by Tommy Smith. The victory meant that City consolidated their position just one point off the top of the table, on a night when the top five teams all recorded wins.

FANS SAY "The last few games have given me great confidence that we can go up this year. We have the cutting edge we lacked last year." – *Gavin Cynan-Jones*

64

THE BREAK DOWN

6 | 4

48 | 52

POSSESSION

2 |

SHOTS

8 ON

3 OFF

post-match reaction of this game from
lkyMackay and
ny Jackett on
diff City Player

CARDIFF CITY Player

wall: Taylor; Dunne,
orne, Lowry, Malone,
ght (Taylor), Abdou,
ter (c); Henry (Batt),
derson (Wood),
gh.
s not used:
de, Shittu,
on,
dman.

Cardiff City:
Marshall;
McNaughton, Hudson
(c), Connolly, Taylor; Smith,
Gunnarsson, Whittingham,
Mutch, Noone (Bo-Kyung);
Maynard (Helguson).
Subs not used: Lewis, Nugent, Mason,
Velikonja, Cowie.

65

A tainted victory. Nicky Maynard tears his anterior cruciate ligament after an awkward fall at the Den.

CRYSTAL PALACE 3
Murray (Pen 52, 62, Pen 72)

CARDIFF CITY 2
Gunnarsson (13), Cowie (15)

SATURDAY ▶ 22ND SEPTEMBER ▶ 3.00PM | Full Attendance 12,757

🏠 **11,622**
🚌 **1,135**

MALKY

"We committed suicide really by gifting Crystal Palace two penalties. We felt fairly comfortable at half-time, but when you give two penalties to a team like that you do deserve to be punished. I don't have any qualms with either penalty decision we gifted both of them"

FREEDMAN

"As a comeback it is the best I've had in my managerial career. Cardiff are a good side and they'll be in the shake-up come the end of the season. That makes me even prouder as a manager that we've stood up to this huge challenge today."

The Bluebirds were denied a fourth successive league victory as they let a two goal lead slip at Selhurst Park.

City were in the driving seat at half-time after they scored two quick-fire goals for the second match in a row. Aron Gunnarsson had scored the opener, breaking into the box past several Palace defenders before slotting the ball calmly past Speroni. And just moments later it was two. An optimistic effort from Craig Bellamy was deflected into the air, with the ball falling to Don Cowie just inside the box. The Scotsman fired it home on the half-volley in similar fashion to his goal on the same ground on the final day of last season.

The second half saw a complete swing in momentum, however, as two penalties helped the Eagles to turn the game on its head. The referee first pointed to the spot after a Palace free kick deflected off Andrew Taylor's hand in the wall. Glenn Murray made no mistake to pull one back for his side. And the striker was involved in the equaliser too, as his goal-bound effort was turned over the line by Matthew Connolly. Finally, Murray completed the comeback, converting another spot kick after Helguson's clumsy challenge, leaving the final score at 3-2.

COWIE

"We were beaten at Bristol City and bounce back with three consecutive wins. We have to do that again on the back of today's defeat. First up is Blackpool this Saturday and then we play Birmingham at home a couple of days later. We are still in good shape."

FANS SAY

"The two penalties were the difference. You could say that Crystal Palace were lucky and we were unlucky on the day. We pushed for more goals when maybe we should have sat on the lead." – *Andrew Morris*

THE BREAKDOWN

REFEREE: Mr. G. Ward

10 4

52 48

POSSESSION

0 1

SHOTS

8 ON 2
7 OFF 4

e post-match reaction of this game from Malky
ackay, Dougie Freedman
d Darcy Blake on
rdiff City Player

CARDIFF CITY Player

ystal Palace: Speroni,
ake, Ramage (Ward),
elaney, Parr; Bolasie
oxey), Dikgacoi, Moritz
Villiams), Jedinak (c),
Zaha; Murray.
bs not used:
ice, Garvan,
oodwillie,
ilbraham.

Cardiff City:
Marshall,
McNaughton, Hudson
(c), Connolly, Taylor, Smith
(Kim), Cowie (Noone),
Gunnarsson, Whittingham, Bellamy
(Mason), Helguson.
Subs not used: Lewis, Turner, Kiss, Velikonja.

69

The master and the student. Helguson celebrates
countryman Gunnarsson's opener at Selhurst.

THE CHAMPIONSHIP

THE WEEK THAT WAS: 'GRANNYGATE'

Life-long Birmingham City fan **Craig Davies** (*pictured*) put his beloved Blues firmly to sword netting four times in Barnsley's remarkable 5-0 victory at St. Andrew's in last Saturday's evening kick-off.

The Tykes had lost their five previous road trips heading into the game, yet left the second city with a first away clean sheet in twenty-four attempts after inflicting Brum's heaviest home defeat for twenty-five years! Davies, a twenty-six year old veteran of eleven clubs, finally looks to have put his career back on track. Touchingly, yet rather confusingly, the surely soon to be re-called Welsh international dedicated his fine feat to his grandmother. That's his Brum supporting grandmother – in a moment which was clearly meant to be sweet, yet could easily have been read as antagonistic by his proud granny!

Burnley striker **Charlie Austin** joined Davies atop the Championship scoring charts after netting the sixth and seventh goals of his season in the Clarets' 2-1 win at Derby on Saturday. The brace raised the former Swindon man's total to seventeen in all competitions for 2012 as he looks to replace Jay Rodriguez in the hearts of the Turf Moor faithful. The result marked the first away win of the season for Eddie Howe's men and the individual success of Austin and Barnsley's Davies could be set to continue a curious recent trend where under fift percent of players to have won the Championshi Golden Boot have come from a side promoted that season.

Peterborough United remain the only club of the whole seventy-two in the Football League to yet pick up a single point. The Posh succumbed to Wolves at London Road on Saturday with a penalty from Sylvan Ebanks-Blake, a two-time winner of the Championship Golden Boot, opening the scoring and Bjorn Sigurdarson's first goal in English football sealing the three points late on. The result stretches Darren Ferguson's winless streak to thirteen Championship matches dating back to a 1-0 win over Leicester last March and leaves them rooted to the base of the table.

And finally, **Leeds United** and **Nottingham Forest** failed to re-enact last season's incredible ten goal thriller at Elland Road, instead playing out a tense 2-1 win for the Whites. In a clash which must have evoked strong nostalgi feelings amongst fans of two sides who represented the pinnacle of British football achievement during the seventies and early eighties, goals from Luciano Becchio and Dominic Poleon secured a much needed three points for Neil Warnock's men.

▶▶ CHAMPIONSHIP LEADING SCORERS 2012/13

#	Player	Club	Goals
1	CHARLIE AUSTIN	BURNLEY	7
2	CRAIG DAVIES	BARNSLEY	7
3	LUCIANO BECCHIO	LEEDS UNITED	6
4	THOMAS INCE	BLACKPOOL	6
5	CRAIG MACKAIL-SM	BRIGHTON	6

GOALS GALORE

The npower Championship is often billed as one of the most exciting leagues in the world, and this has been backed up by the statistics once more in the 2012-13 campaign.

With just 7 matches each played this term, Championship fans have already been treated to 263 goals! That averages out at over 3 goals per game – comfortably more than in the Premier League, League 1 or League 2.

Today's visitors **Blackpool** have certainly played their part in this early goal-scoring spree, topping the list with 16 to their name so far. A 6-0 demolition of **Ipswich Town** as well as their recent 4-1 drubbing of **Middlesbrough** have contributed to this impressive total.

Tangerine winger Thomas Ince has chipped in with his fair share of these – sitting joint second on the top scorers list with six goals. He's joined by Brighton's Craig Mackail-Smith and Luciano Becchio of Leeds United, with Craig Davies and Charlie Austin one above them. **But Ince's unrivalled 6 assists sets him apart from the rest, meaning that he's played a part in 75% of Blackpool's goals this season.**

Of course, City have been no stranger to the back of the net themselves. **Peter Whittingham** is currently the top scoring midfielder of the division having chipped in with 5 goals so far, including his hat-trick against Wolves. He's not just scoring tap-ins either! With 15% of the season now played, let's hope that the free flowing scoring continues as we embrace the autumn.

DID YOU KNOW?

Blackpool fans travelling south for today's game will be making one of the longer journeys of their season, with an almost 500 mile round trip! But, in the past the club have strived to make the players travels from the North West as comfortable as possible. In fact, the 'Pool were the first ever club to travel by plane to a Football League fixture on the day of the game. They set the record back in March 1957, flying down to Cardiff for a Division 1 match at Ninian Park before coming out on top in an exciting 4-3 win in the capital.

LATEST RESULTS

Blackburn Rovers 1–2 Middlesbrough
Blackpool 1–3 Huddersfield Town
Birmingham City 0–5 Barnsley
Crystal Palace 3–2 Cardiff City
Derby County 1–2 Burnley
Ipswich Town 1–2 Charlton Athletic
Leeds United 2–1 Nottingham Forest
Leicester City 3–1 Hull City
Millwall 1–2 Brighton & Hove Albion
Peterborough United 0–2 Wolves
Sheffield Wednesday 1–2 Bolton Wanderers
Watford 2–2 Bristol City

THIS WEEKEND'S FIXTURES
(All games kick-off at 3pm unless otherwise stated)

Saturday 29th September
Barnsley v Ipswich Town
Bolton Wanderers v Crystal Palace
Brighton & Hove Albion v Birmingham City (5.30pm)
Bristol City v Leeds United
Burnley v Millwall
Cardiff City v Blackpool
Charlton Athletic v Blackburn Rovers
Huddersfield Town v Watford
Hull City v Peterborough United
Middlesbrough v Leicester City
Wolves v Sheffield Wednesday

Sunday 30th September
Nottingham Forest v Derby County (1.15pm)

2012/13 NPOWER CHAMPIONSHIP LEAGUE TABLE

Pos	Team	P	W	D	L	GD	Pts
1	Brighton	7	5	1	1	10	16
2	Huddersfield	7	4	2	1	6	14
3	Blackburn	7	4	2	1	4	14
4	**Blackpool**	7	4	1	2	9	13
5	Hull City	7	4	1	2	4	13
6	Wolves	7	4	1	2	4	13
7	**Cardiff City**	7	4	1	2	3	13
8	Leicester City	7	4	0	3	3	12
9	Middlesbrough	7	4	0	3	-1	12
10	Bristol City	7	3	1	3	2	10
11	Nottm Forest	7	2	4	1	1	10
12	Leeds United	7	3	1	3	0	10
13	Barnsley	7	3	1	3	0	10
14	Bolton	7	3	1	3	-1	10
15	Crystal Palace	7	3	1	3	-2	10
16	Burnley	7	3	0	4	0	9
17	Derby County	7	2	2	3	1	8
18	Charlton	7	2	2	3	-1	8
19	Birmingham	7	2	2	3	-6	8
20	Watford	7	2	1	4	-4	7
21	Sheffield Wed	7	2	1	4	-5	7
22	Millwall	7	2	0	5	-6	6
23	Ipswich Town	7	1	2	4	-10	5
24	Peterborough	7	0	0	7	-11	0

CF ELEVEN

THE OFFICIAL CARDIFF CITY FC MATCH PROGRAMME

CARDIFF CITY

—VERSUS—

BIRMINGHAM CITY

TUE 2ND OCT 7:45PM

npower CHAMPIONSHIP   MATCH 09 £3

MATCH SPONSOR: LDS MOTOR FACTORS

MATCH BALL SPONSOR: NATHANIEL CARS

TEAM SPONSOR: PYRAMID HYGIENE LTD

Malaysia   **PUMA**   Player

05

KEEP ON RUNNING

Good evening and welcome to the stadium for today's game against Birmingham City. We come into tonight's match in good shape, having played very well to comfortably beat a very good Blackpool team here on Saturday.

I think it is an indication of the progress we are making that we were able to produce a performance of that level to record a big win against one of the promotion favourites. It was important to bounce back from the disappointment against Crystal Palace the week before, so I was really pleased that we showed no Selhurst hangover.

Last season, we had a similar situation when we went to Peterborough in October and suffered a defeat that was particularly difficult to take – but we responded in the best possible way by going unbeaten in our next eight league matches, winning six of them. That run enabled us to establish ourselves in the middle of the leading pack of promotion contenders – a group which we remained in step with for the rest of the season and saw us eventually finish with a place in the play-offs. So, I'm hoping that we use the disappointment of the Palace match to spur us into another good run.

Looking back at last season, I was reminded that Blackpool came and beat us 3-1 – a match which some people have claimed marked a turning point in our league campaign, so we knew we would have to be at our best on Saturday. To try to combat Ian Holloway's team, we drew up a well-defined game plan that we thought would give us a chance of winning. Obviously, I was delighted to see the players follow our instructions to the letter and to run out such convincing winners – something we will be looking to repeat against a tough Birmingham team tonight.

I'll take this opportunity to welcome Lee Clark, his staff and players who have made the trip from the Midlands for tonight's game on the back of an impressive result of their own. It is worth remembering that the Blues were in the Premier

League only 18 months ago and they still retain a core of players and an infrastructure that reflects that top level heritage. We will not be making the mistake of underestimating the threat Birmingham pose today.

This is our fifth home match of the season and it has been particularly pleasing to have recorded wins in each of the first four. Even more so when you consider the quality of opposition that we have faced here at the CCS since August – Huddersfield, Wolves, Leeds and Blackpool – and I'm sure all of them are more than capable of building on their positive starts to mount a sustained promotion push. Indeed, six of our first eight league matches have been against teams currently in the top half of the Championship table, so we have been matching ourselves against the best the division has to offer, making our decent start all the more satisfying.

Another aspect of our play that I have enjoyed is the variety of types of goal and goalscorer we have seen since August. Matthew Connolly's double on Saturday made him the ninth player to register for us in league action in 2012/13 and no one else in the Championship has had more different scorers thus far. As well as our threat going forward, it is also pleasing that Saturday's clean sheet was our fourth of the season, more than anyone else in the division. If we get to May having kept clean sheets in 50% of our league matches, we'll be in good shape! However, whilst all of these numbers are impressive, what counts is what we do on the pitch from game to game and we have two difficult matches – tonight against Birmingham then a trip to Ipswich on Saturday – before the next international break, so we are looking to build on the start and keep notching up wins.

The levels of support here on Saturday were great and played no small part in our win, so I will be looking for the same tonight – there's always something special about games played under lights and I'll be expecting another cauldron of atmosphere to help push the lads over the line.

Enjoy the game.

" WE WILL NOT BE MAKING THE MISTAKE OF UNDERESTIMATING THE THREAT BIRMINGHAM POSE TODAY "

CARDIFF CITY 3
Connolly (17,57), Whittingham (27)

BLACKPOOL 0

SATURDAY ▶ 29TH SEPTEMBER ▶ 3.00PM | Full Attendance 21,216

🏠 **20,677**
🚌 **539**

MALKY

"It was a really big win for us today. Blackpool remain one of the teams who I think will be up there at the top end of the table at the end of the season. They are a very dangerous team with lots of experience, so I'm delighted with the result and our performance today. We executed our game plan and the decision making was first class."

HOLLOWAY

"Goals change games. If we give away goals as easily as we did today then we're not going to win. I've seen Whittingham bend free kicks in from thirty-five yards out before so you have to say well done to him for that, but the other two were given away too easily from our point of view.

The Bluebirds cruised to their fourth consecutive home win of the season with a convincing 3-0 defeat of Blackpool. In doing so, they matched a feat not achieved by the Club since the promotion year of 1959-60.

It was an evenly matched start to the game, though City soon found their stride and rhythm. Wave after wave of attack soon led to the opener on seventeen minutes, Matt Connolly firing home from inside the area after good work and a smart cut back by the untouchable Craig Bellamy. Injury to Tommy Smith seven minutes later led to the introduction of Joe Mason – and it was his good work that led to City's second. From a seemingly impossible angle and distance, Peter Whittingham fired home a superb free kick that beat Matt Gilks at his near post. It was Whittingham's sixth goal in eight Championship appearances to date this term.

Blackpool came out stronger after the break following a change of formation, though City effectively killed off the game in the fifty-third minute. Admirable work by Bellamy in closing down Blackpool's defenders led to a Whittingham corner that was nodded home with ease by Connolly for his second of the game. There was no way back for Blackpool – and they rarely threatened from there on in.

CONNOLLY

"I've never scored two in a game before and I may not ever again! I think I've only scored five or six in my career since turning professional actually. The important thing is to win games though and who scores the goals doesn't really matter."

FANS SAY

"The perfect response to the disaster at Palace saw City take a massive victory against a strong promotion rival. A super performance and Craig Bellamy back to his best!" – Ned Thomas

THE BREAK DOWN

REFEREE: C. Boyeson

5 ⚑ 4

54% 46%
POSSESSION

3 2

SHOTS
5 **ON** 2
7 **OFF** 7

-match reaction from Malky Mackay,
Holloway and
t Connolly on
iff City Player — **Player**

iff City: Marshall,
laughton, Taylor, Hudson (c),
nolly, Whittingham,
narsson, Smith (Mason
Noone, Bellamy
72), Helguson
owie, 81).
s not used:
s, Kiss,
er,
onja.

Blackpool:
Gilks, Broadfoot,
Crainey, Evatt,
Baptiste (c), Robertson
(Osbourne 59), Phillips.M, Sylvestre
(Delfouneso 45), Martinez, Dicko
(Eccleston 61), Phillips.K.
Subs not used: Halstead, Eardley, Gomes,
Ferguson.

79

Inspirational. Craig Bellamy helps City finally see off their seaside tormentors.

THE CHAMPIONSHIP

TUSSLES AT THE TOP

Brighton and Hove Albion's shiny new home suffered a twenty-five minute power cut on Saturday evening, and the Seagulls' season also suffered a momentary black-out as they missed the chance to open up a three point gap at the top of the Championship table. It was **Birmingham City** who responded to last week's humiliation at the hands of Barnsley to sneak a 1-0 win, thanks to former Cardiff City man **Chris Burke's** twenty-five yard wonder strike. The win was Birmingham's first away from home all season and lifted them into a mid-table position; for Brighton, the defeat leaves them atop a three-team pile with ourselves and Wolves at the Championship summit on goal difference alone.

Wolves' strong run continued in fortuitous fashion at home to Dave Jones' Sheffield Wednesday. **Bakary Sako's** *(pictured)* twice taken free kick was enough to hand Stale Solbakken's side all three points for the fourth match on the bounce. It was also the third consecutive win at Molineux which incredibly matches Wolves' entire home wins total from last season's relegation campaign. Wednesday were aggrieved not to have been handed a penalty in the first half when **Jermaine Johnson** looked to have been felled in the box, but the no-decision from the referee contributed to a sixth straight defeat for the Owls who, prior to this winless run, had been unbeaten in nineteen and for

whom **Jay Bothroyd** has some serious contrition to convey (check Twitter).

Huddersfield Town missed the chance to move into top spot after falling to Gianfranco Zola's **Watford** in wild encounter in Yorkshire. Once again it was an Udinese-inspired victory as **Fernando Foristieri** and **Matteo Cassetti,** two of ten players on loan from the mid-table Serie A counterparts, played a vital role in the late dramatics. Firstly, Foristieri netted in the 68th minute to level up **Oliver Norwood's** early free-kick, and then in the closing moments with the score locked at 2-2 after goals from **Fitz H** and **Alan Lee,** full-back Cassetti surged into the box and was felled. That allowed **Troy Deene** just a week out of prison after serving three months for affray, to power home the spot kick and earn a first win in six for the Horne

Blackburn Rovers began life after **Steve Ke** with a chance at the top spot also, but had settle for a hard fought 1-1 draw at **Charlto Athletic.** Former Fulham man **Dickson Etuh** produced a smart finish from close range to open the scoring in favour of the Lancashir outfit, yet it was **Chris Powell's** newly promoted men who had the final say thro **Johnnie Jackson's** equaliser. In fact, it cou have been even sweeter for the Addicks h the former Tottenham man not missed wi an earlier penalty. The result leaves Rove in fourth place, just a point off top and perfectly placed for whoever their incomin manager may be.

≫ SEPTEMBER FORM GUIDE: THE TOP FIVE

1	2	3	4	5
13	12	12	12	1
≫ **CRYSTAL PALACE** W:4 D:1 L:0 GD:4	≫ **CARDIFF CITY** W:4 D:0 L:1 GD:7	≫ **BRIGHTON** W:4 D:0 L:1 GD:6	≫ **LEICESTER CITY** W:4 D:0 L:1 GD:4	≫ **WOLVES** W:4 D:0 L:1 G

1O PLACE LIKE HOME

...'s 3-0 weekend victory over **Blackpool** secured a fourth win ... of four at Cardiff City Stadium this season, fulfilling Malky ...ckay's desire for the fans and players alike to turn the ground ... a fortress during this campaign.

...cester City are the only other team with a 100% home record ...he Championship. The King Power Stadium continues to be a ...y difficult ground to go to, with impressive recent victories ...r **Hull City** and **Burnley** contributing to this feat. Their ...nparably poor away form has kept the Foxes just one point ...top.

...the other end of the table, **Peterborough United** have lost all 4 ...their home matches this season, conceding 8 goals in the ...cess. Their form will be extremely worrying for fans of the ...sh as they've only managed one victory on the road as well – ...Emile Sinclair hat trick at **Hull City's** KC Stadium on Saturday ...ded a 7 game losing streak in the league.

...o looking for their first home win this term are **Ipswich Town**. ...o wins and two draws from their opening games at Portman ...ad see them join the Posh in the relegation zone. And things ...ven't gone much better away from home. Paul Jewell's ...ctured) men have failed to keep a clean sheet in their last 6

matches in total, a run which includes a 6-0 drubbing at the hands of **Blackpool.**

That convincing win by the Tangerines helped them on their way to topping the home scoring charts, with 13 goals to their name. They are joined, surprisingly, by **Bristol City,** who have also conceded 11 goals at home – the most in the division. Meanwhile, **Charlton Athletic** and **Peterborough United** are at the bottom of the chart, having been able to muster up just 3 goals apiece at their home grounds so far.

DID YOU KNOW?

The last time City started a season this well at home was back in 1959/60. In that campaign the Bluebirds suffered their first defeat in their fifth home match, after securing wins over Liverpool, Middlesbrough, Bristol City and Derby County. In fact, they were in an identical position at the same stage of that campaign as we currently are now. With 8 matches played City found themselves in second place, level on points with first place Aston Villa. This is certainly a good omen as they finished the season in exactly the same position, earning promotion to the top flight.

npower
FOOTBALL LEAGUE

LATEST RESULTS

Brighton & Hove Albion 0–1 Birmingham City
Barnsley 1–1 Ipswich Town
Bolton Wanderers 0–1 Crystal Palace
Bristol City 2–3 Leeds United
Burnley 2–2 Millwall
Cardiff City 3–0 Blackpool
Charlton Athletic 1–1 Blackburn Rovers
Huddersfield Town 2–3 Watford
Hull City 1–3 Peterborough United
Middlesbrough 1–2 Leicester City
Nottingham Forest 0–1 Derby County
Wolves 1–0 Sheffield Wednesday

MIDWEEK FIXTURES
(All games kick off at 7.45pm unless otherwise stated)

Tuesday 2nd October
Barnsley v Peterborough United
Bolton Wanderers v Leeds United (8pm)
Brighton & Hove Albion v Ipswich Town
Bristol City v Millwall
Burnley v Sheffield Wednesday
Cardiff City v Birmingham City
Charlton Athletic v Watford
Huddersfield Town v Leicester City
Hull City v Blackpool
Wolves v Crystal Palace

Wednesday 3rd October
Middlesbrough v Derby County
Nottingham Forest v Blackburn Rovers

2012/13 NPOWER CHAMPIONSHIP LEAGUE TABLE

Pos	Team	P	W	D	L	GD	Pts
1	Brighton	8	5	1	2	9	16
2	**Cardiff City**	8	5	1	2	6	16
3	Wolves	8	5	1	2	5	16
4	Blackburn	8	4	3	1	4	15
5	Leicester City	8	5	0	3	4	15
6	Huddersfield	8	4	2	2	5	14
7	Blackpool	8	4	1	3	6	13
8	Hull City	8	4	1	3	2	13
9	Leeds United	8	4	1	3	1	13
10	Crystal Palace	8	4	1	3	-1	13
11	Middlesbrough	8	4	0	4	-2	12
12	Barnsley	8	3	2	3	0	11
13	**Birmingham**	8	3	2	3	-5	11
14	Bristol City	8	3	1	4	1	10
15	Nottm Forest	7	2	4	1	1	10
16	Burnley	8	3	1	4	0	10
17	Bolton	8	3	1	4	-2	10
18	Watford	8	3	1	4	-3	10
19	Charlton	8	2	3	3	-1	9
20	Derby County	7	2	2	3	1	8
21	Millwall	8	2	1	5	-6	7
22	Sheffield Wed	8	2	1	5	-6	7
23	Ipswich Town	8	1	3	4	-10	6
24	Peterborough	8	1	0	7	-9	3

CF ELEVEN

THE OFFICIAL CARDIFF CITY FC MATCH PROGRAMME

CARDIFF CITY

VERSUS

WATFORD

TUE $^{23RD}_{OCT}$ 7:45PM

npower CHAMPIONSHIP   MATCH 12 £3

MATCH SPONSOR: HEATWISE

one game community
www.kickitout.org

Malaysia PUMA Player

06

MALKY MACKAY

BUILDING HOME

" IT CAN'T ALWAYS BE FLOWING PRETTY PASSING THAT WINS YOU GAMES, SO I AM PLEASED THAT WE HAVE MANAGED TO PICK UP POINTS PLAYING BOTH WAYS "

Good evening and welcome back for what feels like our first home match in ages.

The last time we were here, three weeks ago tonight, we picked up another very useful three points by beating Birmingham City 2-1 on a very wet and windy Welsh night. Lee Clark's team came here on the back of a very useful win at Brighton and they were determined to build on that result so we knew they would be difficult to break down. Craig Bellamy's opportunism was enough to get our noses in front and I was disappointed to allow them back into the game from a set piece. Thankfully parity did not last long as Mark Hudson quickly put us back in front and we went on to create enough good chances to have made the game much safer than it ended up.

We then made it three wins on the trot at Ipswich in the last match before the international break and we had to show plenty of spirit to do so having come from behind to snatch it at the death. It was clear that we were not at our best in the first half, but it was still sickening to concede right on half time thanks to such a bad refereeing mistake. When those kinds of things happen, some teams take the misfortune as a sign that it is not to be their day and capitulate in the game. Thankfully we followed the other path and used it as a spur to get back into the game and then go on to win it.

The Championship is such a difficult league to play in and get out of and there will be plenty of games when teams have to scrap for the points because they are not at their best. It can't always be flowing pretty passing that wins you games, so I am pleased that we have managed to pick up points playing both ways so far this campaign.

It was then disappointing to come back from the break with a defeat at Nottingham Forest on Saturday. It's an old cliché but goals do change games. There was nothing between the teams in the first 25 minutes then we

had a mad five minutes and found ourselves 2-0 down. In order to come back from that, it was important to start the second half well, so I was doubly frustrated to concede so soon after half-time. Finding ourselves 3-0 down against a good team gave us a real mountain to climb but we went on to create enough chances to claw all three goals back. Heidar gave us a lifeline and I felt confident that we had it within us to grab at least a point, but a combination of good goalkeeping and below-par finishing meant we came up short.

The last time we lost we showed an excellent reaction by winning our next three games, so we're glad that the next match has come around so quickly, giving us an opportunity to bounce straight back. Tonight also sees my old team Watford in town, so I bid Gianfranco Zola, his staff and players a warm Welsh welcome. There has been a lot of change at Vicarage Road in the 15 months since I left so there will not be too many familiar faces amongst them tonight but I'd also like to extend my welcome to two former colleagues who remain very good friends – their goalkeeping coach Alec Chamberlain and kit man Will Jones. I look forward to catching up with them after the game.

Continuing the subject of former Watford players, you will have seen that Academy Manager Neal Ardley left us last week to take up the Manager's job at Wimbledon. We wish Neal well in his new job and thank him for his contribution during his five years here. In the meantime, the youngsters are in good hands with Geraint Twose taking over on an interim basis while we open up applications for the permanent job. It's a very important position to be filled, particularly with the advent of the new EPPP regulations, so we have to make sure we appoint the best man and give him the tools to make our academy a vital part of the club's future success.

CARDIFF CITY 2
Bellamy (39), Hudson (57)

BIRMINGHAM CITY 1
Lita (54)

TUESDAY ▶ 2ND OCTOBER ▶ 7.45PM | Full Attendance 20,278

🏠 **19,722**

🚌 **506**

MALKY

"It was always going to be a tough game, but on another day I think we could have scored four or five. The work-rate made the difference, starting with Craig Bellamy at centre forward and working all the way back. We closed down and pressed Birmingham and overall I thought the quality was great."

CLARK

"We deserved at least a point. We passed it around well and got a deserved equaliser, but them getting back in the game so quickly was a blow. I've looked back and Bellamy wasn't offside. We should have dealt with it; Jack should have come and punched it. Now we've just got to push on."

On a night blighted by torrential rain, the Blues initially controlled possession, with Wade Elliott and Leroy Lita combining well early on to force David Marshall into a fantastic save. Heidar Helguson then created a great opportunity for Aron Gunnarsson, though the midfielder directed his shot straight at Jack Butland. But Cardiff were galvanised by Peter Whittingham on 38 minutes. The playmaker lofted a pinpoint pass over the top to the advancing Mark Hudson, who beat the offside trap expertly. Squaring the ball across goal, the skipper laid on the easiest of finishes for Craig Bellamy to slot home for the opener.

Seven minutes into the second half though and Birmingham were level. Hudson was booked for a challenge on Lita, the resultant free kick whipped in by Elliott, for the striker to beat the offside trap and make things all square. But it wasn't long before the Bluebirds were back in control; Bellamy's deflected cross led to a corner, Whittingham as ever put it into the danger zone, before that man Hudson fired off-balance past Butland to restore his side's lead. It was a lead that City wouldn't relinquish – and it ensured them a record fifth successive home victory.

HUDSON

"We knew Birmingham were going to make it difficult for us, on the back of a good result for them on the weekend. We had a slow start but we have ground it out, which is something we've become good at. You need to win your home games then pick up points away from home. We're doing that."

FANS SAY
"City overcame a stubborn Birmingham side who looked as if a draw would have suited them. But the Bluebirds' persistent attacking style wore them down to take three valuable and deserved points." – *Gerry Gill*

THE BREAK DOWN

REFEREE: Mr. K. Friend

POSSESSION
48%   52%

SHOTS
ON 5
OFF 3

The Post-match reaction from Malky Mackay, e Clark and Mark udson on Cardiff y Player

CARDIFF CITY Player

rdiff City: Marshall, cNaughton, Taylor, Hudson , Connolly, Whittingham, one (Kim), Gunnarsson, ason, Helguson, Bellamy (Cowie).
bs not used: wis, Turner, Kiss, nway, likonja.

Birmingham City: Butland, Caldwell, Davies, Spector, Packwood (Hurst), Robinson, Burke, Elliott, Fahey, Løvenkrands (Redmond), Lita (King).
Subs not used: Doyle, Mullins, Ambrose, Zigic.

89

My back yard. Joe Mason out-jumps opposing striker Marlon King.

IPSWICH TOWN 1
Campbell (45)

CARDIFF CITY 2
Helguson (63,87)

SATURDAY ▶ 6TH OCTOBER ▶ 5.20PM | Full Attendance 16,434

🏠 16,181

🚌 253

Malaysia

City remained top of the Championship after coming from behind to pick up a rare three points at Portman Road.

A first half that was absent of major talking points was turned on its head with the final touch of it, as Ipswich took the lead in controversial fashion. Mark Hudson's slip allowed the home side to attack via their left wing, and the resulting cross from Lee Martin was converted via the hand of striker DJ Campbell. The striker seemed shocked at the referee's failure to disallow his effort as he wheeled away in celebration.

But the Bluebirds took just fifteen minutes of the second half to level things. Substitute Craig Conway played a dangerous diagonal cross into the area which Ipswich keeper Scott Loach fumbled to the feet of Heidar Helguson for the easiest of finishes. With the game all square it was the Bluebirds who looked in control for the next twenty minutes. Their dominance was rewarded with the winning goal just a few minutes before full time, as Helguson got between Richard Creswell and Loach to fire a free header into the net.

FANS SAY
"Ipswich away is never an easy place to go, but the side's battling attitude got them one of the best results of the season so far. Even after being cheated for their goal, Helguson took advantage of two mistakes to win it." – *Liam Davies*

MALKY
"I thought we completely dominated the second half. During the first half we didn' make the right decisions or put the balls into the correct areas, but during the second I thought we worked the bal into those areas really well. Craig Conway came on and stretched them – I'm delighted with his overall performance."

JEWELL
"Big errors cost us the game today. We had a bit of fortune with the goal, though we were the better team in the first half. I don't like to single players out but there's no denying that two goalkeeping errors have cost us the game. It was the manner of their goals which saw our heads drop today."

HELGUSON
"This was a great win for us. We're top of the table for two weeks as we go into the international break and that's a good feeling. We have earned three wins on spin now – and six wins out of sever games played, while we all know that we really should have won at Palace as well."

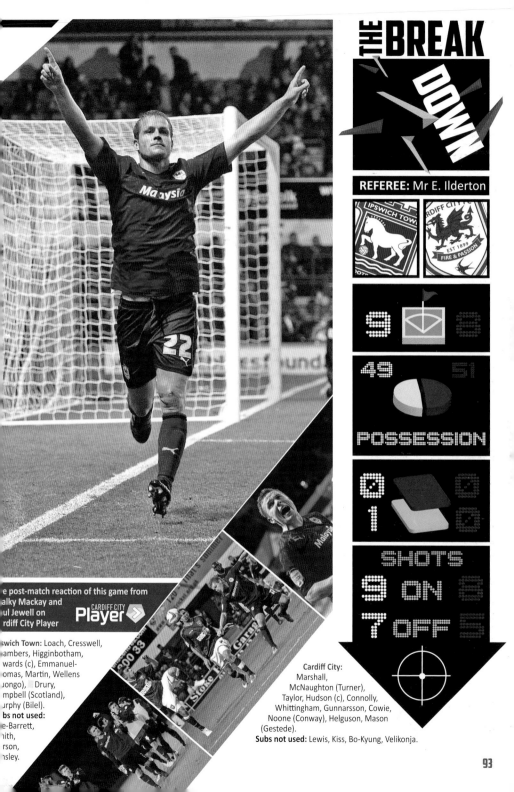

REFEREE: Mr E. Ilderton

9

49   51

POSSESSION

0
1

SHOTS
9 ON
7 OFF

e post-match reaction of this game from
alky Mackay and
ul Jewell on
rdiff City Player

CARDIFF CITY
Player

swich Town: Loach, Cresswell,
ambers, Higginbotham,
wards (c), Emmanuel-
omas, Martin, Wellens
uongo), Drury,
mpbell (Scotland),
urphy (Bilel).
bs not used:
e-Barrett,
hith,
rson,
hsley.

Cardiff City:
Marshall,
McNaughton (Turner),
Taylor, Hudson (c), Connolly,
Whittingham, Gunnarsson, Cowie,
Noone (Conway), Helguson, Mason
(Gestede).
Subs not used: Lewis, Kiss, Bo-Kyung, Velikonja.

Instant Karma. A Helguson brace cancels out DJ Campbell's handled opener at Portman Road.

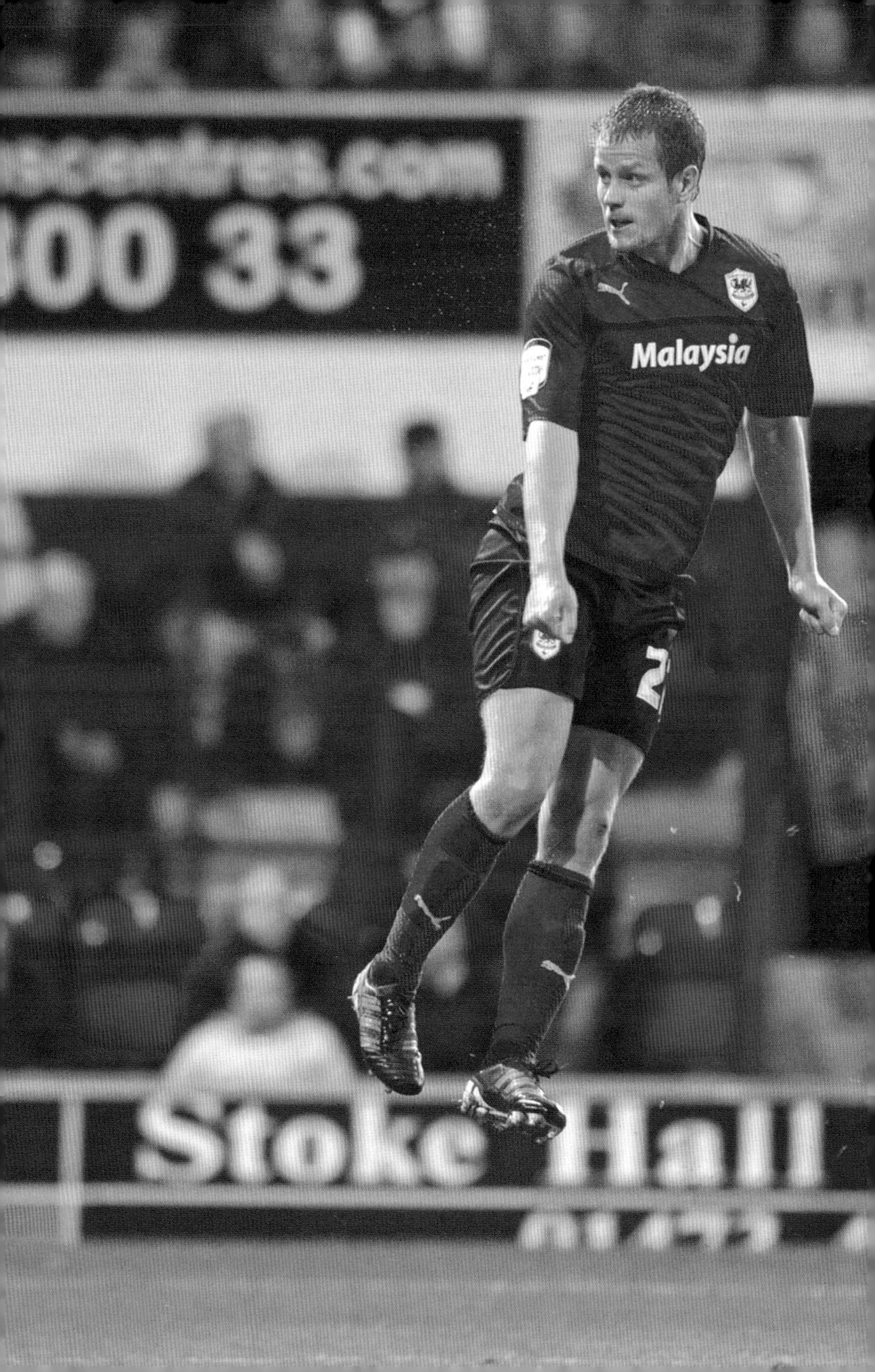

Malaysia
300 33
Stoke Hall

NOTT'M FOREST 3
Reid (25), Ayala (27), Sharp (47)

CARDIFF CITY 1
Helguson (74)

SATURDAY ▶ 20TH OCTOBER ▶ 3.00PM | Full Attendance 21,491

🏠 **19,596**

🚌 **1,895**

MALKY

"We couldn't do much about Andy Reid's free kick but the other two goals were basically defensive errors and something we have to look at. To be fair the players had a go at it ar had thirteen attempts their goal in the seconc half. On another day w might have got someth from the game."

O'DRISCOLL

"We scored good goals today. Andy Reid has been scoring goals like the one he did today throughout his career and it came at a good time. Cardiff went mor direct and were fightin for a lot of balls on the edge of our box, but w dug in and won the gar on the strength of wha we did in the first half."

TAYLOR

"We're disappointed at way we conceded today especially as we started quite well and finished too. We've got to dust ourselves down and get three points at home to Watford on Tuesday nig We took a lot of suppor today and they were brilliant as always."

Forest started well at the City Ground in this one, without causing too much danger to David Marshall. But Andy Reid's pinpoint free kick on twenty-five minutes left the City 'keeper with no chance as it pinged off the crossbar and into the net. Cardiff were then caught out again following the restart, Greg Halford finding Daniel Ayala in the box with a floated cross that the Spanish defender was unable not to profit from.

Into the second half and with Cardiff eager to find a foothold in the game, Forest capitalised in dramatic fashion. Billy Sharp exchanged passes with half-time substitute Radoslav Majewski, beating the offside trap to fire home past Marshall with only eighty seconds of the half gone. At 3-0 down it was going to take something special for City to take anything, though Heidar Helguson's goal sixteen minutes from time set up an exciting closing spell. Had Tommy Smith's excellent effort not struck the upright, then maybe it could have been a different story, especially following the late dismissal of Adlene Guedioura for a second bookable offence. Unfortunately, City would taste defeat for the third time this season.

FANS SAY "We didn't get going until the game was lost. If we had played like we did in the last twenty minutes of the second half for the full ninety I think we would have got something." – *Jon Tucker*

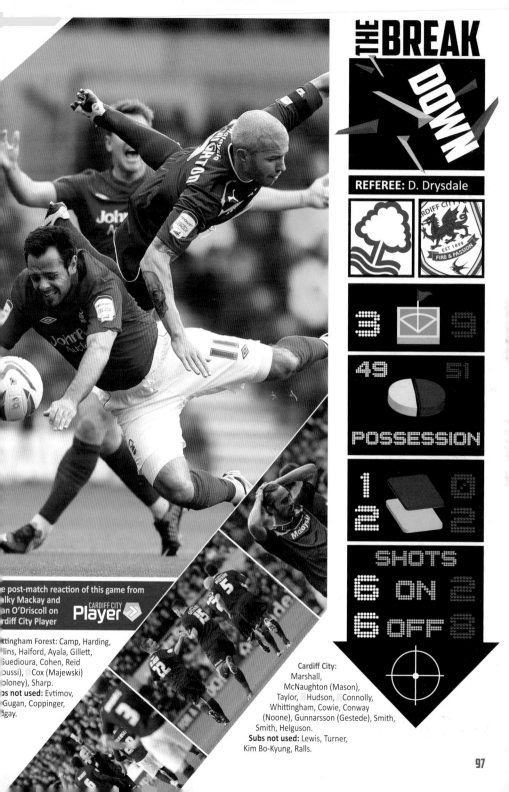

THE BREAKDOWN

REFEREE: D. Drysdale

EST 1899
FIRE & PASSION

3 | 3

49 | 51

POSSESSION

1 | 0
2 |

SHOTS
6 ON 2
6 OFF 3

the post-match reaction of this game from
ilky Mackay and
an O'Driscoll on
rdiff City Player

CARDIFF CITY Player >>

ttingham Forest: Camp, Harding,
lins, Halford, Ayala, Gillett,
uedioura, Cohen, Reid
oussi), Cox (Majewski)
oloney), Sharp.
s not used: Evtimov,
Gugan, Coppinger,
lgay.

Cardiff City:
Marshall,
McNaughton (Mason),
Taylor, Hudson, Connolly,
Whittingham, Cowie, Conway
(Noone), Gunnarsson (Gestede), Smith,
Smith, Helguson.
Subs not used: Lewis, Turner,
Kim Bo-Kyung, Ralls.

97

I'll need that! Gunnar asks a City Ground ball-boy for his towel.

THE CHAMPIONSHIP

TOIL AND TROUBLE

Like strawberries and cream, a burger and fries, or Halloween season and a raft of sub-standard horror movies — Championship football and heartbreak are two things that go hand-in-hand. Life is tough in this division at the best of times, let alone when you're struggling for form and desperate for a win. So, if the old adage about bad luck evening itself out over the course of the season is remotely true, then fans of several clubs should be looking positively towards happier times ahead. Football's never that simple though, is it?

The International break seems to have done little to have changed the fortunes for Paul Jewell and his **Ipswich Town** side, as two weeks after squandering a lead against ourselves, they went and did exactly the same on Saturday. This time it was **Hull City** who benefited, as Steve Bruce's men ensured that Jay Emanuel-Thomas' first half strike counted for little. Nick Proschwitz's late double for the Tigers, the second of those coming in injury time, leaves Town twenty-third in the table with just seven points to their name.

That's one more point than bottom placed **Peterborough United** have though, as they too saw a valuable draw disappear in the ninetieth minute when **Watford's** Matěj Vydra tucked away a penalty after the surging Daniel Pudil has been felled.

The goal handed the Posh their ninth defeat from eleven league encounters so far this season; incredib they are still yet to draw a match and are now five points away from safety.

That deficit could have been larger though, had **Brist City** not fallen to a late goal themselves at manager-less Bolton Wanderers. Steve Davies' early double ha the Robins in command at the Reebok Stadium, yet t Trotters dug deep and eventually dug themselves out of that substantial hole thanks to goals from Chris Eagles and Jay Spearing. Martin Petrov completed the come-back seven minutes from tim to cap a stunning turn-around and pile further misery on Dere McInnes' *(pictured)* team who are now five matches without a win.

It also leaves Bristol just a point behind **Birmingham City,** after they suffered their own share of disappointme on Saturday at home to **Leicester City.** St Andrew's isn't a happy hunting ground at present for Blues, who conceded five there to Barnsley last month and have just two home wins to their name all season. It was Leicester's Ben Marshall who made sure th total didn't rise to three for the time being with a trademark strike from distance. As well as repercussions at the bottom of the league, that goal also lifted the Foxes to the top of the table, taking advantage of our struggles in Nottingham to regain top spot on goal difference.

►► CHAMPIONSHIP LEADING SCORERS 2012/13

1	2	3	4	5
12	**8**	**7**	**7**	**6**
► CHARLIE AUSTIN BURNLEY	► LUCIANO BECCHIO LEEDS UNITED	► CRAIG DAVIES BARNSLEY	► GLENN MURRAY CRYSTAL PALACE	► DARIUS HENDERSON MILLWALL

SEEING RED

The majority of Championship fans will be delighted to get back into the full swing of league football following an international break that brought mixed fortunes for the home nations. However, the Tricebirds' 3-1 weekend defeat at the City Ground came as a disappointment, particularly as we had lost just one of seven previous matches.

With the game all but over, a seemingly insignificant second yellow for Nottingham Forest's Algerian winger **Adlène Guedioura** may have slipped under the radar. It was, however, his second dismissal of the season having already seen red for a petulant kick against Crystal Palace last month. With **Dexter Blackstock's** *(pictured)* recent dismissal against local rivals Derby County to their name as well, Forest have picked up more red cards than any other Championship side this year. They also have a league high of 25 yellow cards, leaving them 5 points adrift at the bottom of the fair play league. This is a somewhat surprising statistic for a team now managed by Sean O'Driscoll – a known advocate of stylish, attractive football.

Tonight's visitors **Watford** are not much higher in the disciplinary standings after two of their players were given their marching orders in successive games this month. **Matěj Vydra**, perhaps the most impressive of the **Hornets'** young loanees, was the victim of a harsh dismissal at the Riverside just one match after **Fernando Forestieri** saw a second yellow for an alleged dive. **Birmingham City** are the only other team to receive more than one red card, although they have recorded ten fewer yellows than Watford's total of 22.

The best behaved in the division to date are **Hull City** and **Derby County** with just 9 yellow cards apiece, while the Tricebirds find themselves in middle of the fair play league having not received a red card since Darcy Blake's dismissal against Barnsley over two years ago!

DID YOU KNOW?

Cardiff City have no fewer than five former Watford players in their regular first team squad who racked up 658 appearances for the Hornets between them. Both **Tommy Smith** and **Heidar Helguson** enjoyed two separate spells at the club – Tommy played around 300 games in the process, while Heidar was their record signing in 2000, joining for £1.5 million from Lillestrøm. **Jordon Mutch** and **Andrew Taylor** both spent a season on loan at Vicarage Road as well, while **Don Cowie** made the move to South Wales with Malky Mackay having been a star man in the Golden Boys' midfield for three seasons.

npower
FOOTBALL LEAGUE

LATEST RESULTS
Burnley 1–0 Blackpool
Birmingham City 1–1 Leicester City
Bolton Wanderers 3–2 Bristol City
Brighton & Hove Albion 0–1 Middlesbrough
Charlton Athletic 0–1 Barnsley
Derby County 1–1 Blackburn Rovers
Huddersfield Town 2–1 Wolves
Hull City 2–1 Ipswich Town
Nottingham Forest 3–1 Cardiff City
Watford 1–0 Peterborough United
Crystal Palace 2–2 Millwall

MIDWEEK FIXTURES
(All games kick off at 7.45pm unless otherwise stated)

Tuesday 23rd October
Barnsley v Crystal Palace
Blackpool v Nottingham Forest (8pm)
Bristol City v Burnley
Cardiff City v Watford
Ipswich Town v Derby County
Leeds United v Charlton Athletic
Leicester City v Brighton & Hove Albion
Middlesbrough v Hull City
Millwall v Birmingham City
Peterborough United v Huddersfield Town
Wolves v Bolton Wanderers

Wednesday 24th October
Blackburn Rovers v Sheffield Wednesday

2012/13 NPOWER CHAMPIONSHIP LEAGUE TABLE

Pos	Team	P	W	D	L	GD	Pts
1	Leicester City	11	7	1	3	8	22
2	**Cardiff City**	11	7	1	3	6	22
3	Huddersfield	11	6	2	3	5	20
4	Crystal Palace	11	6	2	3	1	20
5	Wolves	11	6	1	4	4	19
6	Hull City	11	6	1	4	3	19
7	Middlesbrough	11	6	1	4	0	19
8	Brighton	11	5	3	3	8	18
9	Leeds United	11	5	3	3	2	18
10	Blackburn	11	4	5	2	3	17
11	Nottm Forest	11	4	5	2	3	17
12	Blackpool	11	5	1	5	4	16
13	**Watford**	11	5	1	5	-2	16
14	Derby County	11	3	5	3	2	14
15	Burnley	11	4	2	5	0	14
16	Bolton	11	4	2	5	-2	14
17	Barnsley	11	4	2	5	-2	14
18	Charlton	11	3	3	5	-1	12
19	Millwall	11	3	3	5	-5	12
20	Birmingham	11	3	3	5	-7	12
21	Bristol City	11	3	2	6	-2	11
22	Sheffield Wed	11	2	3	6	-7	9
23	Ipswich Town	11	1	4	6	-12	7
24	Peterborough	11	2	0	9	-9	6

CF ELEVEN

THE OFFICIAL CARDIFF CITY FC MATCH PROGRAMME

CARDIFF CITY

VERSUS

BURNLEY

SAT 27TH OCT 3:00PM

npower CHAMPIONSHIP   MATCH 13 £3

MATCH SPONSOR: eCOSWAY

TEAM SPONSOR:
WALES INTERNATIONAL FREIGHT

Show Racism the Red Card
Wales

Malaysia PUMA Player

07

MALKY MACKAY

ENDEAVOUR DELIVERS

Good afternoon and welcome back to Cardiff City Stadium for today's visit of Burnley.

In my notes for Tuesday's game against Watford I spoke of the need to find ways to win even when the football is not flowing, so I was really pleased that we kept plugging away and were rewarded with a late winning goal for the third time this season.

We were disappointed to have gone behind to a goal from a set piece, but we had already seen enough evidence this season to know that we certainly have both the quality and the necessary battling instincts to overcome an early setback, so I was pleased that we kept our focus and were eventually rewarded.

Three times now we have scored late winners which have turned a haul of three points into nine points and I can't help but think that these small margins are the kind of thing that can prove decisive over the course of a season. As I said, it was also the third time we have won matches after conceding the first goal, which is a testament to both the players themselves and our medical and conditioning staff who have made sure that we'll never be found wanting in the fitness department.

People may point to the fact that Watford finished the game with just nine men, but in some ways that did not make our task any easier. We were already dominating possession when it was 11 v 11 and when the red cards came, it gave their players something to hold on to and fight for. Although I thought the referee got both decisions right, Watford were still fired up by their sense of injustice, making them an even more awkward opponent.

Aron Gunnarsson's winning goal was also a good indication of the spirit we have in the squad. I opted to start with Gunnar on the bench — something I am more able to do with the deeper squad we have this season — but he responded to his disappointment in the most positive fashion, by coming on and grabbing the winning goal.

I'm expecting another tough match here today because Burnley have made the long trip to Wales buoyed by wins in their last two games and scoring plenty of goals in the process. They have a strong squad with lots of good players so it is not a surprise that their results have recently turned around. I welcome Terry Pashley, their caretaker manager, and his staff here today. Terry must think this management lark's easy with maximum points from his two games in charge, so hopefully we'll manage to change that today!

Much has been made in the press of the fact that we have now won all six of our home games this season and I won't deny that these little milestones are nice, but they pale into insignificance against the bigger picture of what we are trying to achieve in taking this club forward. Therefore, I'm not shouting from the rooftops right now – but I hope to be doing so in May.

You may have seen yesterday that we made a move to bring in Fulham youngster Kerim Frei on loan to see us through the next few weeks. Kerim is an exciting talent who we have been following for some time and it speaks volumes for us as a club that Fulham, the player and his representatives felt Cardiff would be a good move for his developing career.

He played sixteen Premier League games last season as well as seven in the Europa League which gives you some idea of his pedigree, particularly considering he's still only 18 years old.

At the time of writing this all of the paperwork had been signed and we were awaiting FIFA ratification to confirm that he is available for today's game, but I'm sure he'll be an asset for us. Please join me in giving Kerim a warm Welsh welcome today.

Enjoy today's game. As always we are counting on and appreciate your continued excellent support.

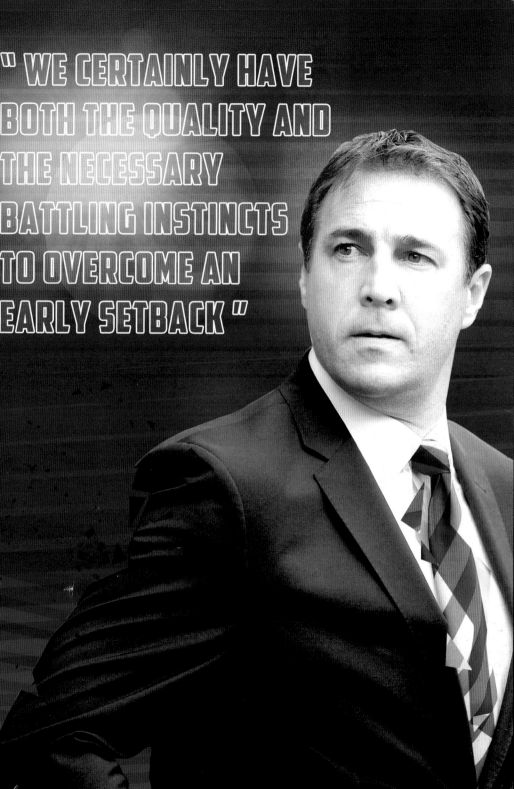

" WE CERTAINLY HAVE BOTH THE QUALITY AND THE NECESSARY BATTLING INSTINCTS TO OVERCOME AN EARLY SETBACK "

CARDIFF CITY 2

Whittingham (Pen 71), Gunnarsson (90+1)

WATFORD 1

Hoban (28)

TUESDAY ▶ 23RD OCTOBER ▶ 7.45PM | Full Attendance 20,077

🏠 **19,653**

🚌 **424**

MALKY

"We knew full well that was going to be a very tough game for us tonight – it's why Watford have won the away games that they have this season, as the sit in there and come ou and attack well on the counter. We knew that we were going to have t be patient to deal with that, which we were."

ZOLA

"I'm very disappointed at that result and I fee sick for my players. It doesn't feel right after a performance like tha for us to come out of i with nothing. Obviously the two red cards changed the game but I did not think that we would lose. We were holding on right to the end."

With Cardiff dominating play and possession, Watford relied on catching the home side on the counter attack. This tactic paid dividends in the twenty-eighth minute, as the Hornets won a corner from a quick break and Tommie Hoban was there to force the ball the ball over the line from close range after David Marshall had initially saved Marco Cassetti's header.

Sixty-three minutes into the tie, Watford were reduced to ten men, after a challenge between Daniel Pudil on Craig Noone. Pudil was alleged to have made contact with the face of the City winger with his hand and thus, given his marching orders. Cardiff equalised in the seventy-first minute when Peter Whittingham scored from the penalty spot, before Watford's fourth red card in as many games was shown to Nathaniel Chalobah for a second bookable offence.

City threw everything at Watford in search of the winner, and that finally came in injury time as substitute Aron Gunnarsson powered home a Noone cross with his head, helping break a sixty-five year-old record in the process.

COWIE

"Obviously we are delighted; we left it late b the most important thing was that we got the three points. As soon as they go down to nine men, people expected us to go and win We had to be patient, but eventually we got the goa and we are still right up there. Our fans supported us to the end and were superb."

FANS SAY "All credit to the boys, they kept going right until the end. That's twice in the last three games that we've been behind at half-time and turned it around to get all three points. Great character and belief." – *David John*

THE BREAKDOWN

REFEREE: M. Heywood

CARDIFF CITY FC · EST 1899 · FIRE & PASSION

WATFORD

0 ⚑ 4

52% 48%

POSSESSION

6 2
1 3

SHOTS

6 ON 6

11 OFF 5

Post-match reaction from Malky Mackay, Gianfranco Zola and Don Cowie on Cardiff City Player

CARDIFF CITY Player ➤

Cardiff City: Marshall, Taylor, Hudson (c), Turner (Gestede, 83), Connolly, Whittingham, Cowie, Noone, Smith Gunnarsson, 84), Helguson, Bellamy Mason, 45).

Subs not used: Lewis, McNaughton, Conway, ...m.

Watford:
Almunia (c), Hall,
Yeates, Hogg, Doyley,
Pudil, Vydra (Anya, 60),
Cassetti (Thompson 71), Hoban,
Geijo (Deeney, 74), Chalobah.
Subs not used: Bond, Murray, Abdil, Forestieri.

107

Agony and ecstasy. Tommy Smith tears a hamstring against Watford that would keep him out until the New Year.

THE CHAMPIONSHIP
SETTLING IN OK?

It often transpires that the bookies' favourites for relegation ahead of each Championship season commencing are the three sides newly promoted from League One.

Favourites for promotion, accordingly, are regularly the triumvirate of clubs demoted from the top flight the previous May. Sometimes there's accuracy in the predictions, sometimes there isn't. Either way, it's a fairly safe starting point for the garden-variety Championship observer.

So let's take a look at how the six newbies are faring on the back of midweek results. In fairness, **Blackburn Rovers** are suggesting that they're in with a good shout of an immediate return to the Premier League, sitting as they are in fifth place. Currently manager-less Rovers – despite all of their off-field dramas – saw off fellow new boys **Sheffield Wednesday** 1-0 on Wednesday evening to bolster a very strong start enjoyed under the now departed (and uber-maligned) Steve Kean. Their form isn't great though – their midweek win was their first in six games. For Dave Jones' Owls however, that was their seventh defeat from their last nine games, leaving them twenty-third in the division. An impressive start, at this moment at least, seems misleading and, potentially, irrelevant.

Wolves look like they could follow the instant return pattern, but their form, too, is suspect. A 2-2 draw with another relegated side, **Bolton Wanderers,** on Tuesday meant they've taken just four points from the last twelve on offer. As for Bolton, they'll be hoping that newly-nabbed manager Dougie Freedman can kick-start a Championship campaign which some thought they would dominate. They sit sixteenth going into the weekend – with just one win in their last five.

Which leaves us with just two remaining newbies formerly of League One – the first of whom is treading water above the relegation zone, the second defying all expectations. **Charlton Athletic** are currently eighteenth after winning the third tier last term, on thirteen points with one win in five and four clear of the relegation zone. But it's Simon Grayson's **Huddersfield Town** who have put a real spanner in the works so far, having won six of their last ten games to sit just outside the Play-Off places in seventh.

Whether the six newbies defy expectations or follow a predictable course come the end of the season is still anyone's guess. What is for certain is that a quarter of the way into the season, the Championship continues to sell itself as one of the most unpredictable and uncompromising divisions in the upper echelons of European football.

⟫ TOP SCORERS BY TEAM

1	2	3	4	5
26	23	22	21	21
⟩ BURNLEY	⟩ BRISTOL CITY	⟩ CARDIFF CITY	⟩ CRYSTAL PALACE	⟩ BLACKPOOL

COMEBACK KINGS

The Bluebirds victory over **Watford** on Tuesday evening set a new club record as we secured an unprecedented sixth home win on the bounce. However, City also created another interesting statistic in doing so – along with **Crystal Palace** and **Hull City** we have now picked up more points from a losing position than any other Championship team, fighting back to win on three separate occasions. Meanwhile, today's visitors **Burnley** have been on the other side of several comebacks this term as only last place (and now manager-less) **Ipswich Town** have let more points slip.

The character shown by City to bounce back has pleased Malky Mackay several times already. A Peter Whittingham hat trick saw off **Wolves** last month as we took the lead just five minutes after falling behind to Bakary Sako's early opener. And the trick was repeated at Portman Road, as DJ Campbell's controversial goal for **Ipswich Town** was cancelled out by a Heidar Helguson brace.

Burnley have drawn twice and lost three times from the eight occasions that they've gone ahead this season, dropping thirteen points in the process. In fact, had they hung on to all of their leads they'd be sitting five points clear at the top of the table! City have shared some of their pain, however, as both sides fell victim to spectacular Palace comebacks – the Eagles turning a two goal deficit into victory on both occasions. City fans will be reassured by the fact that it remains the only time that we have failed to win after taking the lead this campaign.

Elsewhere in the Championship, **Leeds United** and **Wolves** have both surrendered more than ten points from winning positions this season, while on the flip side, **Brighton** and **Leicester City** have won every single game in which they've taken the lead.

DID YOU KNOW?

Up until 2009, Burnley's current man of the moment **Charlie Austin** was playing non-league football in conjunction with his job as a bricklayer. He represented Kintbury Rangers and local club Hungerford Town before moving to play for Poole Town as a semi-professional for the 2008-09 season. His 48 goals in 42 appearances that term attracted the interest of Swindon Town, for whom he signed as a professional for the 2009/10 campaign. 31 Robins goals in 54 appearances preceded a move to Burnley the following season, where he's so far notched up 31 in 56. At just twenty-three years of age, the future appears very bright for Charlie indeed.

MIDWEEK RESULTS

Barnsley 1–1 Crystal Palace
Blackburn Rovers 1–0 Sheffield Wednesday
Blackpool 2–2 Nottingham Forest
Bristol City 3–4 Burnley
Cardiff City 2–1 Watford
Ipswich Town 1–2 Derby County
Leeds United 1–1 Charlton Athletic
Leicester City 1–0 Brighton & Hove Albion
Middlesbrough 2–0 Hull City
Millwall 3–3 Birmingham City
Peterborough United 3–1 Huddersfield Town
Wolves 2–2 Bolton Wanderers

TODAY'S GAMES
(All games kick off at 3pm unless otherwise stated)

Barnsley v Nottingham Forest
Blackburn Rovers v Watford
Blackpool v Brighton & Hove Albion
Bristol City v Hull City (5.20pm)
Cardiff City v Burnley
Ipswich Town v Sheffield Wednesday
Leeds United v Birmingham City
Leicester City v Crystal Palace
Middlesbrough v Bolton Wanderers
Millwall v Huddersfield Town
Peterborough United v Derby County
Wolves v Charlton Athletic

2012/13 NPOWER CHAMPIONSHIP LEAGUE TABLE

Pos	Team	P	W	D	L	GD	Pts
1	Leicester City	12	8	1	3	9	25
2	**Cardiff City**	12	8	1	3	7	25
3	Middlesbrough	12	7	1	4	2	22
4	Crystal Palace	12	6	3	3	1	21
5	Blackburn	12	5	5	2	4	20
6	Wolves	12	6	2	4	4	20
7	Huddersfield	12	6	2	4	3	20
8	Leeds United	12	5	4	3	2	19
9	Hull City	12	6	1	5	1	19
10	Brighton	12	5	3	4	7	18
11	Nottm Forest	12	4	6	2	3	18
12	Blackpool	12	5	2	5	4	17
13	Derby County	12	4	5	3	3	17
14	**Burnley**	12	5	2	5	1	17
15	Watford	12	5	1	6	-3	16
16	Bolton	12	4	3	5	-2	15
17	Barnsley	12	4	3	5	-2	15
18	Charlton	12	3	4	5	-1	13
19	Millwall	12	3	4	5	-5	13
20	Birmingham	12	3	4	5	-7	13
21	Bristol City	12	3	2	7	-3	11
22	Peterborough	12	3	0	9	-7	9
23	Sheffield Wed	12	2	3	7	-8	9
24	Ipswich Town	12	1	4	7	-13	7

CF ELEVEN

THE OFFICIAL CARDIFF CITY FC MATCH PROGRAMME

CARDIFF CITY

VERSUS

HULL CITY

SAT 10TH NOV 3:00PM

npower CHAMPIONSHIP MATCH 16 £3

MATCH SPONSOR: THE VALE RESORT

 LEST WE FORGET

Malaysia PUMA Player

08

MALKY MACKAY

QUALITY COUNTS

Good afternoon and welcome back for today's game with Hull City.

I'll start by extending that welcome to Steve Bruce, his staff, players and everyone who has made the long journey from Humberside today. Last time we were here, two weeks ago today, we produced what I consider to be our most complete performance of the season to date when we beat Burnley 4-0. From the very first whistle, we played with an intensity and aggression which made us very difficult to deal with, particularly when mixed with the quality and skill which we have in abundance in this squad.

On days like that I don't think there is a team in the Championship who can handle us and it was certainly true that the final scoreline in no way flattered us. If anything we could have scored one or two more.

It was also pleasing to see us keep a clean sheet, something I appreciate probably as much as the four goals we managed to score. Coming into the game, Burnley were the division's top scorers, so we had to be at our best to keep them out – and in doing so become just the second team this season to prevent them from scoring.

We then travelled north last weekend for the televised match at Bolton. As has been reported I was very frustrated to come away from the Reebok with nothing, because I thought our performance merited more than we got. For the first hour of the game, we were in total command and deserved the lead which Craig Noone's goal had given us, but we then managed to concede two goals in quick succession which left us with nothing.

I also felt we got the worst of the officiating on the day. We certainly should have had a penalty in the last minute when Mark Hudson was rugby tackled in the area and that would have given us the chance to earn the point, which I felt our efforts deserved.

Tuesday's game at Charlton was a very difficult one

to analyse. Again we started well and were comfortably on top before a series of individual mistakes from us turned the match on its head. Despite all the problems we went through on the night, we still did enough in the last ten minutes to almost recover a three goal deficit and nick a point, so I was encouraged to see that the team kept on going.

What we all know about the Championship is that there's sufficient quality in the league for any team to beat any other on their day. If we are not at our best, we will get turned over, regardless of whether our opponents are top or bottom of the table. There's quality in all twenty-four of the squads, so we will never be accused of or guilty of underestimating our opponents. There will be plenty more surprising results in the league this season, probably continuing this weekend.

Sometimes the best time to learn about the people in your club – players, staff and fans – is when results are not going your way, so it's even more important that we all stick together at the moment and continue to work as hard as possible to bring success to Cardiff. I've said it before, but it bears repeating; there's no limit to what can be achieved by a hard-working group of dedicated people united by a common purpose and I'm pleased we have that here in South Wales.

Since Tuesday night we have sat down as a group, staff and players, and analysed the match in some detail in the knowledge that we have the quality and courage in the squad to go on another winning run and reclaim the leadership of the division quickly. We hope that run starts today, but also realise that we will need to produce another top quality performance to beat a very talented Hull side. We will also need your fantastic support as much as ever, so I look forward to hearing plenty of noise from the stands.

Enjoy the game.

" WE HAVE THE QUALITY AND COURAGE IN THE SQUAD TO GO ON ANOTHER WINNING RUN "

CARDIFF CITY 4

Mason (3), Noone (41), Connolly (82), Gunnarsson (85)

BURNLEY 0

SATURDAY ▶ 27TH OCTOBER ▶ 3.00PM Full Attendance 21,191

🏠 **20,714**

🚌 **477**

MALKY

"We've played against the top scorers in the league and top scorer Charlie Austin so to keep a clean sheet, tak our chances and be clinical at the other en I'm very pleased. The goals were excellent, but we could have had more. We kept going though, even at half-time at 2-0 up."

PASHLEY

"The goals we conceded were self-inflicted. After the first goal we never really recovered. We tried to be positive in the second half to try to get the next goal, but we conceded a third. Cardiff are top of the league and it's no fluke."

NOONE

"We dominated the entire game really. We said at half-time that w needed to keep it goin as we were on the fror foot; it was about doir it again after the break and we managed to do that. Today's performance was a lot better than against Watford."

It took all of three minutes for the Bluebirds to take the advantage in this one. Joe Mason surged from just inside City's half before offloading to Craig Noone out on the right wing. Noone, who looked dangerous throughout the half, produced a shot that smacked Burnley keeper Lee Grant's post and made its way to Mason, who had continued his run into the penalty area, and the striker put Cardiff ahead from close range. It was City who enjoyed the upper hand in most of the first half, and their sustained pressure led to Craig Noone doubling their lead after forty minutes, his shot from outside the penalty area being too hot for Grant to handle and bobbling over the line.

The second half was again a one-sided affair. To Burnley's credit, City had to wait until the eighty-first minute before scoring again though, Peter Whittingham's corner being headed in by Matthew Connolly to put City three in front. Substitute Aron Gunnarsson scored for his second successive game at the death after a good knock down by Rudy Gestede. City had regained top spot in the Championship.

FANS SAY "Don Cowie absolutely BOSSED the midfield. Best performance I've ever seen him play and Kim Bo-Kyung was outstanding as well. In fact, there wasn't a player that didn't impress me." – *Stephen Baker*

THE BREAKDOWN

REFEREE: N. Miller

6 ⚽ 6

60% 40%
POSSESSION

0 ▭ 1
0 ✗ 0
SHOTS
8 ON 6
7 OFF 4

st-match reaction from Malky Mackay,
rry Pashley and
aig Noone on
rdiff City Player

CARDIFF CITY Player

rdiff City: Marshall, Taylor,
dson (c), Turner, Connolly,
n (Gunnarsson),
hittingham, Cowie, Noone
ei), Helguson (Gestede),
ason.
bs not used: Lewis,
cNaughton,
nway,
nnarsson,
s.

Burnley:
Grant, Trippier,
Duff, Shackell (c),
McCann, Marney, Paterson
(Ings), Stanislas (Vokes), Mills,
Stock (Stewart), Austin.
Subs not used: Jensen, Lafferty,
Edgar, O'Neill.

117

A brief encounter. Loanee Kerim Frei impresses as a substitute against the Clarets.

NPOWER CHAMPIONSHIP

BOLTON 2
Petrov (Pen 69), N'Gog (74)

CARDIFF CITY 1
Noone (40)

SATURDAY ▶ 4TH NOVEMBER ▶ 5.20PM | Full Attendance **17,304**

🏠 **15,794**
🚌 **1,510**

MALKY

"Decisions change games. They got a penalty out of nothing and N'Gog was already diving when he was touched. The referee gives it, fair enough, but if he gives that he has to give Mark Hudson's penalty. It was unbelievable and I hope he takes a good look at his performance."

FREEDMAN

"I thought in the first half it was difficult to take that we were 1-0 down. I don't think we deserved that. This set of players had a setback at half-time but we got an excellent response from them. It was nothing magical; we just had a few words about belief."

There was only one shot on goal in the first half at the Reebok, but that one shot produced a goal. Five minutes before the break, Craig Noone found the ball at his feet inside the area, keeping his composure and taking advantage of Bolton 'keeper Adam Bogdan being unsighted to slot home.

Bolton increased intensity after the break in search of an equaliser and the introduction of David N'Gog really changed the game. First he won a penalty from which Martin Petrov scored, N'Gog going to ground after very minimal contact from Kim Bo-Kyung. The former Liverpool man scored the second goal himself, deflecting home a Sam Ricketts strike, before being shown a red card in the dying minutes for a second bookable offence.

Cardiff can rightly feel hard done by though, after being denied a penalty for what appeared to be a cynical foul by Stephen Warnock on Mark Hudson. David Marshall's last gasp strike after coming up for an injury time corner nearly made headlines, but it wasn't to be.

MARSHALL

"We have to grind out results when we need to. Results are going against us. A win today would have opened a gap for us, but Bolton are a tough team to play at their stadium and they made substitutions which made a difference. We have to look to ourselves."

FANS SAY "We dominated the game apart from a ten minute spell when N'Gog came on. I think we deserved at least a point. Marshall was so close to scoring and we were denied a stone wall penalty." – *Gareth Knight*

THE BREAKDOWN

REFEREE: T. Bates

7 | 🚩 | 13

49 | 51

POSSESSION

1 | 0
3 | 1

SHOTS

8 **ON** 5

5 **OFF** 1

post-match reaction of this game from
...lky Mackay and
...ugie Freedman on
...diff City Player

CARDIFF CITY Player ▶

...on Wanderers: Bogdan, Mills,
...les, Andrews, Knight, K.Davies
...(N'Gog), Warnock,
...Davies, Ricketts, Pratley,
...rov) Lee (Ream).
...s **not used:** Afobe,
...dell, Spearing,
...ch.

Cardiff City:
Marshall, Taylor,
Hudson, Turner,
Connolly, Whittingham,
Noone, Cowie, Kim (Gunnarsson)
Mason (Frei), Helguson (Gestede).
Subs not used: Lewis, Kiss, McNaughton,
Conway.

121

Not quite. David Marshall is denied a stoppage time equaliser as Ádám Bogdán saves with his face.

CHARLTON 5

Jackson (39,45), Stephens (54), Haynes (59), Hulse (65)

CARDIFF CITY 4

Helguson (4), Mason (24), Noone (90), Gunnarsson (90)

TUESDAY ▶ 6TH NOVEMBER ▶ 7.45PM Full Attendance **15,764**

🏠 **14,942**

🚌 **822**

Heidar Helguson had headed the Bluebirds into an early lead at the Valley, flicking Peter Whittingham's set-piece into the far corner of the goal. And twenty minutes later, City made it two. This time Whittingham's corner was headed against the bar by Turner after a Hudson flick on. Joe Mason capitalised on the subsequent goal mouth scramble, driving home.

Charlton pulled one back after a mistake by David Marshall. City's number one mispunched a high, looping cross straight to the feet of the home skipper Johnnie Jackson, who powered the ball into the top corner. And just minutes later Jackson equalised, heading home unmarked from a corner kick on the stroke of half-time.

Three Charlton goals in the second half took the game away from the Bluebirds. Dale Stephens inadvertently caught Marshall off his line from a long range free kick before Danny Haynes and Rob Hulse both headed home with the City defence in disarray. Two late consolations from Craig Noone and Aron Gunnarsson almost paved the way for a famous comeback, but it wasn't to be.

MALKY

"To give away five goals is unforgivable. We're 2-0 up and playing really well we make a mistake before half-time and they get their tails up and get back into it. It was a strange evening but it was one or which too many people had an off-night and when that happens then you can be punished — and we were."

POWELL

"We were playing the top of the table side and went 2-0 down, but then you saw resolve and character. Maybe we got the rub of the green with Dale Stephens' goal, but I felt Rob Hulse and Danny Haynes both led the line."

TAYLOR

"Sorry to all the fans for tonight's performance – it wasn't good enough. But we have two massive games at home to bounce back now, starting with Hull on Saturday. We'll stay positive as we know it's a long season."

FANS SAY "This game won't define our season, it's just so disappointing. We've still got to get behind the team on Saturday though – it's why we call ourselves supporters." – *Andrew Jenkins*

124

THE BREAKDOWN

REFEREE: K. Stroud

8  5

 59 41

POSSESSION

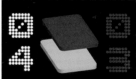

0 4

SHOTS

13 ON 12

3 OFF

e post-match reaction of this game from lky Mackay and tt Connolly on diff City Player

CARDIFF CITY Player

arlton Athletic: Hamer, Solly,
kar, Cort, Morrison; Dervite,
nes (Wright-Phillips),
kson (c), Pritchard,
tephens (Hollands),
se.
s not used:
ton, Taylor, Fox,
en, Azeez.

Cardiff City:
Marshall,
Connolly, Hudson (c),
Turner, Taylor, Frei (Bo-
Kyung), Whittingham, Cowie
(Gunnarsson), Noone, Helguson
(Gestede), Mason.
Subs not used: Lewis, McNaughton, Kiss,
Conway.

125

Damage limitation. Craig Noone rounds Charlton's
Ben Hamer with the game all but lost.

THE CHAMPIONSHIP

ALL ABOARD THE MERRY-GO-ROUND!

Six Championship clubs either welcomed or waved off managers this week, now just fifteen games into the Championship season.

On Saturday, new Ipswich Town boss **Mick McCarthy** *(pictured)* watched on, just hours into the job, as on-loan QPR striker DJ Campbell handed him the perfect start with an eighth minute winning goal at Birmingham City. Three days later and his second game in charge could hardly have been more disastrous. Early on Saturday morning, **Ian Holloway** had been named as the new manager of Crystal Palace and watched on later that afternoon as a Glenn Murray double sunk Blackburn Rovers, themselves handing a managerial debut to former defensive stalwart **Henning Berg.** Come Tuesday, five goals for Palace against McCarthy's Ipswich, including a further hat-trick for Murray, represented the perfect inauguration for Holloway. As for Berg, he was denied a first win as Rovers manager thanks to Lee Novak's injury time equaliser for Huddersfield after a Jordan Rhodes strike and Danny Murphy penalty looked to have set Blackburn on course for all three points.

Former Watford manager **Sean Dyche** was last week named as the new manager at Burnley following Eddie Howe's shock departure the week prior. He's overseen back-to-back victories to begin his Turf Moor reign. Taking charge having watched his Clarets thumped 4-0 at Cardiff the week previously, goals from Martin Paterson and Charlie Austin handed him a huge win on debut over a very strong Wolves outfit and then they followed that up with a single goal victory over Leeds United on Tuesday night with Charlie Austin netting for the twentieth time this season.

Meanwhile **Dougie Freedman**, who vacated the role at Crystal Palace which led to Holloway's appointment, is now at the helm of Bolton Wanderers and he saw his new side scrape past Cardiff in controversial fashion on Saturday evening to hand him a debut victory as Trotters manager. A pair of highly debatable penalty decisions went Wanderers' way and former Liverpool striker David N'Gog enjoyed an action-packed substitution cameo which saw him have a perfectly good goal ruled out for offside, dive to win a penalty, deflect home the eventual Bolton winner, and collect a red card for two bookable offences! On Tuesday, Bolton followed that up with a point garnered from a goal-less draw at home with Leicester giving them four points in the three days from teams that sat at the top of the league just a week ago.

The one manager-less club during this period has been **Blackpool.** With Ian Holloway having departed for Palace last Saturday morning, they entered a tricky encounter away at Derby with emotions evidently raw. They paid the price with a heavy 4-1 defeat, yet responded just three days later with a fine 2-0 win at Dave Jones' Sheffield Wednesday – their first victory in over a month.

» TOP SCORERS

1	2	3	4	5
17	13	9	8	8
» CHARLIE AUSTIN BURNLEY	» GLENN MURRAY CRYSTAL PALACE	» LUCIANO BECCHIO LEEDS UTD	» THOMAS INCE BLACKPOOL	» CRAIG MACKAIL-SMITH BRIGHTON

BANG FOR YOUR BUCK

...esday night's events at the Valley may not have ended with a ...sitive result for City, but it backed up a common cliché about the ...ampionship – that it is one of the most unpredictable and ...citing leagues around.

...t it was all the more surprising that this set of midweek fixtures ...w 3 goalless draws, especially seeing as there had been just 4 all ...ason before Tuesday!

...put that into context – there have already been 7 0-0 draws in ...e Premier League (after just 10 rounds of fixtures) and 9 in ...ague One, while League Two fans have had to endure a grand ...tal of 21 stalemates!

...e Bluebirds have found the back of the net in all but 1 of their 15 ...atches so far – a record surpassed only by Ian Holloway's new ...ub Crystal Palace, who are yet to draw a blank. Their 5-0 mauling ... Ipswich Town on Tuesday means that only we have scored more ...als than the Eagles.

...wever, City did provide one of the few stalemates seen so far, as ...r deadlock with Brighton was the first of the season. In fact, the ...agulls, along with Nottingham Forest, are the only two ...ampionship teams to have been involved in more than one 0-0 ...is campaign. This is perhaps unsurprising when you consider that ...us Poyet's men have failed to score in 6 of their matches so far – ...e worst record in the division, along with Peterborough United.

...d those two teams met on Tuesday night when it took until the ...nd minute for a goal! It fell Brighton's way, meaning that the ...sh have lost every one of the 6 matches in which they've failed to ...tch a goal, conceding 8 in the process. Let's hope for more goals ... the right end) this afternoon!

DID YOU KNOW?

...lull manager Steve Bruce says he's hoping Sone Aluko won't be ...alled up by Nigeria for this year's African Cup of Nations. But, ...aving already turned out for the Super Eagles, Sone is on an ...dd list of siblings who have played for different countries – as ...is older sister, Eni, represents England and Team GB.

...erome and Kevin-Prince Boateng are perhaps the most famous, ...aving played for Germany and Ghana respectively. Meanwhile ...Massimiliano "Max" Vieri, brother of famous ...talian forward Christian, made 6 appearances ...or Australia. Finally, in one of the most bizarre ...amily ties – Croatian playmaker Luka Modrić ...pictured) is a second cousin of former Aussie ...kipper Mark Viduka. Bonkers.

npower
FOOTBALL LEAGUE

MIDWEEK RESULTS
Birmingham City 2–0 Bristol City
Brighton & Hove Albion 1–0 Peterborough Utd
Burnley 1–0 Leeds United
Charlton Athletic 5–4 Cardiff City
Derby County 2–0 Barnsley
Huddersfield Town 2–2 Blackburn Rovers
Hull City 2–1 Wolves
Nottingham Forest 0–0 Middlesbrough
Sheffield Wednesday 0–2 Blackpool
Watford 0–0 Millwall
Bolton Wanderers 0–0 Leicester City
Crystal Palace 5–0 Ipswich Town

WEEKEND FIXTURES
(All games kick off at 3pm unless otherwise stated)
YESTERDAY
Middlesbrough v Sheffield Wed (7.45pm)

TODAY
Barnsley v Huddersfield Town
Blackburn Rovers v Birmingham City
Blackpool v Bolton Wanderers
Cardiff City v Hull City
Ipswich Town v Burnley
Leeds United v Watford
Leicester City v Nottingham Forest (12:45pm)
Millwall v Derby County
Peterborough United v Crystal Palace
Wolves v Brighton & Hove Albion

TOMORROW
Bristol City v Charlton Athletic

2012/13 NPOWER CHAMPIONSHIP LEAGUE TABLE

Pos	Team	P	W	D	L	GD	Pts
1	Crystal Palace	15	9	3	3	9	30
2	Middlesbrough	15	9	2	4	6	29
3	**Cardiff City**	15	9	1	5	9	28
4	**Hull City**	15	9	1	5	4	28
5	Leicester City	15	8	2	5	7	26
6	Blackburn	15	6	6	3	3	24
7	Huddersfield	15	7	3	5	0	24
8	Brighton	15	6	5	4	8	23
9	Derby County	15	6	5	4	5	23
10	Burnley	15	7	2	6	0	23
11	Nottm Forest	15	5	7	3	3	22
12	Blackpool	15	6	3	6	3	21
13	Wolves	15	6	3	6	1	21
14	Millwall	15	5	5	5	2	20
15	Leeds United	15	5	5	5	0	20
16	Watford	15	6	2	7	-3	20
17	Bolton	15	5	4	6	-2	19
18	Birmingham	15	5	4	6	-5	19
19	Charlton	15	4	5	6	-3	17
20	Sheffield Wed	15	4	3	8	-6	15
21	Barnsley	15	4	3	8	-8	15
22	Peterborough	15	4	0	11	-6	12
23	Bristol City	15	3	2	10	-7	11
24	Ipswich Town	15	2	4	9	-20	10

DETAILS PRIOR TO THIS WEEKEND'S GAMES

CF ELEVEN

THE OFFICIAL CARDIFF CITY FC MATCH PROGRAMME

CARDIFF CITY

•—VERSUS—•

MIDDLESBROUGH

SAT 17TH NOV 3:00PM

npower CHAMPIONSHIP   MATCH 17 £3

MATCH SPONSOR: LADBROKES

TEAM SPONSOR: ARUP

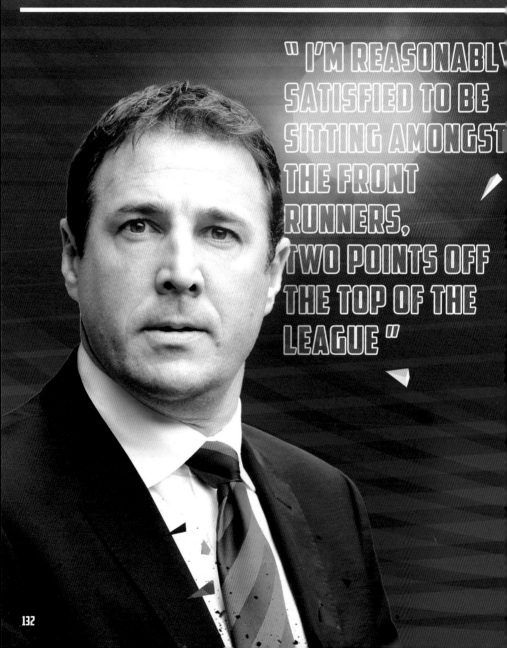

09

MALKY MACKAY

STEADY PROGRESS

" I'M REASONABLY SATISFIED TO BE SITTING AMONGST THE FRONT RUNNERS, TWO POINTS OFF THE TOP OF THE LEAGUE "

Good afternoon and welcome back for today's match with Middlesbrough. It's our second home game in succession and we'll obviously be hoping that it goes the same way as the previous eight! However, we know there is a tough task in front of us as Tony Mowbray brings his team here today in fine form and ahead of us in the league.

I'll start by welcoming Tony, his staff, players and everyone who has made the extremely long trip from the north-east today. Tony is a friend who I have known for a long time – back to the days when we played together at Celtic and continuing on to the time when we were both in East Anglia, Tony at Ipswich during my spell with Norwich.

He's both a man and a manager for whom I have enormous respect and he's doing another excellent job at the Riverside again this season, so I really look forward to the opportunity to pit my wits against him this afternoon.

I was delighted with our performance and result here last Saturday against Hull City. For the third time in our last four outings we were in front in the first three minutes and we went on to totally dominate the opening half hour, creating a string of chances that should have put the game to bed well before half-time.

You'll struggle to find a braver footballer than Heidar Helguson and that was amply demonstrated by the way he put his body and well-being on the line to score that opening goal. He only had eyes for the ball and made sure he had scored before the inevitable clattering came his way. It was no surprise to me to see him bounce back up after some treatment and proceed to throw himself around for another 65 minutes, doing what was necessary to help the team win despite a black eye and blood oozing out of his nose!

After losing Kevin McNaughton to injury we had to reshuffle the side and it took us a little while to reassert ourselves on the match but, even though Hull enjoyed a good ten minutes leading up to half-time, I didn't ever feel that we allowed them a sight of our goal and we always looked totally comfortable.

After a couple of half-time tweaks, we started the second half much as we had started the first, well on top and creating chances that really could have put Hull to the sword. It was, therefore, a relief when we finally went 2-0 up with ten minutes left thanks to a bullet header from captain Hudson from Gunnar's brilliant cross.

We're now virtually a third of the way through the league campaign and I'm reasonably satisfied to be sitting amongst the front runners, two points off the top of the league. We know there are a lot of battles ahead of us over the remaining 31 matches, starting here today, but I feel we're well equipped to meet each challenge as it comes.

As you may have seen yesterday, we were delighted to announce that Andrew Taylor has signed a contract extension that commits him to the club for a further two years beyond his original agreement.

Andrew is one of those players who sometimes goes under the radar when it comes to making headlines, but he is always one of the first names on the teamsheet for me and has been utterly consistent in his attitude, application and performance since he joined us almost 18 months ago.

He is one of the guys I know I can absolutely count on week in, week out so I was really pleased that he is as happy with us as we are with him. Thanks to Andrew and his representatives for working with us to make it a relatively straight forward process.

Finally, it was good to see a large crowd here on Tuesday night for the Development Squad's 2-1 win over Swansea City. I know the fans will take a lot of pleasure in beating our neighbours but, for me, the level of performance was just as important as the result and showed that we have some talented youngsters not far off first team recognition. It was also another step on the road to recovery for Stephen McPhail and he did well to get another 90 minutes in his legs.

As ever, we are counting on your fantastic support today in another big game for us so please make yourselves heard!

Enjoy the game.

CARDIFF CITY 2
Helguson (3), Hudson (82)

HULL CITY 1
Koren (90)

SATURDAY ▶ 10TH NOVEMBER ▶ 3.00PM Full Attendance **20,058**

🏠 **19,626**
🚌 **432**

MALKY

"We started like a house on fire. We looked like we could have scored three or four. We went on the front foot in the second half and didn't give them a breath. I always thought the second goal was coming. I'm very proud of my players."

BRUCE

"I thought Cardiff were the better side and we were nowhere near the level we've been at in recent weeks. But it might have been different had the disallowed goal been given. It was a big turning point in the game. It's a ridiculous decision."

GUNNARSSON

"We managed the game well. We had a meeting after the Charlton game to look at where we'd made mistakes, but you have to focus on the next game every time. We are all in this together and will put our bodies on the line."

Cardiff City Stadium maintained its reputation as a fortress with an eighth successive home victory, the first goal coming after just three minutes. Craig Noone shimmied onto his left and curled in an early cross, Heidar Helguson losing his marker to guide a header past Ben Amos while putting his body on the line.

Thankfully, after lengthy treatment, the Icelandic striker returned to the pitch. Injury to Kevin McNaughton forced a tactical re-shuffle with Aron Gunnarsson slotting in at right back and Filip Kiss coming on in midfield. And Hull thought they'd equalised on the stroke of half-time, only for a Jay Simpson goal to be ruled out for handball.

The second half saw Cardiff rejuvenated and piling on the pressure, with Peter Whittingham's fantastic set piece ability and range of passing causing havoc. Sone Aluko's thirty yard free kick clipped the bar before Cardiff's potency going forward was demonstrated again; Gunnarsson picked out Mark Hudson with a fine cross who made no mistake from a few yards out with a diving header. The final stages were made decidedly more nervy thanks to an injury-time looping wonder goal from Robert Koren, but City held on for the win.

FANS SAY "Boro next at home and if we can beat them then I believe we can beat anybody at Cardiff City Stadium. Blackpool, Leeds, Wolves, Burnley and now Hull – amazing" – *Stephen Baker*

THE BREAK DOWN

REFEREE: I. Williamson

CARDIFF CITY FC — EST 1899 — FIRE & PASSION

THE TIGERS

11 ⚑ 1

52% 48%

POSSESSION

2

SHOTS ON 5

OFF 6

Post-match reaction from Malky Mackay, ...ve Bruce and ...n Gunnarsson on **CARDIFF CITY Player**
...diff City Player

...diff City: Marshall, McNaughton
...s) (Ralls), Taylor, Hudson (c),
...rner, Whittingham, Noone,
...im, Gunnarsson, Mason,
...guson (Gestede).
...s not used: Lewis,
...gent, Conway, Frei.

Hull City:
Amos, Rosenior,
Chester, McShane
(Brady), Faye, Elmohamady,
Evans, Koren, Quinn (McLean),
Simpson (Meyler), Aluko.
Subs not used: Jakupović, McKenna,
Olofinjana, Proschwitz.

135

Battle Born. Heidar displays familiar war wounds after putting City ahead against the Tigers.

THE CHAMPIONSHIP

GOALS GALORE!

There's no doubt where the most astonishing fixture of last weekend's Championship slate took place – Elland Road, Leeds.

With news leaking of an 'imminent' takeover prior to kick-off, spirits were understandably high amongst **Leeds United** fans hopeful of recording their first win in a month to top elevate on-field positivity to match that at board room level. What followed though was something entirely different. Watford's on-loan forward Matěj Vydra grabbed the only goal of a fiercely contested first half which suggested an equally tight encounter in the second forty-five.

The match swayed after the break though, as Whites centre-half Jason Pearce was red-carded and then combative midfielder Rudolph Austin broke his ankle. Neil Warnock *(pictured)* had already made his three substitutions as a way of tactically adapting to their original one man deficit that left Leeds with only nine men to face a now understandably rampant Hornets outfit. Almen Abdi and Mark Yeates made it 3-0 before Michael Tonge was able to pull one back for Leeds from the spot. It was purely consolation though. Vydra grabbed a second, while Sean Murray and Troy Deeney both netted in injury time to pile on the misery, and the score, which ended 6-1 to the visiting Hornets.

Wolves and **Brighton & Hove Albion** were in a free-scoring mood too, as they combined for six at Molineux in a frantic 3-3 draw which ebbed and

flowed incessantly. Goals from Bakary Sako and Craig Mackail-Smith had the sides level at the interval, before a rash challenge from (and subsequent dismissal by) Wolves captain Karl Henry left his side with an uphill challenge for much of the second half. Despite that, a Tongo Doumbia strike had the Black Country outfit briefly ahead again, before Will Buckley leveled things u after seventy-two minutes. Then came the late drama. Christophe Berra was penalised for handball in the fina minute of regular time, and when Stephen Dobbie scored from the spot the match looked done and dusted. Not quite. Former Bluebird Roger Johns has endured a tough time since arriving at Wolves last summer, but he picked an opportune time to net his first gold goal deep into injury time when he rose to power home a header and give his side an unlikely share of the spoils.

Elsewhere, two local derbies provided four goal splits as first **Leicester City** and **Nottingham Forest** and then **Blackpool** and **Bolton Wanderers** played out intriguing 2-2 draws. Simon Cox converted a controversial spot kick after Zak Whitbread was adjudged to have fouled Billy Sharp in the sixty-seventh minute which gave Forest a share of the spoils away at high-flying Leicester. While at Bloomfield Road, Michael Appleton's first match in charge was salvaged by an inspired substitution as thirty-ni year old Kevin Phillips, three years his new manager's senior, came off the bench late on set up Nathan Delfouneso for a deserved sha of the Lancashire spoils. In total we enjoyed forty-two Championship goals last weekend Here's to a similar return this time out!

≫ MISBEHAVING

1	2	3	4	5
5 2	7 0	5 1	4 1	5 0
≫ ADLENE GUEDIOURA NOTTINGHAM FOREST	≫ SHANE LOWRY MILLWALL	≫ DANIEL PUDIL WATFORD	≫ KARL HENRY WOLVES	≫ WILFRIED ZAHA CRYSTAL PALAC

THE ART OF PLAYING AWAY

This afternoon's match against **Middlesbrough** will see **Cardiff City** – the side with the best home record in the Football League – come up against a team in fine form on their travels in recent weeks.

Of their last 5 away games, Boro have won four and drawn one – a record that only high-flying **Crystal Palace** can match, although Tony Mowbray's men have scored more and conceded fewer in the process. However, while City have suffered from a touch of travel sickness in recent weeks, it seems that a few other Championship teams have found the cure.

Gianfranco Zola's **Watford** certainly know how to find the net away from home as their emphatic 6-1 victory at Elland Road last weekend took their away goals tally to 17 – that's 3 more than anyone else in the division. But they're not the first side to have had a goal-fest on opposition turf this year.

Back in September, **Blackburn Rovers** netted 5 times in a bizarre match against **Bristol City**, as Rovers scored twice in stoppage time to win 5-3 at Ashton Gate. Jordan Rhodes *(pictured)* notched his first goals for the club after his £8 million move from Huddersfield Town which, at the time, took them to the top of the Championship table.

And **Barnsley** joined in on the action the very next week, inflicting a shock 5-0 home defeat upon **Birmingham City** in which Welsh international front-man Craig Davies bagged 4 for himself. Oddly enough, 2 of the 3 sides to notch 5 or more goals in an away match find themselves at the foot of the home scoring charts. Watford have been much shyer in front of goal at Vicarage Road, netting just 8 times from the same amount of games. And **Barnsley** have fared even worse – Oakwell season ticket holders have seen a division low of just 6 home goals all season with Cardiff their next visitors on November 24th.

DID YOU KNOW?

News broke in the week that Crystal Palace's **Wilfried Zaha** *(pictured)* had been called up to the England team to face Sweden on Wednesday, in the wake of five high profile dropouts from the squad. Roy Hodgson's decision made the Ivorian born winger the first Championship outfield player to be called up to an England camp since **Jay Bothroyd**, while playing for City back in the 2010/11 campaign. Incidentally, Zaha made his first ever career appearance against Cardiff City the season before, coming off the bench after goals from **Gábor Gyepes** and **Chris Burke** sealed a 2-1 win for City at Selhurst Park.

LAST WEEKEND'S RESULTS

Barnsley 0–1 Huddersfield Town
Blackburn Rovers 1–1 Birmingham City
Blackpool 2–2 Bolton Wanderers
Bristol City 0–2 Charlton Athletic
Cardiff City 2–1 Hull City
Ipswich Town 2–1 Burnley
Leeds United 1–6 Watford
Middlesbrough 3–1 Sheffield Wednesday
Millwall 2–1 Derby County
Peterborough United 1–2 Crystal Palace
Wolves 3–3 Brighton & Hove Albion
Leicester City 2–2 Nottingham Forest

WEEKEND FIXTURES
(All games kick off at 3pm unless otherwise stated)

Saturday 17th November
Birmingham City v Hull City
Bolton Wanderers v Barnsley
Bristol City v Blackpool
Burnley v Charlton Athletic
Cardiff City v Middlesbrough
Crystal Palace v Derby County
Huddersfield Town v Brighton & Hove Albion
Leicester City v Ipswich Town
Nottingham Forest v Sheffield Wednesday
Peterborough Utd v Blackburn Rovers (5.20pm)
Watford v Wolves

Sunday 18th November
Millwall v Leeds United (1.15pm)

2012/13 NPOWER CHAMPIONSHIP LEAGUE TABLE

Pos	Team	P	W	D	L	GD	Pts
1	Crystal Palace	16	10	3	3	10	33
2	**Middlesbrough**	16	10	2	4	8	32
3	**Cardiff City**	16	10	1	5	10	31
4	Hull City	16	9	1	6	3	28
5	Leicester City	16	8	3	5	7	27
6	Huddersfield	16	8	3	5	1	27
7	Blackburn	16	6	7	3	3	25
8	Brighton	16	6	6	4	8	24
9	Derby County	16	6	5	5	4	23
10	Millwall	16	6	5	5	3	23
11	Nottm Forest	16	5	8	3	3	23
12	Watford	16	7	2	7	2	23
13	Burnley	16	7	2	7	-1	23
14	Blackpool	16	6	4	6	3	22
15	Wolves	16	6	4	6	1	22
16	Charlton	16	5	5	6	-1	20
17	Bolton	16	5	5	6	-2	20
18	Leeds United	16	5	5	6	-5	20
19	Birmingham	16	5	5	6	-5	20
20	Sheffield Wed	16	4	3	9	-8	15
21	Barnsley	16	4	3	9	-9	15
22	Ipswich Town	16	3	4	9	-19	13
23	Peterborough	16	4	0	12	-7	12
24	Bristol City	16	3	2	11	-9	11

CF ELEVEN

THE OFFICIAL CARDIFF CITY FC MATCH PROGRAMME

CARDIFF CITY

VERSUS

SHEFFIELD WEDNESDAY

SUN 2ND DEC 3:00PM

npower CHAMPIONSHIP   MATCH 20 £3

MATCH SPONSOR: ARUP

MATCH BALL SPONSOR:
CHARLES M. WILLIE & CO (SHIPPING) LTD

Malaysia PUMA Player

10

SQUAD STRENGTH

Good afternoon and welcome back for today's game with Sheffield Wednesday.

We come into the weekend top of the league which is particularly pleasing after a tough November, with six games in total, four of which were away from home.

I would like to take this opportunity to welcome Dave Jones and his staff as they bring their Wednesday side to South Wales today. Dave obviously had six years here and achieved a lot during that time, so I hope that today he gets the warm welcome that his success here deserves.

There has been a bit of stick flying around about our results away from here this season, but I felt we went a long way towards putting that right in the last week by picking up four points from two difficult games at Barnsley and Derby County.

There have been three games in succession when we have had to battle against considerable adversity to pick up points, starting from the win over Middlesbrough here two weeks ago. To lose two of your back four to injury in the first twenty minutes of the game – with Kevin McNaughton already on the injury list – meant that we had to undergo considerable readjustment in the course of the match.

It also meant we had to ask a couple of our young teenagers, Ben Nugent and Joe Ralls, to do a man's job by filling in against what is, I think, a very good 'Boro team. Knowing the characters of both lads and seeing how they have developed over the last eighteen months, I had little fear that they would be up to the task and so it proved.

It was particularly pleasing to beat Middlesbrough as it gave us our ninth successive win here as well as picking up three points at the expense of a team which is likely to challenge at the top of the league as the season goes on. We were called on to do some defending to protect our clean sheet but I never really felt that Tony Mowbray's team carved out real chances to score and the win was absolutely what we deserved on the day.

The injuries that we had picked up, particularly across

the back four, meant that we had to bring Simon Lappin in on loan from Norwich to offer us more cover down the left side. Simon is an experienced player who played a significant role in Norwich's promotion to the Premier League two years ago, so we were lucky to be able to sign him and I'd like to take this opportunity to formally welcome him to the club.

Simon was signed in time for last Saturday's trip to Barnsley and I was really pleased to make it three straight wins and return to the top of the league. Oakwell is never an easy place to go and get a result and Keith Hill had boosted his squad with four signing in the week leading up to our match, so we knew we weren't in for an easy afternoon.

Ben Nugent getting on the score sheet was a bonus for us and, once Aron Gunnarsson had doubled our lead, the win was never in doubt, despite having to do it the hard way through Simon Lappin's red card in the closing stages.

The resulting suspension again meant that we had to plug a few round pegs into square holes for the tough trip to Derby on Tuesday and, again, I couldn't fault the effort and application of the lads at Pride Park.

Bearing in mind that we went to Derby with Kevin McNaughton, Ben Turner, Andrew Taylor, Don Cowie, Tommy Smith, Simon Lappin, Nicky Maynard and Kadeem Harris unavailable, it makes the result all the more impressive.

Craig Noone's sending off left us with a very difficult job to do because there was still more than thirty minutes to go and Derby are a team who are capable of doing damage. However, I was very proud of the way we stubbornly kept our shape and denied them real goal scoring opportunities. Every point we gain is vital and Tuesday was one of those draws that felt like a win.

We're focused on chalking up our tenth straight win here and making sure that we end this weekend where we started it – top of the league and looking forward to an exciting future.

Enjoy the match.

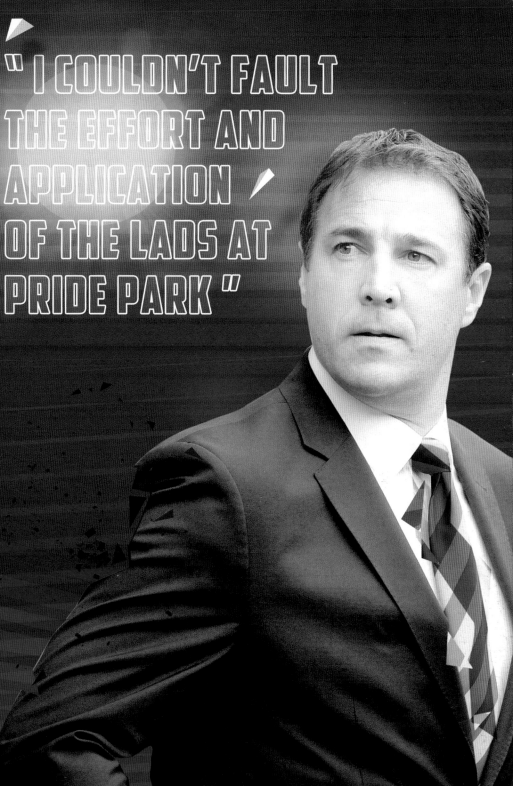

" I COULDN'T FAULT THE EFFORT AND APPLICATION OF THE LADS AT PRIDE PARK "

CARDIFF CITY 1
Connolly, 19
MIDDLESBROUGH 2

SATURDAY ▶ 17TH NOVEMBER ▶ 3.00PM Full Attendance **21,578**

🏠 **20,839**

🚌 **739**

MALKY

"I thought our fans were fantastic. They knew it was a tough game against a good team that would come and test us. They are beginning to really embrace this winning record, this run and are enjoying playing good football

MOWBRAY

"I'm heartened. I enjoyed watching the team in the second half with th way we played, the way we moved the ball. No team goes through the season without defeats. You've got to take it on the chin."

CONNOLLY

"We made changes we dug in and we won the game. The year I went up with QPR we won countless games lik that. Physically it was a very hard game, but we've go three points."

Starting well and controlling the game, Cardiff won a corner following good work from Craig Noone, Joe Mason and Aron Gunnarsson. Peter Whittingham delivered to the back post and Matt Connolly headed home for his fourth goal this season. However, both Andrew Taylor and Ben Turner had to leave the pitch due to injury, Malky choosing to hand Ben Nugent his début and throwing midfielder Joe Ralls on at left back. Boro's best chance came in the dying moments of the first half, Scott McDonald wasting a golden opportunity created by Emmanuel Ledesma.

City injury-hit squad were further rocked after the break, with Mark Hudson needing stitches, before returning to marshal the makeshift defence. Gunnarsson was then forced to leave the field of play with a back strain; however, he was replaced by the returning Craig Bellamy, who within a minute created a fantastic chance and galvanised the attack. Mason was then denied a concrete penalty that would have put the game to bed, giving 'Boro hope. The atmosphere was electric inside CCS as Cardiff stoutly defended their lead for the remainder of the game, Nugent and Ralls never looking out of place. As the final whistle blew to signal nine home victories out of nine – the best record in Europe – the stadium erupted.

FANS SAY
"Great intensity, atmosphere and a fantastic performance from fans and players alike. For the players to keep it at 1-0 under pressure raised us to our feet. Awesome." – *Jordon Davies*

REFEREE: O. Langford

3 🚩 7

42% 58%

POSSESSION

1 📔 2

SHOTS

2 ON 10

4 OFF 9

st-match reaction from Malky Mackay,
y Mowbray and
tt Connolly on
diff City Player

CARDIFF CITY Player ❯

diff City: Marshall, Taylor (Ralls),
dson, Turner (Nugent),
nnolly, Whittingham, Kim
Kyung, Noone,
nnarsson (Bellamy),
son, Helguson.
s not used: Lewis,
way, Frei,
tede.

Middlesbrough:
Steele, Hoyte, Bikey,
Friend (Bailey), Hines,
Leadbitter, McEachran, Haroun
(Smallwood), Ledesma, Jutkiewicz
(Emnes), McDonald.
Subs not used: Leutwiler, Thomson,
Williams, Miller.

145

Nuge potential. 19-year-old Ben makes his League debut;
he'd go on to become the Club's Young Player of the Season.

BARNSLEY 1
Mellis (76)

CARDIFF CITY 2
Nugent (22), Gunnarsson (51)

SATURDAY ▶ 24TH NOVEMBER ▶ 3.00PM | Full Attendance **8,227**

🏠 **7,558**

🚌 **669**

MALKY

"It was good to get another three points at a tough ground against a resolute team who have had fresh influx of player this week. We knew would be difficult an conditions got worse as the game went or so I'm delighted."

City took the early initiative in this one, creating more attacking threats than Barnsley at a very cold and wet Oakwell. This attacking play paid off on twenty-two minutes when Ben Nugent headed home a brilliantly struck Peter Whittingham corner. The goal was Nugent's first at senior level and a perfect way to mark his first senior start. Cardiff took this 1-0 lead into half-time with no major scares.

With just over five minutes played of the second period, Cardiff scored from yet another perfectly delivered Whittingham set piece. This time Aron Gunnarsson was there to power home the corner into the bottom left of the net to give City a 2-0 cushion. Barnsley did get themselves back into the game with quarter of an hour left as Jacob Mellis found himself unmarked at the back post to calmly slot the ball across goal and into the bottom corner.

This resulted in the Tykes pushing for an equaliser and their optimism grew stronger when on loan Simon Lappin got shown a second yellow and received his marching orders on his City debut. But Cardiff held on to end their away days hoodoo and return to the top of the Championship.

HILL

"We have let Luke Steele down. He has made two match-winning saves and w conceded from both corners; the players are responsible for the individual mistakes they have made. The individua errors cost you."

GUNNARSSON

"We needed to take what we've been doi at home into away games and we did tha We could have won b more and in the end we put pressure on ourselves. We're glad because we knew Barnsley would fight."

FANS SAY "This was a good game, though it got a bit scrappy towards the end. Our strikers played very well and we definitely deserved to take all three points." – *Josh Richards*

REFEREE: D. Whitestone

8   6

49%   51%

POSSESSION

0   1
2   3

SHOTS

8 ON 7

7 OFF 5

e post-match reaction of this game from Malky
ackay, Keith Hill and
on Gunnarsson on
rdiff City Player

CARDIFF CITY
Player

rnsley: Steele, Wisemen,
olbourne, McNulty, Cranie,
wson (Buzsaky), Done
oble-Lazarus), Mellis,
eening, Davies, Tudgay
nclair).
bs not used:
lakevicius,
ster, Stones,
Brien.

Cardiff City:
Marshall,
Connolly, Hudson,
Nugent, Lappin, Noone,
Whittingham, Gunnarsson
(Mutch), Kim, Mason (Bellamy),
Helguson (Gestede).
Subs not used: Lewis, Conway, Ralls, John.

149

Starting a trend. Gunnarsson's winner at Oakwell begins a nine game unbeaten away run.

NPOWER CHAMPIONSHIP

DERBY COUNTY 1
Robinson (69)

CARDIFF CITY 1
Helguson (11)

TUESDAY ▶ 27TH NOVEMBER ▶ 7.45PM | Full Attendance 20,911

🏠 **20,134**

🚌 **777**

MALKY

"To dog it out and to play like that against a team who have won the last three, scored nine goals and have only been beaten once at home this season was very pleasing. Up to that point (the sending off I was very, very happy with my team."

CLOUGH

"We've generally played very well at home this season. This performance was a continuation of that really. We huffed and puffed (in the) second half, but they are extremely difficult to break down, with ten or eleven men."

MARSHALL

"It was always going to be difficult playing with ten men for the last half hour – Derby are very good at home. I think if we could have seen out ten or fifteen minutes though we may have held on to win."

Cardiff City took an early lead at Pride Park when Heidar Helguson scored his eighth of the season after eleven minutes. Craig Noone had provided the cross into the box for Mark Hudson who remained up field after the long throw in. His header forced Derby keeper Legzdins to tip onto the bar, but only for brave striker Helguson to head home – once again taking a blow to the face for his troubles.

The second half started in the same vein as the first, with no side really taking the initiative. However, just after the hour mark the game took a turn for the worse for the visiting City fans. Craig Noone picked up his second yellow card in a matter of minutes, giving Derby confidence that led to their equaliser after sixty-nine minutes.

Craig Bryson had darted his way into the left hand side if the box, squared a great pass across the goal mouth where Theo Robinson was there to simply tap home. Derby dominated the rest of the game, though City held firm for a very decent away point that kept them top of the npower Championship.

FANS SAY "Quality players able to play in multiple roles shone through for us against Derby. Credit to Malky and the players who will not accept defeat." – *Gavin Gray*

REFEREE: M. Brown

DERBY CO   CARDIFF CITY
EST 1884   EST 1899 FIRE & PASSION

11   2

63%   37%
POSSESSION

0   1
2   2
SHOTS
9 **ON** 2
10 **OFF** 5

he post-match reaction of this game from
alky Mackay and
gel Clough on
rdiff City Player

CARDIFF CITY Player

rby County: Legzdins, Brayford,
berts (O'Connor), Keogh,
xton, Bryson, Coutts,
cobs (Tyson), Hughes,
binson (Hendrick),
mmon.
bs not used:
elding, O'Brien,
vies,
eeman.

Cardiff City:
Marshall, Connolly,
Hudson, Nugent, Ralls,
Noone, Whittingham,
Gunnarsson (Conway), Kim,
Bellamy (Mutch), Helguson (Mason).
Subs not used: Parrish, Kiss, Gestede, John.

153

Whatever it takes. Joe Ralls steps in at left-back for the injured Andrew Taylor at Pride Park.

AUGUST – NOVEMBER: THE TALE OF THE TAPE

As we approach the halfway point of the season, this afternoon's game gives us a chance to analyze how the division has shaped up between August and the end of November. Here are the findings!

DISCIPLINE IS KEY

The past week has seen two City streaks of minor gravitas come to an end. Not since our second league outing of the season at the AMEX Stadium against Brighton had we seen a Cardiff match end all square; but perhaps more unusually no City players had received marching orders from a referee for nearly a hundred games prior to Simon Lappin's dismissal at Barnsley – way before manager Malky Mackay even arrived at the club!

So how does City's disciplinary record compare with the chasing pack in the Championship? There are no City players among the top twenty-five worst disciplined in the league – a testament indeed to our character and style of play. Watford's **Daniel Pudil** *(pictured)* holds the unfortunate honour of being the league's dirtiest player to date, already with eight yellow cards and a red to his name.

NETBUSTERS

City's joint top scorers, **Heidar Helguson** and **Peter Whittingham,** each have seven league goals to their name. But, heading into this weekend, they were ten goals behind the league's top scorer **Charlie Austin.** Burnley's goal machine already had seventeen goals under his belt despite his side's modest 14th place position!

Speaking of goals, up until the end of November, City had scored more than anyone else in the division with thirty-seven – accumulating the highest average goals scored per game with 1.94. We have the best record against teams currently in the top half of the table too – picking up on average 1.88 points per game against the league's high-fliers. Over the first four months of the season it was Huddersfield Town who had the best record against teams in the lower half

CHAMPIONSHIP ASSISTS

1 **CHRIS EAGLES** BOLTON — 10
2 **PETER WHITTINGHAM** CARDIFF CITY — 7
3 **JACOB MELLIS** BARNSLEY — 7
4 **CRAIG NOONE** CARDIFF CITY — 7
5 **THOMAS INCE** BLACKPOOL — 7

the Championship, taking twenty-three points ahead of City's
~enty-one over nineteen games.

ƆME SWEET HOME

~ widely reported last week, Cardiff City have the best home
:ord in not only the Championship but across the major leagues
Europe, winning all nine of our fixtures at Cardiff City Stadium to
~te. Middlesbrough and Leicester had both won seven home
~mes ahead of this weekend, while Nottingham Forest and Crystal
~lace had achieved the most away wins with five apiece.

~KING A LEAD

~rdiff City have scored the game's opening goal in thirteen out of
~neteen games played, while opponents Sheffield Wednesday
~ve the lowest total with six. On only one occasion (the 0-0 draw
Brighton) have Cardiff failed to score, while Wednesday have not
~und the target in 36.8% of their fixtures. If
~ games finished at half-time, City would
~ll have topped the table at the end of
~vember with 1.84 points per game,
~ile if the second half was all that
~unted Leicester City would have
~en nine points clear with forty-four
~d Cardiff would be joint-third with four
~her teams on thirty-one!

~ will come as no surprise to City fans that
~ter Whittingham and Craig Noone
~oth 7) are near the summit of the
~ole of assists, with only Bolton's
~ris Eagles (10) having more
~an the City playmakers. David
~arshall's six clean sheets
~eanwhile
~e
~aten
~ly by
~sper
~hmeichel's *(pictured)*
~ght for Leicester.

~ll in all, the statistics tables
~ve a distinctly Cardiffian
~el to them – and long
~ay that continue.

TODAY'S GAMES

Burnley v Blackburn Rovers (12.30pm)
Cardiff City v Sheffield Wednesday (3.00pm)

NEXT WEEKEND'S FIXTURES

Friday 7th December
Blackburn Rovers v Cardiff City (7.45pm)

Saturday 8th December
(All games kick off at 3pm unless otherwise stated)

Charlton Athletic v Brighton & Hove Albion
Crystal Palace v Blackpool
Derby County v Leeds United (1.00pm)
Huddersfield Town v Bolton Wanderers
Ipswich Town v Millwall
Leicester City v Barnsley
Nottingham Forest v Burnley
Peterborough v Middlesbrough
Sheffield Wednesday v Bristol City

2012/13 NPOWER CHAMPIONSHIP LEAGUE TABLE

Pos	Team	P	W	D	L	GD	Pts
1	**Cardiff City**	19	12	2	5	12	38
2	Crystal Palace	19	11	4	4	12	37
3	Middlesbrough	19	11	2	6	8	35
4	Leicester City	19	10	3	6	14	33
5	Millwall	19	9	5	5	7	32
6	Hull City	19	10	2	7	3	32
7	Brighton	19	8	7	4	11	31
8	Watford	19	9	3	7	6	30
9	Nottm Forest	19	7	8	4	3	29
10	Blackburn	19	7	7	5	3	28
11	Huddersfield	19	8	4	7	-3	28
12	Derby County	19	7	6	6	2	27
13	Charlton	19	7	6	6	2	27
14	Burnley	19	8	3	8	-1	27
15	Leeds United	19	7	5	7	-4	26
16	Blackpool	19	6	7	6	3	25
17	Bolton	19	6	7	6	-1	25
18	Wolves	19	6	4	9	-2	22
19	Birmingham	19	5	6	8	-7	21
20	Barnsley	19	4	5	10	-10	17
21	Ipswich Town	19	4	5	10	-23	17
22	Bristol City	19	4	3	12	-9	15
23	**Sheffield Wed**	**19**	**4**	**3**	**12**	**-14**	**15**
24	Peterborough	19	4	1	14	-12	13

DETAILS PRIOR TO THIS WEEKEND'S GAMES

ƆID YOU KNOW?

~The side top of the Championship table at the end of December has gone on to earn promotion to the top flight in
~each of the past seven seasons. **Ipswich Town** were the last team to fail to do so, slipping to third place back in the
2004-05 campaign before losing out to **West Ham United** in the playoffs. Paul Jewell's **Wigan Athletic** pipped them
~o second place that year, as the division's two top scorers **Nathan Ellington** and **Jason Roberts** fired them into the
Premier League for the first time in the club's history – the lethal strike partnership netting forty-five goals between
~hem. We're well placed – but there's a long way to go!

CF ELEVEN

THE OFFICIAL CARDIFF CITY FC MATCH PROGRAMME

CARDIFF CITY

VERSUS

PETERBOROUGH UNITED

SAT 15TH DEC 3:00PM

npower CHAMPIONSHIP

MATCH SPONSOR:
DRS FURNACES CIVIL ENGINEERING

MATCH BALL & TEAM SPONSOR:
GLJ RECYCLING

Malaysia PUMA Player

11

KEEP IT UP

" I CONSTANTLY PREACH PATIENCE TO THE PLAYERS SO IT WAS GREAT TO SEE TH REWARD COME WITH CRAIG CONWAY'S LAT WINNER "

Good afternoon and welcome back for today's game with Peterborough United.

I'll start off by extending a warm welcome to Posh manager Darren Ferguson, along with his staff, players and all those who have made the long journey from Cambridgeshire for today's game. I guess the hours on the motorway were a useful way of escaping the grind of Christmas shopping!

Darren has done a fantastic job at London Road, taking the club up to the Championship twice and ensuring comfortable survival last season. It's been an impressive achievement at a place with a budget dwarfed by a lot of clubs at this level, so I have enormous respect for Darren and the way he has gone about his task.

Obviously we come into today's game in fantastic form and coming off what was probably our best display of the season at Blackburn last Friday. We've now won five of our last six and picked up 16 of the last 18 points which means we are sitting proudly on top of the table. However, all of that will count for very little if we do not approach today's game properly and apply ourselves in the manner which has allowed us to win our previous ten matches here at home. We all saw two weeks ago how difficult it can be to break down an obdurate opponent when Sheffield Wednesday came here determined to keep their shape and hoping to nick a point.

I was pleased with the way we kept going, kept playing football and didn't let the frustration get the better of us. I constantly preach patience to the players so it was great to see the reward come with Craig Conway's late winner. To win promotion, teams have to chalk up all kinds of victories during the course of the season and I think we have already done that here including resounding beatings for the likes of Burnley, Blackpool and Wolves as well as clinical, efficient triumphs over Middlesbrough and Hull and then 'ugly' wins where we have had to scrap till the very end – Sheffield Wednesday, Huddersfield and Watford.

Last Friday at Ewood Park was a contrast to the Wednesday game because I thought we were at our fluent best and managed to comfortably beat a team which I expect to feature at the top end of the league come May. We started very well and

should probably have been more than 1-0 up at half-time, but I was also pleased that we showed the necessary resilience to weather Blackburn's strong start to the second half and then go on to fully impose ourselves on them and run out 4-1 winners. It was a real team victory with four different scorers and Heidar Helguson leading the line magnificently up front. I had no doubt that he deserved a goal, but had to be satisfied with assists on three of the ones we did score!

It has been a very good week for the club as you will have seen the news in the last couple of days that Ben Turner has agreed to extend his stay here and signed a new deal. He follows Andrew Taylor in committing himself to Cardiff City and we are really pleased to have him under contract for an extra two years. Ben has been an important part of what we set out to achieve when I first came to Cardiff 18 months ago – identify and sign young talent and then create an environment in which that talent continues to develop and improve, creating a significant asset for the club.

From the day Ben arrived from Coventry, he has displayed a first-rate attitude to everything he has been asked to do and I am sure we will all enjoy seeing his development continue – hopefully becoming a Premier League player in a Cardiff City shirt. I'd also like to thank his representatives for their help in both bringing Ben here and then agreeing to extend his contract with us.

We are now entering the hectic Christmas period of fixtures and we have some mouth-watering matches coming up but before we can let our focus drift to the near future, we will need to be fully concentrated on today's task because, as we have seen so often in this division, any team is capable of beating any other one an any given day.

As these are my last notes before Christmas Day, I'd like to take this opportunity to wish you all a very merry festive period. The warmth and support I have experienced since I came to Wales has been one of the most enjoyable features of managing this great club, so I hope that everyone has a fantastic Christmas and New Year period. I look forward to seeing you all back here on Boxing Day.

Enjoy the game.

CARDIFF CITY 1
Conway (80)
SHEFFIELD WED. 0

SATURDAY ▶ 2ND DECEMBER ▶ 3.00PM | Full Attendance **22,034**

🏠 **21,028**
🚌 **1,006**

MALKY

"I thought we applied ourselves right from the start we knew they were a big team that would come and tr to apply pressure a set-pieces – but I thought we dealt with that really well."

JONES

"That's happened t us too many times this season where they've worked hard, but that lapse of concentration at certain times of the game has cost us. I think they need a little bit of luck."

CONWAY

"Everyone's really happy and I think w played some good stuff. Obviously it was frustrating at times as they played defensively, but we had to break them down and show gre patience."

Cardiff had dominated the first half against the visiting Owls, but failed to turn their slick passing into clear cut chances. Both Matt Connolly and Mark Hudson threatened to continue their excellent scoring form from defence, while Jordon Mutch saw his effort deflect just wide on his 21st birthday.

The second half continued in a similar manner as several chances went unconverted after some solid build up play. Indeed City did have to rely on David Marshall to save well after Gary Madine had been put through on goal, but Rudy Gestede then went closest as his header flew agonisingly wide of Chris Kirkland's post.

However, the strength of City's squad proved vital as Craig Conway, deputising for the suspended Craig Noone, fired a left-footed half volley into the bottom corner with just ten minutes remaining. The goal extended City's home record to an unprecedented ten wins out of ten as they regained their place at the top of the table.

FANS SAY | "Hard work but thoroughly deserved. We out-played them, but they were hard to break down. We were not at our best, but still got the points. Well done lads." – *Paul Stevens*

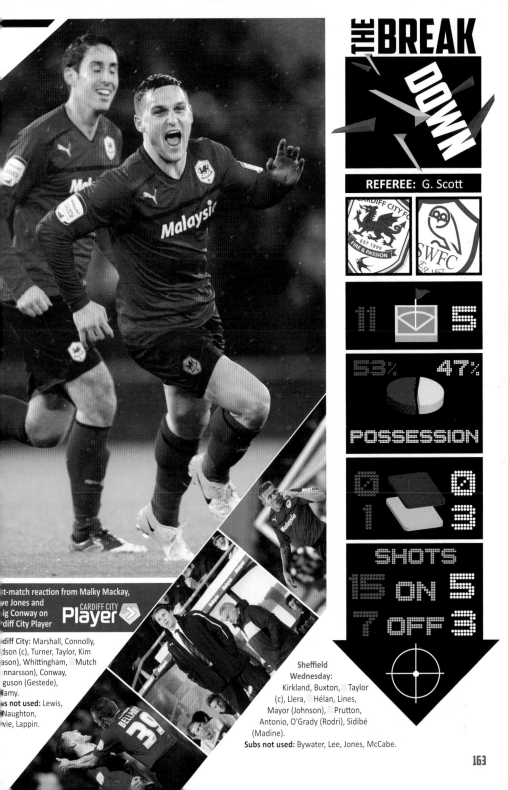

REFEREE: G. Scott

11   5

53% 47%

POSSESSION

1   0
    3

SHOTS
15 ON 5
7 OFF 3

t-match reaction from Malky Mackay,
ve Jones and
ig Conway on
diff City Player

CARDIFF CITY Player

diff City: Marshall, Connolly,
dson (c), Turner, Taylor, Kim
ason), Whittingham, Mutch
nnarsson), Conway,
guson (Gestede),
amy.
s not used: Lewis,
Naughton,
vie, Lappin.

Sheffield
Wednesday:
Kirkland, Buxton, Taylor
(c), Llera, Hélan, Lines,
Mayor (Johnson), Prutton,
Antonio, O'Grady (Rodri), Sidibé
(Madine).
Subs not used: Bywater, Lee, Jones, McCabe.

163

Bullish Behaviour. Craig Conway makes a glorious return to the starting eleven with the winner v Wednesday.

BLACKBURN ROVERS 1
King (51)

CARDIFF CITY 4
Hudson (30), Bellamy (55), Mason (84), Kim (85)

FRIDAY ▶ 7TH DECEMBER ▶ 7.45PM | Full Attendance 12,460

🏠 11,866
🚌 594

MALKY

"It's potentially the best result of the season, in terms of the goals scored and the fact that we were playing a team who had just come down from the Premier League. We now have people coming on who can make a real impact."

BERG

"Cardiff were the better team all over the pitch, although maybe not by as much as the score-line suggested. They were more experienced than us, had far better finishing and also defended better than we did."

Facing perhaps their biggest test away from home, Cardiff took the lead through inspirational captain Mark Hudson's fine header on the half hour mark from a Craig Noone cross. City were in complete control and Craig Bellamy nearly doubled their advantage before seeing his effort strike the bar.

The second half brought an equaliser, with substitute Colin Kazim-Richards playing Joshua King through for the striker to slot home. But Cardiff soon re-asserted their dominance, the warrior-like Heidar Helguson linking up neatly with Bellamy who made no mistake with his second chance. David Marshall, who had little to do, then made a fantastic reaction save to deny Dickson Etuhu before Mauro Formica blazed over from close range.

Cardiff put the game beyond doubt in the final ten minutes through substitutes Joe Mason and Kim Bo-Kyung – Mason coolly finishing from Helguson's flick-on and Kim grabbing his first Cardiff goal after winning the ball in midfield, exchanging passes with Helguson and burying an eighteen yard effort to give the Icelander his third assist of the game.

HELGUSON

"That's now seven points taken from the last three difficult away games – that (away hoodoo) has been put to bed now. If we continue playing like we did tonight then no team will want to face us."

FANS SAY "We were amazing and the response to conceding was brilliant. The two experienced lads Bellamy and Helguson showed their value and it was good to see Kim score too." – *Mohammed Suudy*

166

THE BREAKDOWN

REFEREE: S.Hooper

7 ⚑ **2**

49% **51%**
POSSESSION

3

SHOTS
7 ON **4**
6 OFF **5**

post-match reaction of this game from
ky Mackay and
ning Berg on
iff City Player

CARDIFF CITY Player

kburn Rovers: Robinson,
on, Dann, Henley, Hanley,
we, Formica (Nunes),
sson (Kazim-Richards),
u (Rochina), Rhodes,

s not used: Kean,
t, Pedersen,
cevic.

Cardiff City:
Marshall, Taylor,
Hudson (c), Turner,
Connolly, Whittingham,
Cowie, Conway, Noone (Kim
Bo-Kyung), Helguson (Gestede),
Bellamy (Mason).
Subs not used: Lewis, McNaughton,
Gunnarsson, Lappin.

167

'Keep your head down!' Malky shares a lighter moment with former Rover, Bellamy.

THE CHAMPIONSHIP

THE LATE, LATE SHOW

This weekend saw widespread late drama re-shape the top of the Championship table as a stream of dramatic goals in the dying moments had a big bearing on the promotion places.

This was, most helpfully, the case at Selhurst Park where **Blackpool's** Nouha Dicko banged home a last minute equaliser to deny **Ian Holloway** *(pictured)* victory over the club he acrimoniously departed just thirty-five days before. On-loan Aston Villa striker Nathan Delfouneso had given the Seasiders a first half lead, before **Crystal Palace's** winged wonders Wilfried Zaha and Yannick Bolasie took flight. They picked out Owen Garvan and Glenn Murray respecively for two well taken headed goals, Murray's marking his eighteenth strike of the season.

Less helpful to City's cause was Jamie Vardy's last minute turn and strike for **Leicester City** which saw them escape with a point from a home tie with **Barnsley.** Anthony Knockaert had the Foxes on course for what some considered to be a routine victory, only for Stephen Dawson and Reuben Noble-Lazarus to put the Tykes into a surprise lead by half-time. Yet Vardy, a million pound summer singing from Fleetwood Town, grabbed the point and the headlines with his first goal since September.

Middlesbrough meanwhile very nearly let three points slip away at **Peterborough United,** only to be rescued by Ishmael Miller's long-range effort fifteen minutes from time. A Faris Haroun double had the Teessiders in firm control of the match after just twenty minutes. Yet bottom placed Posh had other ideas and a Dwight Gayle double had them back on level terms, and in the ascendancy, before the hour mark. Darren Ferguson's men will be left to rue some slack defending for the defeat though, as they let Miller, with his first touches of the match, to turn outside the area and fire home low and hard past a disappointed Robert Olejnik.

The biggest drama of the day was reserved for the relegation battle though, as **Sheffield Wednesday** and **Bristol City** met at Hillsbrough, both desperate for a win. Dave Jones' men will regret their indiscipline as they twic lost the lead from the spot. Firstly, Miguel Llera handled i the area to allow Sam Baldock to score and cancel out the Spaniard's own third minute header. Then the same two tangled in the box four minutes from time to allow Baldock to convert for a second time and equalise Gary Madine's seventy-ninth minute goal. Tw minutes from time a foul on the edge of the box allowed Albert Adomah to curl home a free kick and give Bristol City a seemingly decisive 3-2 lead a such a late stage.

There was still time for the Owl to launch one final attack though, and incredibly as referee Andre Marriner allowed advantage to be played despite what seemed a clear-cut penalty, Madine turned the ball home amongst a melee for what looked like the leveller. Astonishingly though, Marriner pulled play back against Wednesday, claiming Llera had pushed him in his penalty appeal. It was a decision that saw the points flutter away to the west country.

>> LEADING SCORERS

1	2	3	4	5
42	41	38	37	37
> CARDIFF CITY	> CRYSTAL PALACE	> WATFORD	> MIDDLESBROUGH	> BLACKPOOL

FINISH WHAT YOU'VE STARTED!

statistical look at the late goal effect

...ty have scored late in each of their last two games. Craig Conway's ...inner to prolong our 100% home run came 10 minutes from the ...eath, before Joe Mason and Kim Bo-Kyung chipped in even later to ...ub salt in the wounds at Ewood Park last Friday.

...kipper Mark Hudson had set the tone for late goals with his injury ...me winner against Huddersfield on the opening day. But after Aron ...unnarsson repeated the trick against Watford in October, City went ...n to open the scoring within 5 minutes in 3 of the next 4 matches!

...o City have certainly spread the goals – both around the team ...even different players have scored four or more league goals in a ...ardiff shirt so far) as well as across the 90 minutes. But some of our ...hampionship rivals have found consistency over the full 90 minutes ...arder to come by.

...ake **Huddersfield Town** for example. If the table were drawn up after only 45 minutes, the Terriers would be sitting pretty in second place. Simon Grayson's men have been leading at the break on no fewer than 11 occasions – an achievement matched only by ourselves. Meanwhile lowly **Wolves** and **Burnley,** currently in 16th and 17th position respectively, would be putting pressure on the Yorkshiremen challenging for an automatic spot.

And it's been a similar story for today's visitors **Peterborough United.** Despite going in to the half-time break behind in just 6 of their 21 matches, only once have they outscored their opponents in the second half. If all of their matches had ended at the half-time whistle they would currently be in mid-table safety, 14 points better off than their actual position 5 points adrift in the drop-zone.

DID YOU KNOW?

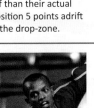

City rewrote history in their last outing at the CCS as an unprecedented 10th win on the bounce broke a club record. But which feat exactly did they surpass?

Well, City have recorded 9 successive home wins in 2 separate campaigns – both of which ended in automatic promotion. In 1951-52, Cardiff went up in second place to Sheffield United thanks, in part, to the firepower of forward **Wilf Grant.** Then in the 2000-01 season, a young **Robert Earnshaw** *(pictured)* finished as top scorer in his first full season for the senior side, having just returned from a loan spell at Scottish Division One side Greenock Morton!

npower FOOTBALL LEAGUE

LATEST RESULTS
7/8th December
Blackburn Rovers 1–4 Cardiff City
Charlton Athletic 2–2 Brighton & Hove Albion
Crystal Palace 2–2 Blackpool
Derby County 3–1 Leeds United
Huddersfield Town 2–2 Bolton Wanderers
Ipswich Town 3–0 Millwall
Leicester City 2–2 Barnsley
Nottingham Forest 2–0 Burnley
Peterborough United 2–3 Middlesbrough
Sheffield Wednesday 2–3 Bristol City
Watford 1–2 Hull City
Wolves 1–0 Birmingham City

TODAY'S GAMES
(All games kick off at 3pm unless otherwise stated)
Barnsley v Sheffield Wed (5:20pm)
Birmingham City v Crystal Palace
Blackpool v Blackburn Rovers
Bolton Wanderers v Charlton Athletic
Brighton & Hove Albion v Nottingham Forest
Bristol City v Derby County
Burnley v Watford
Cardiff City v Peterborough United
Hull City v Huddersfield Town (12:30pm)
Leeds United v Ipswich Town
Middlesbrough v Wolves
Millwall v Leicester City

2012/13 NPOWER CHAMPIONSHIP LEAGUE TABLE

Pos	Team	P	W	D	L	GD	Pts
1	**Cardiff City**	21	14	2	5	16	44
2	Crystal Palace	21	12	5	4	15	41
3	Middlesbrough	21	12	2	7	8	38
4	Hull City	21	12	2	7	5	38
5	Leicester City	21	11	4	6	17	37
6	Watford	21	10	3	8	8	33
7	Millwall	21	9	6	6	4	33
8	Brighton	21	8	8	5	8	32
9	Nottm Forest	21	8	8	5	4	32
10	Derby County	21	8	6	7	1	30
11	Blackpool	21	7	8	6	6	29
12	Charlton	21	7	8	6	2	29
13	Blackburn	21	7	8	6	0	29
14	Leeds United	21	8	5	8	-4	29
15	Huddersfield	21	8	5	8	-5	29
16	Wolves	21	8	4	9	2	28
17	Burnley	21	8	4	9	-3	28
18	Bolton	21	6	8	7	-2	26
19	Birmingham	21	6	6	9	-7	24
20	Ipswich Town	21	6	5	10	-19	23
21	Bristol City	21	5	3	13	-11	18
22	Barnsley	21	4	6	11	-13	18
23	Sheffield Wed	21	4	3	14	-16	15
24	Peterborough	21	4	1	16	-16	13

CF ELEVEN

THE OFFICIAL CARDIFF CITY FC MATCH PROGRAMME

CARDIFF CITY

—VERSUS—

CRYSTAL PALACE

WED 26TH DEC 3:00PM

npower CHAMPIONSHIP — MATCH 24 £3

MATCH SPONSOR: FIX AUTO

TEAM SPONSOR: DAVID GALLIGAN

Malaysia **PUMA** Player

12

WE'RE HALF WAY THER

Good afternoon and a festive welcome back to Cardiff City Stadium for today's match with Crystal Palace. I'd also like to welcome Ian Holloway, his staff, players and everyone from Selhurst Park who have made the trip from London today. It's the second time Ian has been here this season and matches against him are rarely humdrum affairs, so I look forward to taking him on again today.

I really hope you all had a wonderful Christmas yesterday and managed to enjoy yourselves without too much excess!

We were all in at the training ground preparing for today's match, but I made sure the players got away early enough to spend some quality time with their families. Obviously, spirits were high because Saturday's win and performance at Leicester were very, very good. We showed a maturity and determination that are hallmarks I always expect to see in any of my teams, particularly as we were under considerable pressure in the opening stages of the game.

During that period, it was vital that we defended properly, concentrated on the basics – hard work, concentration, application and keeping our shape – and didn't lose our belief. As a team we stuck to the task and, once we had gone in front via that excellent goal from Craig Bellamy, I thought we comfortably handled what Nigel Pearson's men threw at us.

Indeed, once we got our noses in front, I felt that we looked by far the more likely side to score the next goal and, with a bit more care, could have had a more comfortable last ten minutes. However, it was a clinical display against what I believe to be one of the very best teams in this league this season. Leicester have invested considerable sums in their squad going back over the last two years and have a lot of good players at their disposal. To beat them and move ten points ahead of them meant that Saturday will have to go down as a good day for us.

It was also an excellent indication of the spirit and determination amongst everyone at the club to bounce back so decisively from the disappointment of the Peterborough United game here ten days ago. Obviously we were very frustrated with the way we played on the day and couldn't have too many complaints that we didn't chalk up our eleventh straight home win, although I did feel that we created enough chances to grab a point.

Other teams would have dwelled on that loss and perhaps let it colour their next match, particularly when the fixtures called for us to make that difficult trip to Leicester, but we took the loss on the chin, learned lessons from it and bounced straight back with an outstanding victory.

We are now at the precise half way point of the Championship season with 23 matches played and 23 still to go. We have also now played every team in the league and I have to be satisfied to be sitting on top of the table despite having to do without players of the calibre of Nicky Maynard and Tommy Smith for long spells.

I know I say it often but it always bears repeating; only by having everyone in the club pulling together with the same determination and belief will we be able to achieve what we set out to do so I have been very pleased with the progress we have made.

If you consider that we brought in nine new players in the summer, they have bedded in really well and we have come together nicely as a team and a squad. At this time of year, people's thoughts often turn to January and what might happen when the transfer window opens, but before we start dealing with that, we have a very tough match here today and another one on Saturday.

Palace, like ourselves, have had an excellent first half of the season and have not let the departure of their manager unsettle them. Therefore, we know that they will come here today believing that they can beat us and get themselves back into the top two where they have spent the majority of the last few months. We know we will have to match their hard work and their ability to pick up another three points and we will also need your fantastic support again. More than 2,000 of you made the trip to the East Midlands on Saturday and put on a wonderful display of support for the team – the clichéd twelfth man in the stands – and I'm sure today's atmosphere will match that. Enjoy the game.

" WE TOOK THE LOSS ON THE CHIN, LEARNED LESSONS FROM IT AND BOUNCED STRAIGHT BACK WITH AN OUTSTANDING VICTORY "

NPOWER CHAMPIONSHIP

CARDIFF CITY 1
Gestede (89)

PETERBOROUGH 2
Bostwick (22), Gayle (47)

SATURDAY ▶ 15th DECEMBER ▶ 3.00pm Full Attendance **26,073**

🏠 **25,809**
🚌 **264**

City started with intent in this one and inside four minutes, Heidar Helguson's header was in the back of Peterborough's net – only for the linesman's flag to cut celebrations short. Another controversial refereeing decision gifted Posh a free kick on the edge of the Cardiff area on twenty-two minutes and Michael Bostwick made no mistake, pile-driving an unstoppable laid-off shot into the roof of the net. This early advantage allowed Peterborough to sit back and absorb pressure, counter attacking with pace and danger.

Renewed City optimism was cut short two minutes into the second half, Peterborough catching Cardiff at the back with a devastating attack that left Kevin McNaughton in no-man's land as Lee Tomlin squared to on-loan Dwight Gayle for a simple finish.

On another day, Helguson could have bagged a hatrick, but the striker shot wide from twelve yards before a lob agonisingly fell the wrong side of the post. Substitute Rudy Gestede gave Cardiff hope late on with six minutes of injury time left to play, but Posh held on for the unlikely away win.

FANS SAY
"Mark Hudson was definitely missed yesterday. It does happen in this league though, bottom beating top, and a defeat at home was always going to come at some point." – *David Richard Lewis*

MALKY
"On another day, Heidar could have scored five. We did everything but score and we weren't clinical. We were beaten and can play much better. We have to be as consistent as possible, and the league table shows that."

FERGUSON
"We've come to the best team in the league at the moment – a team that I think will get promoted automatically – and beaten them. This is the best victory I've had in the Championship for Peterborough."

WHITTINGHAM
"It was really frustrating for us; I felt that if we had got the goal a little sooner we would have definitely been in with a shout. It's very disappointing but it's all about kicking on from here."

THE BREAK DOWN

REFEREE: D. Coote

13 | 7

55% | 45%

POSSESSION

4 | 4

SHOTS

7 ON 11

13 OFF 4

st-match reaction from Malky Mackay
d Darren
rguson on
diff City Player

CARDIFF CITY Player

diff City: Marshall, McNaughton
nnarsson), Connolly,
urner, Taylor, Conway
stede), Whittingham (c),
owie (Mutch), Noone,
elguson, Bellamy.
s not used: Lewis,
Kyung,
nnarsson,
pin.

Peterborough
United: Olejnik,
Zakuani, Little,
Bostwick, Rowe (c) (Brisley),
Newell (Ferdinand), Knight-
Percival (Alcock), Thorne, Tomlin,
Boyd, Gayle.
Subs not used: Day, Swanson, McCann,
Gordon-Hutton.

177

A familiar pose. Darren Ferguson's men call time on City's record run of home wins.

LEICESTER CITY 0

CARDIFF CITY 1

Bellamy (25)

SATURDAY ▶ 22ND DECEMBER ▶ 3.00PM | Full Attendance 25,055

🏠 22,943

🚌 2,112

MALKY

"I talked to them about their last away performance where we were exceptional but this tops that. As the half wore on, the calmness we showed was incredible against a very good team."

PEARSON

"When you create as many goal scoring opportunities as we did, you would expect to score. But today we came up against a side that, to be fair to them, defended well and had a lot of experience."

Leicester started the game much the brighter but some fine goalkeeping and a little help from the woodwork saw that City didn't fall behind early on. Just after the midway point of the first half Cardiff caught the Foxes on the counter, as Craig Bellamy managed to escape his markers and slot home from a Craig Conway pass.

Leicester then increased the tempo once more and were unlucky not to equalise through Wales international Andy King. The Foxes also came close to equalising through Wes Morgan and David Nugent, but David Marshall was at hand once again.

After the break Leicester started as they had finished the first, but again City nearly caught the hosts on the counter. Bellamy laid the ball off to Heidar Helguson who was denied by a last ditch Morgan interception. The second half saw Malky's men looking a lot more comfortable. As Leicester chased the game there were chances for both sides, but Cardiff City were to hold on for an impressive win to reach Christmas as number one.

CONWAY

"Leicester threw a lot at us in the first half but we weathered the storm well. In the second half I thought we were calm and protected our lead. We're very happy to win here."

FANS SAY

"This was a huge win – Leicester are no mugs. Great to bounce back like that away from home after the Peterborough defeat. Well done lads." – *Elliot Lugg*

THE BREAKDOWN

REFEREE: G.Salisbury

6

65% 35%

POSSESSION

0 0

SHOTS
13 ON 3
5 OFF

e post-match reaction of this game from
alky Mackay and
gel Pearson on
rdiff City Player

CARDIFF CITY Player

cester City: Schmeichel, De Laet,
ncheskey, Morgan, Whitbread,
nkwater, King, Dyer
ngard), Knockaert
arshall), Vardy
aghorn), Nugent.
bs not used:
gan, Moore,
nes, Futacs.

Cardiff City:
Marshall,
Connolly, Hudson (c),
Turner, Taylor, Kim (Cowie),
Whittingham, Mutch
(Gunnarsson), Conway, Helguson
(Gestede), Bellamy.
Subs not used: Lewis, McNaughton,
Noone, Mason.

181

A key scalp. Bellamy's strike at King Power Stadium would set the tone for what would follow.

THE CHAMPIONSHIP

CHRISTMAS CRACKERS

Today is one of the few days of the year where the masses can feasibly show sympathy for the handsomely paid professional footballer! While we take our position in our seats, relaxed and merry from festive cheer, and with our bodies still attempting to digest yesterday's excesses – football players across the land are back in work. In fact, they've never not been in work; the majority of clubs still train, or at least travel, on Boxing Day, and now they're tasked with putting on a top notch display for us fans. Let's hope they deliver!

Last season it was us doing the traveling with a visit to **Watford** and a 1-1 draw after Adrian Mariappa, now at Reading, helped us to the point by netting past his own 'keeper with just ten minutes to go and cancel out Prince Buaben's opener. The result kept City in fourth place and in touch with the top three who were all also in action. Leaders **Southampton** edged out today's opponents **Crystal Palace** thanks to a Guly do Prado double and that gave them a three point advantage after second placed **West Ham** were held to a 1-1 draw at struggling **Birmingham City.** Meanwhile, **Reading's** 3-0 home win over **Brighton** marked their third on the bounce and would prove to be the catalyst that eventually propelled them to win seventeen from their next twenty-three fixtures on their way to promotion.

Back in 2010/11 the Championship played host to a truncated fixture list, but the top three remained in action and again Cardiff were heavily involved. Seyi Olofinjana and Craig Bellamy netted in a 2-0 home win over **Coventry City** which lifted City into second place in the table and above **Leeds United** who dropped a spot following a 2-2 draw with **Leicester City** when a Paul Gallagher penalty and Andy King's goal pulled the Foxes back from two-goal down. It was QPR who remained top after a resounding 4-0 win over **Swansea City** at Loftus Road with Adel Taarabt netting twice and Alan Tate and Clint Hill each seeing red cards.

On Boxing Day 2009 Cardiff were on the end of a shock defeat to lowly **Plymouth Argyle** when Gary Sawyer's deflected finish left City frustrated. The result also left us back in fifth place and level on points with **Swansea City** who were held to a 1-1 draw at **Reading.** League leaders **Newcastle United** were also left frustrated after a 2-2 draw at twenty-third placed **Sheffield Wednesday** which allowed **West Brom** to pull within eight points of the Magpies as they beat bottom-placed **Peterborough United** 2-0. **Blackpool,** who would eventually go on to gain promotion, were at this point sat back in eighth after a 2-away win at **Derby County,** whilst **Crystal Palace** fired three past **Ipswich** in a 3-1 win at Selhurst Park.

›› TOP AT CHRISTMAS

1 2012	2 2011	3 2010	4 2009	5 2008
› CARDIFF CITY	› SOUTHAMPTON	› QPR	› NEWCASTLE UTD	› WOLVES

3 DOWN ... 23 TO GO!

 look at the halfway mark of previous Championship
 easons.

 turday's trip to **Leicester City** marked the half-way point of this
 ason's Championship. By this point every team has had ample
 portunity to stamp their mark on the division but, although the
 ble certainly doesn't lie by now, there always seems to be at least
 e team that defies all expectations in the second half of the
 mpaign to either clinch promotion, reach the Play-Offs or streak
 vay from the relegation picture.

 st season that team was **Reading.** This time last year, the Royals
 ere 11 points adrift of leaders Southampton, who were showing
 w signs of faltering. But a remarkable run in the New Year, spurred
  by the shrewd acquisition of Blackburn front-man Jason Roberts,
 w McDermott's men lose just one of seventeen games, en route
  their finish as champions.

 ading's heroics last season were reminiscent of
 inderland's dramatic ascent back in 2006-07.
 ving notched up just 15 points in the Premier
 ague the season before, their first campaign
 der new manager Roy Keane *(pictured)*
 oked set to be another disappointing
 e, as they sat almost as close to the
 egation zone as the summit of the
 ble. But come the final day, the
 ack Cats were crowned champions.
  the second half of the season the free
 oring outfit boosted their goal difference
  27, and their final position by 10.

  the other end of the table, perhaps the
 ost spectacular second half revival was
 at of **Doncaster Rovers** in 2008-09,
 th current Forest boss Sean
 Driscoll at the helm. It was not
 oking good for Donny after 23 games as
 st 4 wins left them rooted to the bottom
  the league. But an incredible streak of
 rm at the business end of the season left
 e final table looking somewhat different –
 nny had leapt up ten places and more
 an tripled their points tally, leaving them
 t just safe, but comfortably in mid-table.

DID YOU KNOW?

 City eventually slipped up at the CCS after an incredible 10 wins
 on the bounce against Peterborough – but did you know that
 Southampton did exactly the same last year? The Saints also
 stumbled in their eleventh home fixture, having to settle for a
 draw against Blackpool courtesy of a 93rd minute Rickie
 Lambert equaliser. Coincidentally, the team that they faced on
 Boxing Day in their very next home match was Crystal Palace!
 A 2-0 win over the Eagles got them back to winning ways at St.
 Mary's. The City faithful will be hoping that history repeats
 itself this afternoon.

LATEST RESULTS
21st/22nd December
Birmingham City 2–2 Burnley
Blackburn Rovers P–P Brighton & Hove Albion
Blackpool 1–2 Wolves
Crystal Palace 1–1 Huddersfield Town
Ipswich Town 1–1 Bristol City
Leeds United 2–1 Middlesbrough
Leicester City 0–1 Cardiff City
Millwall 1–2 Barnsley
Peterborough United 5–4 Bolton Wanderers
Sheffield Wednesday 2–0 Charlton Athletic
Watford 2–0 Nottingham Forest

TODAY'S GAMES
(All games kick off at 3pm unless otherwise stated)

Charlton Athletic v Ipswich Town
Barnsley v Birmingham City
Bolton Wanderers v Sheffield Wednesday
Bristol City v Watford
Burnley v Derby County
Cardiff City v Crystal Palace
Huddersfield Town v Blackpool
Hull City v Leicester City
Middlesbrough v Blackburn Rovers
Nottingham Forest v Leeds United (12:15pm)
Wolves v Peterborough United

2012/13 NPOWER CHAMPIONSHIP LEAGUE TABLE

Pos	Team	P	W	D	L	GD	Pts
1	**Cardiff City**	23	15	2	6	16	47
2	Hull City	23	14	2	7	8	44
3	**Crystal Palace**	23	12	7	4	15	43
4	Middlesbrough	23	13	2	8	9	41
5	Leicester City	23	11	4	8	15	37
6	Watford	23	11	4	8	10	37
7	Millwall	24	10	7	7	4	37
8	Leeds United	23	10	5	8	-1	35
9	Brighton	23	8	10	5	8	34
10	Derby County	23	9	6	8	2	33
11	Nottm Forest	23	8	9	6	2	33
12	Blackpool	23	8	8	7	7	32
13	Wolves	23	9	4	10	1	31
14	Burnley	23	8	6	9	-3	30
15	Huddersfield	23	8	6	9	-7	30
16	Bolton	23	7	8	8	-1	29
17	Blackburn	22	7	8	7	-2	29
18	Charlton	23	7	8	8	-2	29
19	Birmingham	23	6	8	9	-7	26
20	Ipswich Town	23	6	6	11	-21	24
21	Sheffield Wed	23	6	3	14	-13	21
22	Barnsley	23	5	6	12	-13	21
23	Bristol City	23	5	4	14	-13	19
24	Peterborough	23	6	1	16	-14	19

CF ELEVEN

THE OFFICIAL CARDIFF CITY FC MATCH PROGRAMME

CARDIFF CITY

VERSUS

MILLWALL

SAT 29TH DEC 3:00PM

npower CHAMPIONSHIP   MATCH 25 £3

MATCH SPONSOR: CIRCLE IT

MATCH BALL SPONSOR:
WILLIAMS CONTRACTORS

13

MALKY MACKAY

MOMENTUM MATTERS

Happy New Year and welcome back to Cardiff City Stadium for the final match of 2012, coming only three short days after what was a gruelling encounter and positive Boxing Day result against one of our promotion rivals in Crystal Palace. I would also like to extend a warm welcome to Kenny Jackett and the travelling Millwall players, staff and supporters who have made the one hundred and fifty mile festive trip from the Den. I have no doubt that they will offer another big test to our players this afternoon, yet again requiring the very best from us if we are to see a positive result to maintain pressure on those around us.

As you may have seen in the Palace programme, the backroom staff have worked tirelessly in preparing the squad over the last two days and remain a credit to this football club.

Playing a high volume of Christmas games isn't without its issues, though a spring in our step has been added thanks to what was a very good result on Wednesday against Crystal Palace. The early goal conceded was frustrating for all of us, but on and off the pitch there was a sense of momentum being built by us after that, which I strongly believe led to our equaliser close to the break. And from there onwards you all played a big part in making Cardiff City by far the superior side in the second half, which is something we talked about after the game. Trust us, it's very much appreciated and is a big factor, something that will hopefully remain the case over what will be a difficult second half of the season.

For the fourth time this season, on Wednesday we won a match after having gone a goal behind, a statistic that has yet to be reached by any of our league rivals. Against a very strong opponent I was hugely encouraged by the way my players responded to what was an early setback to turn the game into a positive result, which for me outlines the character, belief and commitment to the club from all of my players and staff. Yet again, the positives of a stronger, if not larger squad could be seen by the quality options on the bench, allowing us, even when we are missing one or two players due to injury or suspension, to turn to players who can change games.

The same can be said of both players and backroom staff when it comes to the overall blend of the group. As a manager you search for the best possible quality, both on and off the field, taking the form of professional excellence and strength of character from the individuals concerned. Finding the right mix, which I believe we continue to do here, can help everything to mesh without the complications of egos and as a result makes this club bigger than the sum of its parts.

Today we have another test of our credentials, while knowing that Millwall will present a huge challenge for us. Some people would say they're surprised that Millwall are up there and challenging for promotion, but I'm not so sure about that. Kenny has built a good squad there over the last few years, so it's going to be a very tough game for us today, but we knew this period was going to be like that.

As I close my final notes column of the calendar year I would, on behalf of all of us at Cardiff City, thank you sincerely for your amazing support in 2012, while asking you all to keep up the sterling work in 2013. I've no doubt that you'll make yourselves heard today and will continue to, forgive the cliché, be our twelfth man out there. Rest assured we'll do all we can to bring you all the success you deserve.

Happy New Year. Enjoy the match.

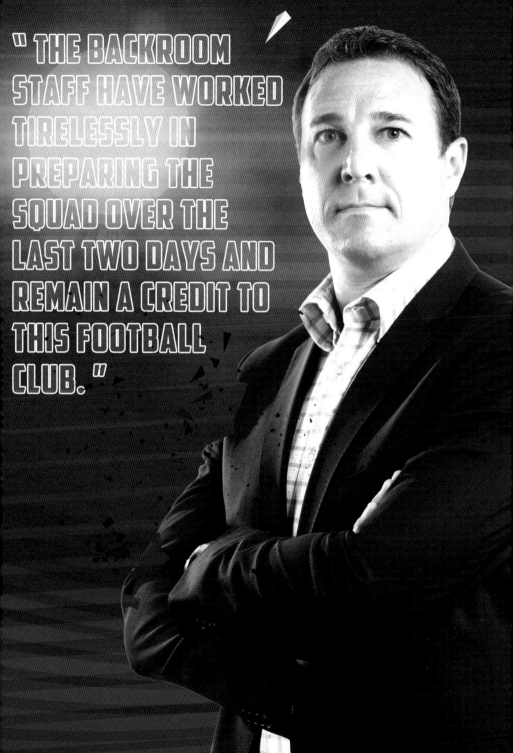

" THE BACKROOM STAFF HAVE WORKED TIRELESSLY IN PREPARING THE SQUAD OVER THE LAST TWO DAYS AND REMAIN A CREDIT TO THIS FOOTBALL CLUB. "

189

CARDIFF CITY 2

Noone (44), Gunnarsson (72)

CRYSTAL PALACE 1

Jedinak (4)

WEDNESDAY ▶ 26TH DECEMBER ▶ 3.00PM | Full Attendance 26,098

🏠 **24,908**
🚌 **1,190**

MALKY

"It took until the half hour mark for us to really get into the game and get on the front foot. From then on I thought we were excellent. It is about patience and doing the correct things and that is what they did."

HOLLOWAY

"We started well and ended terribly. I thought we stopped creating chances and in these games you can't do that, you have to keep going. If either side looked like they were going to score again it was Cardiff."

City boosted their promotion credentials as they opened up a five point gap at the top of the Championship table with a comeback win over Crystal Palace.

Goals were guaranteed in this encounter as both sides had failed to score on just one occasion this season – and it was the visitors who struck first. Eagles' skipper Mile Jedinak hooked in from a corner to stun the sell-out crowd after just four minutes. Wilfried Zaha and Glenn Murray both went close soon after as Palace applied plenty of first half pressure. But City pulled level on the stroke of half-time as Craig Noone hammered the ball home following some good attacking work from Craig Bellamy.

The second half saw City up their game, aided by the half-time introduction of Aron Gunnarsson. And it was the Icelander himself who would win it for Cardiff with less than 20 minutes remaining, heading home from an in-swinging Bellamy corner kick delivery to ensure that City got back to winning ways at the CCS.

NOONE

"It was a great win for us today, especially after having gone a goal down early on; the lads showed great character to get a goal back before the break."

FANS SAY "This was a good, hard win today against Crystal Palace. Well done Cardiff for going five points clear at the top of the Championship." – *Anthony Covington*

REFEREE: P. Gibbs

3 ⚑ 5

46% 52%

POSSESSION

🟥 0 3 🟨 0 4

SHOTS
6 ON 3
OFF 7

st-match reaction from Malky Mackay,
Holloway and
ig Noone on
diff City Player

CARDIFF CITY Player

diff City: Marshall, McNaughton,
Iudson (c), Turner, Taylor,
Joone (Mason),
ittingham, Mutch
innarsson), Conway,
guson (Gestede),
lamy.
s not used:
vis, Cowie,
-Kyung,
pin.

Crystal Palace: Speroni,
Parr (Easter),
Gabbidon, Ramage, Moxey,
Dikgacoi, Garvan, Jedinak (c),
Zaha, Murray, Bolasie (Moritz).
Subs not used: Price, Martin, Williams,
O'Keefe, Appiah.

191

In the pocket. City's full-backs out-smart Manchester United-bound Wilfried Zaha on Boxing Day.

THE CHAMPIONSHIP

BOXING DAY – PULLING NO PUNCHES

The game of the day was undoubtedly played out at the City Ground, where **Nottingham Forest** and **Leeds United** clashed with seismic ramifications again.

With the memory of last season's 7-3 thriller still fresh in the mind, the two former British football heavyweights produced six goals this time out and a subsequent managerial casualty. A Billy Sharp double, Rudolph Austin's own goal and a brilliant Dexter Blackstock header all in the space of sixteen minutes dramatically overturned Paul Green's opener for the visitors. By the time David Somma had turned in a last minute consolation, the game was well and truly buried. Yet, despite an impressive 4-2 win over bitter rivals that left Forest just one point shy of the Play-Off places, it was announced by the club's owner that manager **Sean O'Driscoll** *(pictured)*, recruited only five months previously, had been relieved of his position.

While City were holding off Crystal Palace at a sodden CCS, another big result was going our way on Humberside. **Hull City's** run of four straight wins came to an end in the form of a goalless draw with fellow promotion hopefuls **Leicester City**. The result leaves Hull in second, five points back from Cardiff, while Leicester, who have not scored in their last three fixtures, sit fifth and a further seven points adrift. **Middlesbrough** did keep up the pressure though. They moved into third, six points off the summit with a 1-0 win over **Blackburn Rovers** at Riverside Stadium. Lukas Jutkiewicz was the scorer of the only goal – and Rovers boss

Henning Berg would lose his job at Ewood Park the next day.

Peterborough United, with a spring in their step following their win at Cardiff City Stadium and their frenetic victory in a nine goal thriller over Bolton, made it three wins on the bounce to rightfully move themselves off the foot of the table. **Wolverhampton Wanderers** were comfortably dispatched by three goals to nil as Stale Solbakken's men's home turf struggles continue. Lee Tomlin netted his second in two matches with a seventeenth minute opener, and Tommy Rowe had doubled the advantage at half-time. Almost inevitably Dwight Gayle, fresh off announcing his permanent switch from Dagenham & Redbridge, made it six from seven in Posh jersey to seal the win with a near post finish midway through the second half.

Sheffield Wednesday also recorded their third straight win to move out of the relegation zone. Mamady Sidibe's first half finish was enough to see off **Bolton Wanderers** at the Reebok Stadium and for Dave Jones' men's momentum to continue. In the basement battle, it was Wednesday and Peterborough who were the big winners in more ways than one as **Barnsley** fell to a 2-1 defeat to **Birmingham City** thanks to Curtis Davies' double. **Bristol City** meanwhile saw their match with **Watford** postponed due to a severely waterlogged pitch. The Robins are now five points adrift from safety at the bottom of the pile.

►► LEADING SCORERS

1	2	3	4	5
46	45	41	41	41
► CARDIFF CITY	► CRYSTAL PALACE	► WATFORD	► MIDDLESBROUGH	► BLACKPOOL

ACE FOR THE GOLDEN BOOT

ook at the Championship's top-scorers

e festive period is a time when some Championship goal-scorers
y be checking their pre-season targets to see if they're still on
ck. This year's current hot-shots include the likes of **Glenn**
rray and **Charlie Austin,** who have both reached the 20 goal
rk already. But will they keep it up as we embark upon the
:ond half of the season?

th of those men are on track to surpass the record 27 goals
tched by last season's top scorer **Rickie Lambert**. The Saints'
get man had scored a respectable 12 goals by the turn of the
ar, but hat-tricks against both **Watford** and **Millwall** post-
cember helped him on the way to his huge final haul.

nbert's main golden boot rivals both scored their goals for two
ferent clubs last year. **Billy Sharp** and **Ricardo Vaz Tê** secured
uary transfers to the top two teams in the division, having
ught the eye with ten league goals each for **Doncaster Rovers**
d **Barnsley** respectively. Both were models of consistency in the
:ond half of the season as well, doubling their tallies with their
w clubs.

e of the most remarkable goal-scoring turnarounds in recent
ars was that of **Andy Carroll** (pictured) during **Newcastle's** term
the second tier. He had more yellow cards than
als by Christmas, having mustered up just 4
gue strikes. But he went on to quadruple his
ring record, finishing up with 17 goals to
name.

d what about those who
ve gone off the boil?
lish front-
n
zegorz Rasiak
ked a favourite for the golden boot in
07-08 having netted 17 times for the Saints
the end of January. But just two goals in his
maining 15 matches saw him drift down the
ring charts. Five men surpassed him,
:luding **Michael Chopra** and
bert Earnshaw, then plying his trade
Norwich.

DID YOU KNOW?

The race for the Championship golden
boot is as competitive as ever this year –
but the award is not necessarily an
ndication of league success for the
winner's club. Only four of the eight
golden boot winners since the formation
of the Championship have done so as
part of a promotion winning side. And in
fact, the only time a golden boot winner's club has been
crowned champions was in the 2008-09 campaign as
Wolverhampton Wanderers, fired on by **Sylvan Ebanks-Blake's**
25 goals, finished in 1st place.

npower FOOTBALL LEAGUE

LATEST RESULTS
26th December
Nottingham Forest 4–2 Leeds United
Charlton Athletic 1–2 Ipswich Town
Barnsley 1–2 Birmingham City
Bolton Wanderers 0–1 Sheffield Wednesday
Burnley 2–0 Derby County
Bristol City P–P Watford
Cardiff City 2–1 Crystal Palace
Huddersfield Town 1–1 Blackpool
Hull City 0–0 Leicester City
Middlesbrough 1–0 Blackburn Rovers
Wolves 0–3 Peterborough United

TODAY'S GAMES
(All games kick off at 3pm unless otherwise stated)
Barnsley v Blackburn Rovers
Bolton Wanderers v Birmingham City
Brighton & Hove Albion v Watford (5:20pm)
Bristol City v Peterborough United
Burnley v Leicester City
Cardiff City v Millwall
Charlton Athletic v Derby County
Huddersfield Town v Sheffield Wed. (12:30pm)
Hull City v Leeds United (12:30pm)
Middlesbrough v Blackpool
Nottingham Forest v Crystal Palace
Wolves v Ipswich Town

2012/13 NPOWER CHAMPIONSHIP LEAGUE TABLE

Pos	Team	P	W	D	L	GD	Pts
1	**Cardiff City**	24	16	2	6	17	50
2	Hull City	24	14	3	7	8	45
3	Middlesbrough	24	14	2	8	10	44
4	Crystal Palace	24	12	7	5	14	43
5	Leicester City	24	11	5	8	15	38
6	Watford	23	11	4	8	10	37
7	**Millwall**	24	10	7	7	4	37
8	Nottm Forest	24	9	9	6	4	36
9	Leeds United	24	10	5	9	-3	35
10	Brighton	23	8	10	5	8	34
11	Blackpool	24	8	9	7	7	33
12	Derby County	24	9	6	9	0	33
13	Burnley	24	9	6	9	-1	33
14	Wolves	24	9	4	11	-2	31
15	Huddersfield	24	8	7	9	-7	31
16	Bolton	24	7	8	9	-2	29
17	Blackburn	23	7	8	8	-3	29
18	Charlton	24	7	8	9	-3	29
19	Birmingham	24	7	8	9	-6	29
20	Ipswich Town	24	7	6	11	-20	27
21	Sheffield Wed	24	7	3	14	-12	24
22	Peterborough	24	7	1	16	-11	22
23	Barnsley	24	5	6	13	-14	21
24	Bristol City	23	5	4	14	-13	19

CF ELEVEN

THE OFFICIAL CARDIFF CITY FC MATCH PROGRAMME

CARDIFF CITY

—•— V·E·R·S·U·S —•—

IPSWICH TOWN

SAT 12TH JAN 3:00PM

npower CHAMPIONSHIP MATCH 27 £3

MATCH SPONSOR: BRT INTERNATIONAL

MATCH BALL SPONSOR:
DRS CIVIL ENGINEERING

TEAM SPONSOR: CV SHIPPING

Malaysia **PUMA** Player

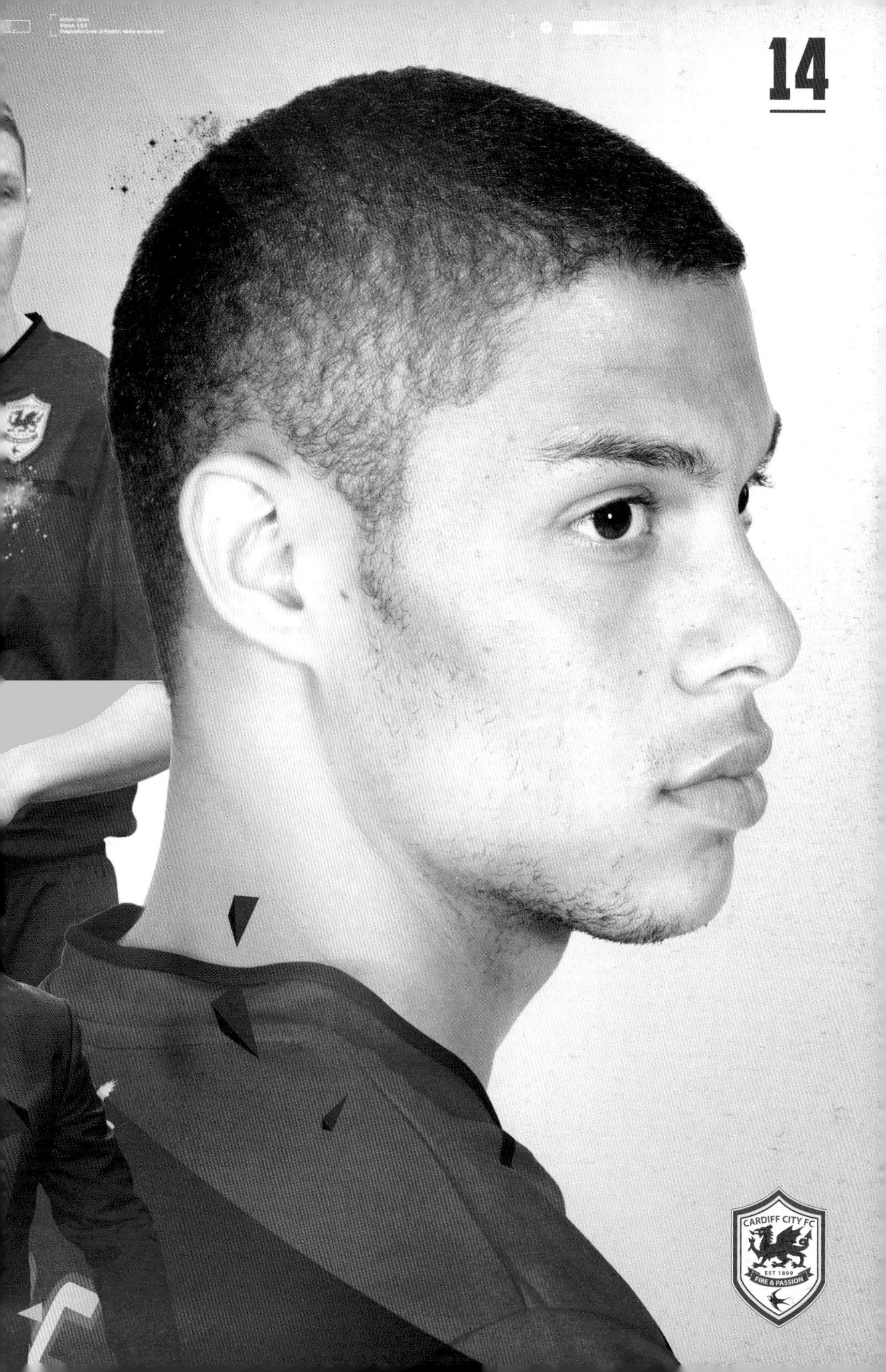

14

CARDIFF CITY FC
EST 1899
FIRE & PASSION

MALKY MACKAY

BACK IN ACTION

Good afternoon and welcome to the Cardiff City Stadium for today's game with Ipswich Town. Today is the third game for us in the new calendar year – 2012 was a year in which we made significant progress as a club and 2013 could be an exciting year too.

I look forward to seeing Town boss Mick McCarthy here today. Mick has done a good job stabilising the club since he arrived a couple of months ago and he's a good man too, so it'll be good to chat to him after the game today. I'd also like to extend that welcome to Mick's staff, players and all fans of Ipswich who have made the long trip to South Wales this afternoon; I hope you had a smooth journey and wish you a safe ride home.

It's been an interesting start to the New Year with the win at Birmingham on 1 January – our fourth successive league victory – and then the F.A. Cup exit at Macclesfield last Saturday.

Starting with the game at St Andrews, it was another good day for us. We had been forced into some late changes to the line-up when Andrew Taylor fell ill on the morning of the match, but that's exactly the reason why we had brought in Simon Lappin on loan. Simon stepped in and did a very good job for us against Birmingham's most dangerous player – Rob Hall on loan from West Ham – and managed to nullify his threat, which meant we kept it very tight at the back.

The pitch at St Andrews makes it hard to play flowing football and, with it being the fourth match in little more than ten days, both teams found it hard to play with a great deal of quality, so it was obvious from the start that we would have to battle to get the points.

A moment of anticipation and a cool head from Joe Mason ended up deciding the match, enabling us to complete the league double over Birmingham for the first time in almost half a century. It showed the quality in our squad that we were able to win a tough

away match against a team which is only eighteen months removed from the Premier League while we were missing Peter Whittingham, Heidar Helguson and Tommy Smith.

Last week at Macclesfield was another opportunity to rotate the squad. I had long planned to use the match as an opportunity for the majority of our development players to stake a claim for more first team inclusion and some of them did just that. It's also important to note that we picked a team which we felt was capable of winning the match and getting into the fourth round of the F.A. Cup and the fact that we were 1-0 up with five minutes remaining more than backs that up.

As we were so young, with eight players aged under 21 on the pitch for the last fifteen minutes, it was a good test and frustrating that they did not manage to see it through. Despite the result, there were still plenty of positives to take from the afternoon – assured performances from Declan John, Ben Nugent and Deji Oshilaja at the back as well as quality on the ball from Joe Ralls in midfield – so it was still a worthwhile exercise. In a similar situation in the future, I would do exactly the same again.

To suggest that our line-up was disrespectful to the tradition of the F.A. Cup was both wrong and also an insult to the eighteen professional players who were on our team sheet, including two full internationals. Instead, we learned what we can from the game whilst congratulating Macclesfield on their win and wishing them all the best for the next round.

I'm happy to be returning to league action today and also know that there is a stiff test in front of us. There has been considerable turnover of players and staff at Ipswich this season, but you can always be certain that Mick's team will be well organised and will give their absolute all to get a result, so we will have to be at our best if we want to maintain our recent winning run.

Enjoy the game.

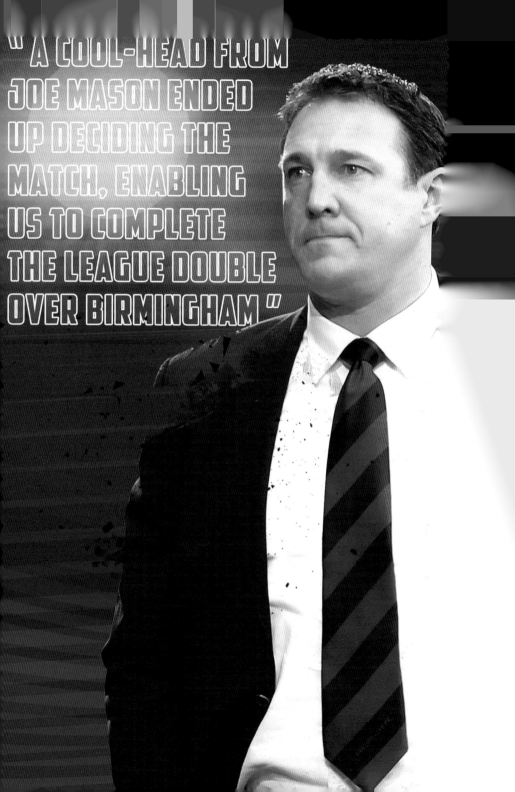

" A COOL-HEAD FROM JOE MASON ENDED UP DECIDING THE MATCH, ENABLING US TO COMPLETE THE LEAGUE DOUBLE OVER BIRMINGHAM "

CARDIFF CITY 1
Gestede (7)

MILLWALL 0

SATURDAY ▶ 29TH DECEMBER ▶ 3.00PM | Full Attendance 24,263

🏠 **23,778**
🚌 **485**

Cardiff City maintained their five point lead at the top of the nPower Championship thanks to a 1-0 victory over Millwall at Cardiff City Stadium.

City took the lead in the early stages of the first half and comfortably held their lead up to the break. The goal came through Rudy Gestede, who was making his first start of the season, as he finished from a right-sided Craig Noone cross. Aron Gunnarsson, also brought into the side following his winner against Crystal Palace on Boxing Day, was forced off by an injury just before half-time, with Jordon Mutch on in his place.

Mark Hudson tried his luck from the halfway line in the second half, but with few real chances in the second period, the league leaders defended solidly to earn the three points. When Millwall did throw bodies forward and strike at goal from long-range, fans Man of the Match David Marshall was more than capable of thwarting the visitors' largely hopeful efforts.

FANS SAY "Despite having only played three days prior, the team battled on to a good win. Three points are three points – well done the City!" – *John Mogford*

KERSLAKE
"We knew that we had a really tough month ahead of us coming into the festive period, but we've applied ourselves the way that the manager expects us to – and we've been delighted with the results."

JACKETT
"It was a good performance and the positive was the amount of chances we created. You need to finish those off. But we didn't go down easily at all."

GESTEDE
"I'm really happy; I've scored on my first start so that's great for the team. We worked hard – Millwall are a tough team so we did well to get three points from them today."

THE BREAKDOWN

REFEREE: M. Halsey

6 ⊽ 3

53% 47%

POSSESSION

1 ▪️▫️ 1

SHOTS

9 ON 6

5 OFF 8

t-match reaction from David Kerslake, nny Jackett and dy Gestede on diff City Player

CARDIFF CITY Player »

diff City: Marshall, McNaughton, lor, Hudson (c), Turner, ittingham, Conway, stede (Helguson), Noone wie), Gunnarsson utch), Bellamy. s not used: Lewis , nolly, Kim, son.

Millwall:
Forde, Shittu (c),
Trotter, Henderson,
Lowry, Henry, Beevers,
N'Guessan (Batt), A. Smith, Abdou,
Malone (Feeney).
Subs not used: Taylor, Dunne, Wright,
J. Smith, Obsorne.

201

Gallic Guile. Rudy opens his seasonal account in the final game of 2012.

BIRMINGHAM CITY 0
CARDIFF CITY 1

Mason (41)

TUESDAY ▶ 1ST JANUARY ▶ 3.00PM | Full Attendance **17,493**

🏠 **15,223**
🚌 **2,270**

MALKY

"We knew we had to battle and fight for everything we got today. To come away with our tenth clean sheet of the season was outstanding and we were very comfortable in the second half."

CLARK

"It's horrible because we are in a business where picking up points is vitally important. The performance collectively was very good against a side that will be promoted."

MARSHALL

"It's been the perfect start to the year for us; we couldn't have hoped for much more than what we've got. Winning four on the bounce over this spell has been fantastic."

On New Year's Day Cardiff City achieved their first win at St. Andrew's since 1966.

The home side dominated much of the first half, but there were very few chances for either team. A shot from Nathan Redmond was comfortably dealt with by David Marshall, while a Wade Elliott strike whistled past the goalkeeper's upright.

Despite these early efforts it was Cardiff City who found themselves securing the breakthrough, after Craig Conway's stinging shot was parried to the feet of Joe Mason who tapped home to make it 1-0.

The second half was free of any major drama for either 'keeper and a period in which City got a larger foothold in the game. Rudy Gestede and Mark Hudson had late efforts which could have sealed the points, though the score remained 1-0 as City held on to go seven points clear at the top of the nPower Championship.

FANS SAY "This was an absolutely awesome away win against Birmingham. We're now seven points clear; I just love it when a plan comes together!" – *Julian Riddiford*

THE BREAKDOWN

REFEREE: R.Madley

3 🚩 **4**

43% **57%**
POSSESSION

0 **0**
3 🟥 **0**

SHOTS
2 ON **3**
3 OFF **3**

e post-match reaction of this game from
alky Mackay and
e Clark on
rdiff City Player

CARDIFF CITY Player ⏩

mingham City: Butland, Caldwell,
vies, Spector, Packwood
ancox), ▮ Robinson,
orrison, Elliott (Jervis),
dmond, Reilly
Gomis), Hall.
bs not used: yle, Pablo,
rke, Henry-
ancis.

Cardiff City:
Marshall, Connolly,
Hudson (c), Turner,
Lappin, Kim (Noone), Mutch
(Cowie), Gunnarsson, Conway,
Mason (Gestede), Bellamy.
Subs not used: Lewis, McNaughton,
Ralls, Helguson.

Hit the road Jack! Mason nets past Butland for a New Year's Day victory.

MACCLESFIELD TOWN 2
Barnes-Homer (85,88 pen)

CARDIFF CITY 1
Jarvis (57)

SATURDAY ▶ 5TH JANUARY ▶ 3.00PM Full Attendance 3,165

🏠 2,524

🚌 641

MALKY

"We picked a team that we felt was capable of winning th game and ended up with nine youngsters under twenty years old out there. I thought the three youngsters at the bac in particular were exceptional."

KING

"This group of players, regardless of whatever happen this season, have made history at the football club. People wrote Barnes-Home off and said he wasn going to score – but believed in him."

Malky Mackay made wholesale changes to face Macclesfield Town in the F.A. Cup, eleven in all from the side that beat Birmingham on New Year's Day. Despite this, it looked like the young City side were heading through when Nat Jarvis prodded home from close range after some brilliant work by Declan John down the left flank. John showed great speed to collect Joe Ralls' pass and slide the ball to Jarvis for the opener.

It didn't seem like a comeback was on the cards for the Silkmen, but Matthew Barnes-Homer, who had been quiet all game equalised with only five minutes left of the tie. Jack Mackreth produced a pinpoint cross to find the striker on the back post who neatly finished past Joe Lewis. The tie looked destined for a replay, but in the eighty-eighth minute the referee gave a penalty against Jarvis for an apparent tug of the shirt. Barnes-Homer stepped up and fired home for his brace, putting Macclesfield Town in the fourth round draw for the very first time.

McPHAIL

"We had a lot of youngsters on the pitc but it's disappointing to throw away such a good lead and all of the hard work that we'd put in up to the eighty-fifth minute. We think we should have won the game."

FANS SAY
"Never mind lads – a great performance and fantastic to see McPhail back out there and Harris on the wing. We have to share Wembley with the clubs at some stage!" – *Jonathan James*

REFEREE: A. Madley

MACCLESFIELD SINCE 1874 — CARDIFF CITY EST 1899 FIRE & PASSION

7 ⌂ 4

40% 60%

POSSESSION

☑ 1   1

SHOTS

4 **ON** 6

7 **OFF** 2

e post-match reaction of this game from
lky Mackay and
phen McPhail on
diff City Player   **CARDIFF CITY Player →**

cclesfield Town: Cronin, Brown,
ham-Barrett, Martin (Winn),
ls, Murtagh, Wedgbury,
ry (Mackreth), Kissock,
nes-Homer, Morgan-
th (Fairhurst).
s not used: Mills,
gne, Konadu-
dom,
ahoua.

Cardiff City:
Lewis,
McNaughton
(Coulson), Nugent, Oshilaja,
John, Harris (O'Sullivan), Kiss
(Wharton), Ralls, McPhail, Velikonja,
Jarvis.
Subs not used: Parish, Mansaray, Darko, Hill.

209

I'll Be There. City fans soak up some Cup magic at Moss Rose.

THE CHAMPIONSHIP

THE 'MAGIC' OF THE CUP?

For all the talk of what the F.A. Cup 'no longer is' over the weekend, the one criticism that certainly couldn't be levelled at it is a lack of drama or excitement. When the dust settled just eight Championship teams made it through unscathed into Round Four, though a further six could follow suit after next week's replays.

In the end it wasn't just ourselves who felt the wrath of the romanticism of the cup, surrendering to the wishes of the neutral fan baying for favourite blood on the most nostalgic of all days in the British football calendar! Ståle Solbakken even paid with his job, with **Wolves'** defeat to **Luton Town** of the Blue Square Premier proving the final straw for the Wolverhampton hierarchy. After overseeing an underwhelming start to the Championship season and now suffering the ignimony of a cup defeat to non-league opposition, Solbakken, appointed in the summer following the club's relegation from the Premier League, was relieved of his duties. **Dean Saunders** *(pictured)* was plucked from Doncaster Rovers in quick-fire fashion, himself a victim of relegation last year, now charged with recuperating the ailing canine at Molineux.

Alex McLeish's spluttering start to life as **Nottingham Forest** manager continued with a high-scoring defeat at home to Paul Dickov's **Oldham Athletic.** Former Everton prodigy Jose Baxter's low free-kick eventually proved to be the seperator in a 3-2 defeat which also saw Robbie Simpson score twice for the League One strugglers. High flying **Hull City** and Dave Jones' **Sheffield Wednesday** will require replays in order to progress. Steve Bruce's second placed Tigers barely escaped with a 1-1 draw at home to **Leyton Orient** when Nick Proschwitz's goal deep into injury time spared the Humber from blushing. Wednesday, meanwhile, were held to a 0-0 bore draw at home to **MK Dons.**

As for the success stories, the Championship recorded one outright victory over Premier League opposition, with a further three forcing replays, albeit from winnable positions late-on. Most culpable of this were **Bolton Wanderers** who led 2-0 at home to **Sunderland** just minutes into the second half, when Marvin Sordell's header had added to Chung-Young Lee's early opener, gifted to him by Carlos Cuellar's suicidal pass across his box. A neat close-range finish from Connor Wickham provided the Mackems with hope though, before Craig Gardener's twenty-five yard screamer completed the come-back. **Blackpool** also found themselves a goal to the good inside the final ten minutes away at **Fulham** only to also be pulled level by a spectacular strike. Greek international legend Giorgos Karagounis' sweet dipping shot into the far corner cruelly cancelled out Ludovic Sylvestre's opener to force a re-set in this one. **Crystal Palace** and **Stoke City** meanwhile played out a goalless encounter at Selhurst Park.

The lone top flight topple came courtesy of **Brighton & Hove Albion** who kicked off the F.A. Cup weekend with comfortable victory over a depleted **Newcastle United** outfit. Short of numbers and quality, the Magpies fell to goals from Andrea Orlandi and Will Hoskins in front of a TV audience.

⟩⟩ MANAGERIAL MASTERS (CHAMPIONSHIP WINS THIS SEASON)

1	2	3	4	5
18	15	15	13	12
⟩ MALKY MACKAY	⟩ STEVE BRUCE	⟩ TONY MOWBRAY	⟩ NIGEL PEARSON	⟩ GIANFRANCO ZOL

SIX-POINTERS

A statistical look at City's record against their top half rivals

The festive period could not have gone any better for City as four consecutive victories boosted the gap from third place up to nine points. But it was the back-to-back wins over **Leicester City** and **Crystal Palace** which really caught the eye and, more importantly, took vital points away from sides that could be promotion rivals come May.

However, those wins should have come as no surprise given **City's** record in previous 'six-pointers' this season. Malky's men have collected more points against top half sides than anyone else in the division. What's more, City have now beaten each of the top eight teams at some point in this campaign. Ninth placed **Brighton,** who we take on at the CCS next month, are the highest ranked team yet to fall victim to City. In fact, our 0-0 draw at the AMEX remains the only time we have failed to find the net all season.

Boxing Day's opponents **Crystal Palace** have had less success in their top of the table clashes. The Eagles have gained just nineteen of their forty-seven points against teams in the top twelve of the division. And this is matched on an individual level – young starlet **Wilfried Zaha** *(pictured)*, for example, is yet to score against a top seven side.

Finally, Dean Saunders' new club **Wolverhampton Wanderers** have an excellent record against their fellow strugglers, as only three Championship teams have picked up more points against bottom half sides. However, it's their performances against the teams at the top which explain their current eighteenth place position. The West Midlands club have notched up just five points against top twelve opponents – their September win over Leicester City remains the only one they have triumphed over a top half side.

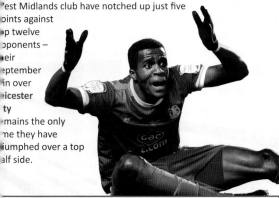

DID YOU KNOW?

This afternoon's visitors **Ipswich Town** have recruited no fewer than 13 loanees over the course of the season. Their tally is surpassed only by **Watford's** 14 – all but two of whom were signed from Giampaolo Pozzo's other clubs, Granada and Udinese. Five of the Tractor Boys' loanees have now returned to their parent clubs. But Mick McCarthy will be hoping that newest recruits **Aaron McLean** and **David McGoldrick** – who has already netted 18 in 25 on-loan at **Coventry** this season – will help to steer them further away from the drop zone.

npower
FOOTBALL LEAGUE

LATEST RESULTS
1st January 2013
Watford 3–4 Charlton Athletic
Birmingham City 0–1 Cardiff City
Blackburn Rovers 3–0 Nottingham Forest
Blackpool 0–0 Hull City
Crystal Palace 3–1 Wolves
Derby County 3–1 Middlesbrough
Ipswich Town 0–3 Brighton & Hove Albion
Leeds United 1–0 Bolton Wanderers
Leicester City 6–1 Huddersfield Town
Millwall 2–1 Bristol City
Peterborough United 2–1 Barnsley
Sheffield Wednesday 0–2 Burnley

TODAY'S GAMES
(All games kick off at 3pm unless otherwise stated)
Barnsley v Leeds United
Bolton Wanderers v Millwall
Brighton & Hove Albion v Derby County
Bristol City v Leicester City
Burnley v Crystal Palace
Cardiff City v Ipswich Town
Charlton Athletic v Blackpool
Huddersfield Town v Birmingham City
Hull City v Sheffield Wednesday (5:20pm)
Middlesbrough v Watford
Nottingham Forest v Peterborough United

2012/13 NPOWER CHAMPIONSHIP LEAGUE TABLE
DETAILS PRIOR TO THIS WEEKEND'S GAMES

Pos	Team	P	W	D	L	GD	Pts
1	**Cardiff City**	26	18	2	6	19	56
2	Hull City	26	15	4	7	10	49
3	Crystal Palace	26	13	8	5	16	47
4	Middlesbrough	26	15	2	9	10	47
5	Leicester City	26	13	5	8	21	44
6	Watford	25	12	4	9	11	40
7	Millwall	26	11	7	8	4	40
8	Leeds United	26	11	5	10	-4	38
9	Brighton	25	9	10	6	9	37
10	Derby County	26	10	7	9	2	37
11	Nottm Forest	26	9	10	7	1	37
12	Burnley	26	10	6	10	0	36
13	Blackburn	25	9	8	8	2	35
14	Blackpool	26	8	10	8	5	34
15	Charlton	26	8	9	9	-2	33
16	Bolton	26	8	8	10	-1	32
17	Huddersfield	26	8	8	10	-12	32
18	Wolves	26	9	4	13	-6	31
19	**Ipswich Town**	26	8	6	12	-21	30
20	Birmingham	26	7	8	11	-9	29
21	Peterborough	26	8	1	17	-12	25
22	Sheffield Wed	26	7	4	15	-14	25
23	Bristol City	25	6	4	15	-12	22
24	Barnsley	26	5	6	15	-17	21

CF ELEVEN

THE OFFICIAL CARDIFF CITY FC MATCH PROGRAMME

CARDIFF CITY

VERSUS

BRISTOL CITY

SAT 16TH FEB 1:00PM

npower CHAMPIONSHIP — MATCH 31 £3

MATCH SPONSOR: LADBROKES

TEAM SPONSOR:
WILLIAMS CONTRACTORS LTD

Malaysia   **PUMA**   Player

15

PITCH PERFECT

Good afternoon and welcome back to Cardiff City Stadium for our early kick-off against Bristol City. It's been a long time since we've had the opportunity to play at home and it's good to be back here with you all today. I would also like to offer a warm welcome to Sean O'Driscoll, along with the staff, players and supporters from Bristol following their short drive over the bridge to be here with us.

Before I cover recent events I'd like to place on record my thanks, respect and appreciation to Alan Whiteley who has stepped down from his position on the board since my last notes. Alan was instrumental in my coming here and remains a close friend. I wish him well in future endeavours.

After over four weeks away we've been looking forward to resuming our run of home games, at a place which over the last eighteen months really feels more and more like home. Our recent trips to Blackpool, Leeds and Huddersfield have all been played on varying degrees of pitch, obviously due in part to the weather and time of year, while today we're back at home in our beautiful stadium. The pitch here has been first class again this season, thanks to Phil Williams and his team who have worked so hard, while receiving the help that they asked for in terms of Tan Sri Vincent Tan investing in our lights, which are vital during winter months. I'm delighted that my players can get back to our surface again today.

Tan Sri has also, since our last home game, allowed us to take the squad away for a warm weather training camp in Dubai, the reasons for which he completely understood when we chatted about it. We are all extremely grateful to him for being able to take a working trip with full sessions every day, the players all buying into what we were doing and working hard. We were also fortunate with the timing of the trip as we were away while conditions in South Wales were arctic to say the least, weather that would have prevented us from training outdoors for the entire week.

Our last match here was a tough encounter against Ipswich for the nil-nil draw. It's something that you have to come to terms with as league leaders that some teams can play against you in a certain fashion. Huddersfield also for example last weekend went from

playing a diamond formation in recent games to a 4-5-1 against us, playing like the away team at home. That's the choice of every team of course and is something we'll have to deal with if we come up against it again. That said my squad are confident, professional and business like in the way they have gone about their job in recent matches.

We followed Ipswich with a good return from three difficult away games, each of them long and tough trips for supporters to make, so I was delighted to pick up seven points from the nine available. It continues our solid away form of six wins and two draws, while any point on the road is a good one in this division, something I know all about. I'm very proud of the mental strength of my squad, which shows in recent form on the road in how they've applied themselves.

Today we face both Bristol City and Sean O'Driscoll for the second time due to the changes at Ashton Gate. Sean is someone I know well and brings a wealth of experience to Bristol, while today is also the Severnside derby, a game which is always interesting and enjoyable for fans on both sides of the bridge, with bragging rights on the table. We're expecting big numbers here today, added to with two thousand travelling from Bristol, in all the crowd possibly eclipsing the twenty-five thousand mark.

I'm in awe at times to the fervour and passion of Cardiff City supporters, including full respect and admiration for the money they spend supporting their home team, home and away. The investment they make, not just in their heart but in their pocket, drives me on and makes the squad want to bring them success all the more. To see as many twenty-five plus thousand gates as possible for our remaining home games would be fantastic, while our away support goes without saying for the continued immense backing that we see week in week out on the road. We'd love to see high numbers continue here, helping to make our stadium an intense atmosphere for visiting teams. It continues on Tuesday and I hope to see you all with us again for another big fixture. For now though our focus is firmly on Bristol. As always it should be a great occasion with your help.

Enjoy the match.

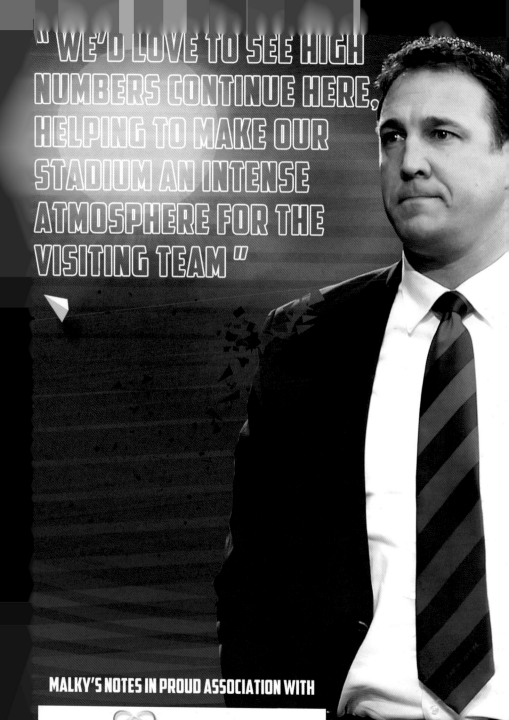

"WE'D LOVE TO SEE HIGH NUMBERS CONTINUE HERE, HELPING TO MAKE OUR STADIUM AN INTENSE ATMOSPHERE FOR THE VISITING TEAM"

MALKY'S NOTES IN PROUD ASSOCIATION WITH

CARDIFF CITY 0
IPSWICH TOWN 0

SATURDAY ▶ 12TH JANUARY ▶ 3.00PM Full Attendance 22,727

🏠 **22,202**
🚌 **525**

MALKY

"We knew it was going to be tough as Mick has a team who have lost just two games in ten and are on a really good run. I'm delighted with the clean sheet and the way we dug in."

McCARTHY

"I'm very pleased with a point and with the fact that we are only the second team this season to prevent Cardiff from scoring. Our away form is improving and this is a terrific point."

Ipswich were the first to test goal in this one, with Guirane N'Daw's stinging thirty yard drive crashing into David Marshall's crossbar. David McGoldrick then fluffed a good opportunity, before a Mark Hudson header from a Craig Bellamy free kick dropped the wrong side of the post.

The second half started with a great opportunity, as Craig Noone showed good awareness to find Bellamy, but Chambers reacted and blocked the striker's effort. Michael Chopra then received a warm reception as he returned to CCS, on the hour mark.

Aron Gunnarsson nearly put Cardiff ahead through fortune when his deflected cross had Scott Loach back-pedalling, but then a golden chance to win the game fell to Town in the dying moments. Frank Nouble's quick feet won him space in the Cardiff area, but the forward's effort fell wide of the far post.

GUNNARSSON

"It was a tough match today. We know that teams are going to come here and want to beat us because we are top of the league. That is just the way it is."

FANS SAY "We were the only team in the top four to get any points today and as such increased our overall advantage as league leaders. It wasn't pretty, but the weather didn't help." – *David Harris*

THE BREAKDOWN

REFEREE: S. Mathieson

10 · 4

53% · 47%

POSSESSION

0 · 2

SHOTS

ON 2

OFF 4

ost-match reaction from Malky Mackay, ick McCarthy and on Gunnarsson on **Cardiff City Player** ardiff City Player

ardiff City: Marshall, Taylor, Hudson, rner, Connolly, Whittingham, onway, (Helguson), Noone, unnarsson, Gestede Mason), Bellamy.
ubs not used: Lewis, cNaughton, Cowie, m Bo-Kyung.

Ipswich Town: Loach, Cresswell, Chambers, Smith, Orr, Edwards, N'daw, Martin (Nouble), Hyam, McGoldrick (Murphy), Mclean (Chopra).
Subs not used: Lee-Barrett, Hewitt, Kisnorbo, Drury.

Stand and never yield. Another shut-out for Marshy and co. against Ipswich.

BLACKPOOL 1
Taylor-Fletcher (60)

CARDIFF CITY 2
Kim (54), Smith (64)

SATURDAY ▶ 19TH JANUARY ▶ 3.00PM Full Attendance 13,998

🏠 13,068
🚌 930

Cardiff City headed to Dubai with a ten point lead at the top of the nPower Championship after taking all three points at Bloomfield Road.

David Marshall smartly stopped an effort from Tom Ince in the most clear-cut chance of the first half, shortly before Gary Taylor-Fletcher questioned the referee's decision not to award the home side a penalty. Tommy Smith, on his first start since the home game with Watford in October, had his shot tipped over the bar by 'Pool keeper Gilks in City's best chance of the period.

Things did not look good for City as captain Mark Hudson was forced off through injury, but they soon took the lead through Kim Bo-Kyung's second goal for the club.

Blackpool fired back via Gary Taylor-Fletcher's header, but a Cardiff counter attack four minutes later concluded with Tommy Smith's excellent winner – the volley his fourth goal in seven games against Blackpool and his first goal for City.

MALKY
"It's our fourth away win in a row and it shows the steeliness and determination of our team. I'm delighted for everyone; it's a very well earned three points."

THOMPSON
"I don't want to change the way we play just because of the pitch, but I think we got a lesson off them today in them helping it over our back four, chasing it down and going for the second ball."

SMITH
"It was nice to see th goal go in. It's great t be back and involved after a long time out which was very frustrating for me. I felt quite sharp and I'm delighted we tool the three points."

FANS SAY
"I'm a Birmingham fan for my sins but I went to our home match with Cardiff. Your fans are great and I hope you go up as Champions. It will be deserved." – *Dave Burrons*

THE BREAKDOWN

REFEREE: M. Naylor

4 ⚑ 2

55% 45%

POSSESSION

☑ ▬ 0
☑ ▬ 3

SHOTS
10 ON 7
4 OFF 5

post-match reaction of this game from
lky Mackay and
ven Thompson on
diff City Player

CARDIFF CITY Player

ckpool: Gilks, Basham, Cathcart,
adfoot (c), Harris, Osbourne
artínez), Sylvestre, Gomes
Phillips), Taylor-Fletcher,
e, Delfouneso.
s not used:
stead, Eastham,
ertson, Caton,
eston.

Cardiff City:
Marshall,
McNaughton, Taylor,
Hudson (c) (Nugent),
Whittingham, Conway, Connolly,
Kim (Cowie), Smith (Helguson),
Gunnarsson, Mason.
Subs not used: Gestede, Noone, Mutch, Lewis.

223

Digging it. Tommy signals his return with a wonder strike at soggy Blackpool.

LEEDS UNITED 0
CARDIFF CITY 1
Campbell (64)

SATURDAY ▶ 2ND FEBRUARY ▶ 3.00PM | Full Attendance **19,236**

🏠 **18,790**
🚌 **446**

MALKY

"We played really we today and came here with a game plan. Th win is a positive, as is another clean sheet - something the near five hundred long travelling fans can enjoy on the way home tonight."

WARNOCK

"It's a cruel game sometimes. I though we played some good stuff today against the side at the top of the table and all of their big names, so I'm really proud of all of the lads today."

CAMPBELL

"We've not played a game for two weeks, but we dug in deep and got the result in the end. When you g to a new club you want to start well, ar I couldn't have asked for much more."

An instant impact from Fraizer Campbell on his debut stretched City's unbeaten run against Leeds United to fifteen matches.

The first half was a fairly even contest in which both sides found it difficult to carve out clear-cut goal scoring chances. Craig Bellamy did have the ball in the net in the closing stages, however, his effort was correctly ruled out for offside, while David Marshall had to be on hand to deny Everton loanee Ross Barkley from close range.

In the second half City moved up a gear, and the introduction of Fraizer Campbell made all the difference. Just a couple of minutes after entering the fray, the former Sunderland man netted a typical poacher's strike – diverting Bellamy's drive past Paddy Kenny. The goal was enough to seal the win for the City, but not before Marshall was called upon once more to palm away Tom Lees' powerful header in the final minutes.

FANS SAY | "Thanks for the great birthday present today Cardiff City! Another three points!!!!" – *Nathaniel Freeman*

REFEREE: M. Dean

6 | 4

62% | 38%

POSSESSION

0 | 3
1

SHOTS

7 ON 3

6 OFF

For post-match reaction of this game from Malky
ckay, Neil Warnock
d Fraizer Campbell
Cardiff City Player

CARDIFF CITY Player

ds United: Kenny, White, Lees,
tier, Byram; Brown, Austin,
ney, Barkley; Diouf
abibou), McCormack.
os not used: Ashdown,
arce, Warnock,
rris, Green, Tonge.

Cardiff City:
Marshall,
Connolly, Hudson,
Turner, Taylor; Conway
(Helguson), Gunnarsson,
Whittingham, Kim (Campbell); Smith,
Bellamy.
Subs not used: Lewis, McNaughton, Cowie,
Noone, Mason.

227

My time. Fraizer marks his City debut with a winning goal at Elland Road.

HUDDERSFIELD TOWN
CARDIFF CITY

SATURDAY ▶ 9TH FEBRUARY ▶ 3.00PM | Full Attendance 15,265

🏠 **13,538**
🚌 **1,727**

MALKY

"It was a tough, uncompromising game. We remain undefeated in our las eight away games though and secured a clean sheet today against a side now unbeaten in their las six at home."

LILLIS

"We've got to look at today as 'points on the board'. Points like today's are important and sometimes you have to set the stall and be happy with a point."

GUNNARSSON

"We fight for each other in every game and I think you can see that. Today was a toug game against a side battling for their lives. But we're unbeaten in eight away now and take the positives."

A draw at Huddersfield was enough for City to extend their lead at the top of the table to eleven points and their unbeaten run to eight games in the Championship.

This was a game of very few clear cut chances, with Huddersfield having no legitimate efforts on target. The Terriers did have the ball in the net in the first half, only for James Vaughan's effort to be disallowed for a foul on David Marshall.

Cardiff's best chance came in first half stoppage time when Matt Connolly saw his audacious strike hit the woodwork.

Cardiff started the second half the dominant team and remained the side most likely to snatch a winner right to the end. But some gritty defending from the home side ensured that the spoils were shared and Malky Mackay's men returned to South Wales with what could prove to be an important point.

FANS SAY "It's 227.5 miles from Cardiff to Huddersfield so even if we'd taken 500, that would be excellent support. Wherever we go, we go in large numbers!" – Stephen Baker

THE BREAK DOWN

REFEREE: M. Brown

4 ⚑ **6**

50% **50%**
POSSESSION

0 **2** **3**

SHOTS

0 ON **3**

3 OFF **4**

e post-match reaction of this game from
lky Mackay and
rk Lillis on
rdiff City Player

CARDIFF CITY Player

ddersfield Town: Smithies,
ods, ▢ Lynch, Gerrard,
4unt, Clayton, Danns,
rwood (Atkinson), Arfield,
nnell, Vaughan (Lee).
bs not used:
nnett, Dixon,
llace, Crooks,
nott.

Cardiff City:
Marshall,
McNaughton
(▢ Nugent), Hudson, ▢ Taylor,
Connolly, Kim (Helguson), Conway,
Gunnarsson, Whittingham, ▢ Bellamy,
Smith (Campbell).
Subs not used: Lewis, Cowie, Noone, Mason.

231

In the wars. McNaughton receives treatment after another full-blooded personal performance at Huddersfield.

THE CHAMPIONSHIP
SINCE LAST WE MET...

A whole calendar month has passed since we last convened at **Cardiff City Stadium, thirty-four days to be precise**, and understandably the landscape of the Championship has shifted during that time. Managers have come and gone, players have moved on to pastures new and points have been won and lost with wild abandon! To what extent? Read on ...

Headline news of course is that Cardiff City's lead at the top over second placed Hull City remains at eight points – as it did following our last home game against Ipswich on January 12th. In fact, the top three stand in the same order that they did thirty-four days ago – **Cardiff City, Hull City, Leicester City** – the only substantial change in the top six has seen **Watford** vault from sixth up to fourth courtesy of a ten point haul from their five matches played in the period. **Crystal Palace** and **Middlesbrough** each lose a place, sitting fifth and sixth respectively, yet 'Boro are somewhat fortunate not to have lost further ground still having picked up just one win in the period (in fact Mowbray's men had lost five straight in the league prior to Tuesday's 1-0 win over Leeds).

Millwall and **Nottingham Forest** suffered most last month. The Lions failed to pick up a single league point during the period, losing each of their four matches, falling five places in the table to twelfth and, probably more damagingly losing the services of two front-line strikers, namely Chris Wood and Darius Henderson to Leicester and Forest. Forest themselves lost three matches, four places in the table and their manager, Alex McLeish. Where they once were just three points shy of a play-off spot, they are now nine. Can the returning **Billy Davies** *(pictured)*, save their season?

The significant drama over the last month has occurred in the division's basement where three relegation threatened outfits recorded a better than 2.00 points per game ratio and Bristol City came mightily close to being a fourth. **Barnsley** were the biggest earners; spurred on by their loan capture of Jason Scotland (three games, three vital goals) they recorded three wins and a draw in their last four matches to lift them up one position to twenty-second. The team, barely holding them off, is Dean Saunders' **Wolves** who managed just two draws from their four matches and have slipped further into the mire.

Elsewhere, our opponents this afternoon have had a fruitful month with new manager Sean O'Driscoll overseeing a nine point gain for **Bristol City.** Surprisingly that has only seen them move up one spot from the foot of the table (where they leap-frog **Peterborough United** despite the latter's unexpected triumph over Leicester and that's down to the incredible fighting spirit shown recently by many of the troubled sides. **Sheffield Wednesday** and **Birmingham City** also grabbed a 2.00 ppg record for the month to give themselves breathing space. It's not getting any clearer down there.

➤➤ LEADING SCORERS

1	2	3	4	5
60	54	52	51	5
➤ WATFORD	➤ CRYSTAL PALACE	➤ LEICESTER	➤ CARDIFF CITY	➤ MIDDLESBROUGH

THERE'S NO 'I' IN TEAM

statistical look at the value of team spirit

...ackpool caretaker boss Steve Thompson admitted that his side ...ve relied too much upon the goals of star man **Thomas Ince** after ...e winger netted his 17th of the season against Millwall on ...turday. Dependence upon one player can, of course, prove risky if ...nd when their goals dry up – but there have been no such worries ...r Cardiff City this season.

...alky's men have shared the goals, with not one player in the top ...3 scorers in the division. In fact, 15 different players have netted ...r City in this Championship campaign, and 8 of those have scored ...least 4 times.

...anfranco Zola's **Watford** are another side blessed with a number ...f regular goal scorers. Matěj Vydra may have stolen some ...adlines with his haul of 19, but the pressure has been taken off ...m by Troy Deeney and fellow Udinese loanee Almen Abdi, who ...ve 20 between them. The only other teammates with 10 or more ...als each to their name are Lukas Jutkiewicz ...d Scott McDonald of **Middlesbrough.**

...owever, you needn't look any further ...an **Burnley** to see the pitfalls of heaping ...e goal-scoring burden on one man's ...oulders. Other than Charlie Austin, only ...artin Paterson has hit the five goal mark ...r the Clarets this campaign. In fact, Sean ...yche's men have only won one game in ...hich Austin has failed to score, proving ...eir dependency on the former Swindon ...an.

...'s a similar story with Glenn Murray at ...rystal Palace. Although the likes of Wilfried ...aha and Brazilian playmaker André Moritz ...ave chipped in with 5 goals apiece, Murray ...as scored 5 times as many for the Eagles. ...espite having exceptional and consistent ...rwards, the goals that such teams may ...ave missed out on from elsewhere in ...e side could prove vital as the end of ...e season draws ever nearer.

DID YOU KNOW?

From the Estadio Azteca to Ashton Gate – **Bristol City's** Jamaican international **Marvin Elliot** *(pictured)* had a taste of the jet setter lifestyle last week. The midfielder helped the 'Reggae Boyz' to a 0-0 draw in a World Cup Qualifier at Mexico's 105,000-seater stadium on Thursday 7th. But just 24 hours after making the 5,000 mile trip home, Elliot made his 200th start for the Robins, and scored in their win over **Nottingham Forest!** Meanwhile **Kim Bo-Kyung** made a shorter journey east than you might have expected while on duty with South Korea, as their match against Croatia was held at Fulham's **Craven Cottage!**

LATEST RESULTS

8/9th February
Blackburn Rovers 1–0 Ipswich Town
Blackpool 2–1 Millwall
Bolton Wanderers 2–1 Burnley
Bristol City 2–0 Nottingham Forest
Charlton Athletic 1–1 Birmingham City
Huddersfield Town 0–0 Cardiff City
Middlesbrough 2–3 Barnsley
Peterborough United 2–1 Leicester City
Sheffield Wednesday 2–2 Derby County
Wolves 2–2 Leeds United
Brighton & Hove Albion 1–0 Hull City
Watford 2–2 Crystal Palace

12th February
Brighton 1–1 Blackburn Rovers
Hull City 2–1 Derby County
Middlesbrough 1–0 Leeds United

TODAY'S GAMES
(All games kick off at 3pm unless otherwise stated)

Cardiff City v Bristol City (1pm)
Birmingham City v Watford
Burnley v Huddersfield Town
Crystal Palace v Middlesbrough
Derby County v Wolves
Hull City v Charlton Athletic
Ipswich Town v Blackpool
Nottingham Forest v Bolton Wanderers

2012/13 NPOWER CHAMPIONSHIP LEAGUE TABLE

Pos	Team	P	W	D	L	GD	Pts
1	**Cardiff City**	30	20	4	6	21	64
2	Hull City	31	17	5	9	9	56
3	Leicester City	30	16	5	9	26	53
4	Watford	31	16	5	10	18	53
5	Crystal Palace	31	14	10	7	15	52
6	Middlesbrough	31	16	2	13	4	50
7	Brighton	31	11	13	7	9	46
8	Blackburn	31	11	11	9	4	44
9	Burnley	31	12	7	12	1	43
10	Derby County	31	11	9	11	3	42
11	Leeds United	31	12	6	13	-7	42
12	Millwall	31	11	8	12	-2	41
13	Nottm Forest	31	10	11	10	-4	41
14	Blackpool	31	10	10	11	4	40
15	Charlton	31	10	10	11	-2	40
16	Birmingham	31	9	11	11	-7	38
17	Bolton	30	9	10	11	-1	37
18	Huddersfield	31	9	10	12	-18	37
19	Sheffield Wed	31	10	6	15	-9	36
20	Ipswich Town	31	9	8	14	-19	35
21	Wolves	31	9	7	15	-8	34
22	Barnsley	31	9	7	15	-11	34
23	**Bristol City**	31	9	4	18	-14	31
24	Peterborough	30	9	3	18	-12	30

235

CF ELEVEN

THE OFFICIAL CARDIFF CITY FC MATCH PROGRAMME

CARDIFF CITY

VERSUS

BRIGHTON & HOVE ALBION

TUE 19TH FEB 7:45PM

npower CHAMPIONSHIP   MATCH 32 £3

MATCH SPONSOR:
TERRY HOWELL
TIMBER & BUILDERS' MERCHANTS LTD

TEAM SPONSOR: HEATWISE

Malaysia   PUMA   Player

16

MALKY MACKAY

DEFENSIVE SOLIDITY

Good evening and welcome back for today's game with Brighton & Hove Albion.

After going through a particularly long time without a home match, it feels great to be back here so soon after Saturday's win over Bristol City. Obviously we are pleased to have taken ten points out of twelve on offer in our last four league games, having only conceded two goals in that run. We are playing with a defensive solidity which we have worked hard to bring to our game. With the attacking options we have, I feel we are always likely to score, so clean sheets definitely mean points.

As you will have seen, we also brought in three new faces during the January window and I have not had the opportunity to fully explain to you the thinking behind each move. As a staff, we acknowledged going into the window that we had two main areas to address – another decent striking option was important to fill the gap left by Nicky Maynard's unfortunate injury and also a bit more depth at the back, particularly on the left side.

I was pleased that in both situations we managed to sign our first choice target. Fraizer Campbell was, I felt, the best striker available on the market within our price range and it is a tribute to the work we have done that he so readily opted to drop out of the Premier League for the chance to come to play for Cardiff. Obviously, his career in a City shirt could not have got off to be a better start with a winning goal at Leeds with only his second touch – 45 seconds after coming on as a substitute and then another two in his first start for us on Saturday.

We had also been really impressed with Simon Lappin's professionalism, attitude and demeanour when he came here on loan earlier in the season and when we were alerted that he would be available from Norwich on a free we moved immediately to bring him here permanently.

Simon is such a positive force around the dressing room and brings with him the know-how of having played an important role in Norwich's promotion two years ago. It goes without saying that he is also a very good player with a fine left foot giving us another option at both left back and on the left of midfield.

The third signing may have been slightly under the radar but many of you will have seen that we took 18-year-old Rhys Healey from Connah's Quay in the Welsh Premier League. When I joined the club, I made it one of my goals to make sure CCFC's imprint was felt across Welsh football and to that end we have stepped up our scouting of that level of the game. Rhys scored lots of goals at just 17 years old and he caught the eye of our scouting staff, which eventually led to him joining us in January. He will start his career with us training with the under 18s (his current age group) and we will gauge his progress from there.

So, I'm sure you'll join with me in issuing a belated Cardiff welcome to Fraizer, Simon and Rhys and wishing them every success during their time with us.

I'm looking forward to seeing Brighton manager Gus Poyet here today. He is always one of the more engaging characters in the Championship and I have a huge respect for the work he has done down on the south coast. Welcome also to all of Gus' players, staff and fans who have made the long trip over from Sussex.

After three long trips north, today is the second of two big home games for us this week and it goes without saying that the season is entering a crucial stage and we'll be counting on your support as ever to help the lads achieve results on the pitch.

Enjoy the game.

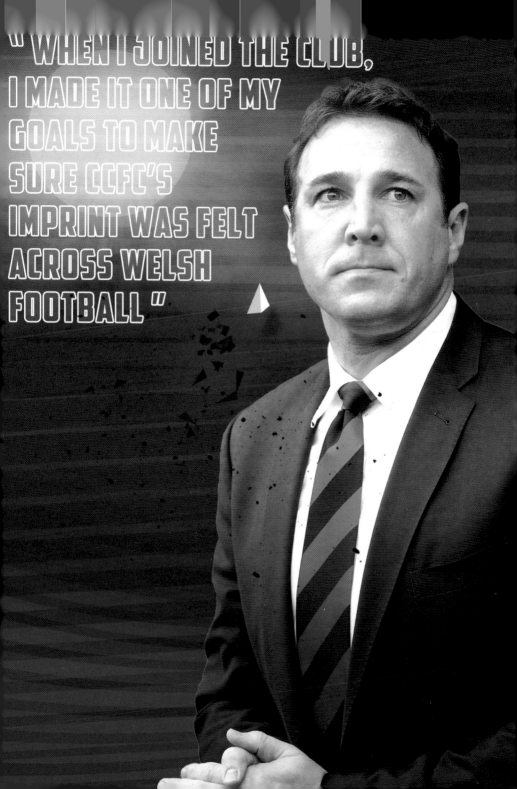

" WHEN I JOINED THE CLUB, I MADE IT ONE OF MY GOALS TO MAKE SURE CCFC'S IMPRINT WAS FELT ACROSS WELSH FOOTBALL "

CARDIFF CITY 2
Campbell (45,58)

BRISTOL CITY 1
Nugent (o.g 90)

SATURDAY ▶ 16TH FEBRUARY ▶ 1.00PM | Full Attendance 25, 858

🏠 23,804
🚌 2,054

MALKY

"We were more than business like today, it was high quality on show. Our group are trying to go forward and do the best we can for the Football Club – and what fantastic support we had today."

O'DRISCOLL

"We knew coming in they were probably going to be the best team we've played and they showed why they are where they are. Their movement and interchanging were good."

Cardiff City marked their return to Cardiff City Stadium with three points as they defeated Bristol City 2-1 in a dominant performance.

It was Fraizer Campbell's first start for City and it was he who broke the deadlock on the stroke of half time. A perfect pass from Tommy Smith opened the defence and the striker dinked home.

Cardiff started the second half as they ended the first and it was not long until they doubled their lead, again through Campbell. An Aron Gunnarsson long throw evaded the defence and landed at the feet of Campbell who smashed home from close range.

The only blip on City's complete performance was an own goal from Ben Nugent in the dying minutes. The game finished 2-1 – unquestionably a score-line which flattered the visitors.

CAMPBELL

"Tommy Smith played a great pass into my stride for the first goal and I just had to run on to it and finish it really. It was perfectly timed just before the break, killing off some of their momentum."

FANS SAY "Well done again boys from CCFC Supporters Club in Waterford, Ireland. We will be over in the next few weeks!" – *Shane Kehoe*

THE BREAKDOWN

REFEREE: E. Ilderton

6 — 3

58% — 42%

POSSESSION

1 — 1

SHOTS

11 ON 6

2 OFF 3

Post-match reaction from Malky Mackay, [Ia]n O'Driscoll and [Quin]izer Campbell on [Car]diff City Player

CARDIFF CITY Player

[Car]diff City: Marshall, Connolly, [Hu]dson, Taylor, Nugent, Noone [(...)m], Gunnarsson, [Wh]ittingham, Bellamy, [Sm]ith (Cowie), Campbell [(Fer]lguson). [Sub]s not used: Lewis, [...]Naughton, [...]son, Mutch.

Bristol City:
Heaton, Foster, Fontaine, Nyatanga, Moloney, Kelly (Kilkenny), Pearson (Howard), Anderson (Adomah), Elliott, Stead, Davies.
Subs not used: Gerken, Wilson, Reid, Burns.

241

Feet under the table. Campbell marks his CCS debut with a severnside brace.

THE CHAMPIONSHIP

TIGHT AT THE TOP

With the past weekend scheduled for F.A. Cup Fifth Round action, the Championship ploughed ahead with a skeleton crew as just seven fixtures were fulfilled. The main talking points and ramifications came in the top six shake-up, as the concertina-like nature of the automatic promotion and Play-Off places continued.

Thanks to the 2-1 win over Bristol City in the early kick-off, Cardiff City initially re-opened an eleven point gap at the summit of the Championship table.

But by the end of play that lead was back down to eight though through Hull City's narrow victory over Charlton Athletic. January signing Mohamed Gedo (pictured) grabbed the only goal, the Egyptian International's second in as many matches, bundling the ball home from close range to move his side back into solitary possession of second place in the table. Leicester City do still have the opportunity to reclaim second spot, should they win their two games in hand, one of which is at Cardiff City Stadium on April 9th.

The Play-Off spots are looking equally unsecured. Watford continued their incredible recent run with a convincing 4-0 win over beleaguered Birmingham City at St. Andrew's. This win, Watford's latest in a run which has seen them lose just once in their last seven matches, moves them into third

in the table, just three shy of Hull, and with a goal difference equal with our own and only bettered by Leicester. Troy Deeney netted twice in this one, whilst Ikechi Anya and Almen Abdi also struck for a Hornets side who have now scored seventeen times in their last seven matches.

Crystal Palace moved into fourth spot with a 4-1 win over Middlesbrough at Selhurst Park that had a huge impact on the shape of the top six. Glenn Murray's twenty-third and fourth Championship goals of the season helped the Eagles on their way to back-to-back home wins which moved them five points clear of th beaten 'Boro who have now lost six of their last seve Championship matches and have fallen behind their rivals in a b for automatic promotion.

At the foot of the table, Wolves earned a valuable poin with a much needed clean sheet i a goalless draw at Derby County. The stalemate keeps Dean Saunders' men marginal outside the relegation zone – a point ahead of Barnsley who do have a game in hand thanks to their 3-1 win over MK Dons and continued involvement i the Cup.

Talking of which, Championship performance of the day honours undoubtedly go to Blackburn Rovers who overcame Arsenal at the Emirate Stadium on Saturday. Arsène Wenger's eigh year wait for a trophy goes on after Colin Kazim-Richard's scuffed shot found its way i off the inside of the far post midway through the second half to earn Michael Appleton's me a much deserved 'cup-set' and a quarter-final t at Millwall.

>> CHAMPIONSHIP HOT SHOTS

1	2	3	4	5
24	21	21	19	17
> GLENN MURRAY	> CHARLIE AUSTIN	> JORDAN RHODES	> MATĚJ VYDRA	> THOMAS INCE

START WITH A BANG!

statistical round-up of some stand-out January recruits

Fraizer Campbell's stats in a City shirt read: 118 minutes, 3 goals. There's no doubt that the England international has shown his pedigree already, but he isn't the only January capture to make an instant impact in the division.

Hull City's loan signing of **Mohamed Nagy 'Gedo'** from Al Ahly may have slipped under the radar of some fans, however, the 31 cap Egyptian has made an early impression for the Tigers. He netted less than 2 minutes into his second appearance, before repeating the trick on Saturday, with the only goal in a 1-0 win over Charlton.

A face better known to Championship supporters is that of **Kevin Phillips** *(pictured)*. The veteran poacher made the deadline day loan move from **Blackpool** to join up with former boss Ian Holloway at **Crystal Palace.** Having scored just twice in 18 games for the Tangerines this season, the 39-year-old already has 2 in 3 for the Eagles, including a vital equaliser against former club Watford.

Elsewhere in the top 6, **Leicester** did their business early, snapping up **Chris Wood** on the first day of the window. Their faith in the New Zealander has been repaid with an astonishing 7 goals in 6 league and cup games for the Foxes.

But it isn't just at the top that January signings have already made a splash. **Jason Scotland,** for example, has scored 3 vital goals in 3 Championship games for 22nd placed **Barnsley** — two of them late winners over Blackpool and Middlesbrough.

Such signings can have a crucial say in the remainder of the season. Last year, Reading's capture of **Jason Roberts** was seen as the catalyst in their promotion bid. Let's hope that, with a few more games under his belt, Fraizer can kick on and play a vital role for City in the remainder of the season — and beyond.

DID YOU KNOW?

In our previous meeting with tonight's visitors **Brighton**, we shared the spoils in a 0-0 draw at the AMEX. Looking back, the result is no surprise, as the Seagulls are the draw specialists of the division, with 13 to their name so far. However, after that match it took 25 Championship fixtures until City next failed to find the back of the net. In fact, Malky's men have only drawn a blank in a league record 3 matches this season, the other two being **Ipswich** at home, and **Huddersfield** away – all of which were goalless draws.

npower FOOTBALL LEAGUE

LATEST RESULTS
16th February
Cardiff City 2–1 Bristol City
Birmingham City 0–4 Watford
Crystal Palace 4–1 Middlesbrough
Derby County 0–0 Wolves
Hull City 1–0 Charlton Athletic
Ipswich Town 1–0 Blackpool
Nottingham Forest 1–1 Bolton Wanderers

TONIGHT'S GAMES
*(All games kick off at 7:45pm
unless otherwise stated)*
Barnsley v Wolves
Birmingham City v Sheffield Wednesday
Burnley v Middlesbrough
Cardiff City v Brighton & Hove Albion
Crystal Palace v Bristol City (8pm)
Derby County v Bolton Wanderers
Hull City v Blackburn Rovers
Ipswich Town v Watford
Leicester City v Charlton Athletic
Millwall v Peterborough United
Nottingham Forest v Huddersfield Town

2012/13 NPOWER CHAMPIONSHIP LEAGUE TABLE

Pos	Team	P	W	D	L	GD	Pts
1	**Cardiff City**	31	21	4	6	22	67
2	Hull City	32	18	5	9	10	59
3	Watford	32	17	5	10	22	56
4	Crystal Palace	32	15	10	7	18	55
5	Leicester City	30	16	5	9	26	53
6	Middlesbrough	32	16	2	14	1	50
7	**Brighton**	31	11	13	7	9	46
8	Blackburn	31	11	11	9	4	44
9	Derby County	32	11	10	11	3	43
10	Burnley	31	12	7	12	1	43
11	Nottm Forest	32	10	12	10	-4	42
12	Leeds United	31	12	6	13	-7	42
13	Millwall	31	11	8	12	-2	41
14	Blackpool	32	10	10	12	3	40
15	Charlton	32	10	10	12	-3	40
16	Bolton	31	9	11	11	-1	38
17	Birmingham	32	9	11	12	-11	38
18	Ipswich Town	32	10	8	14	-18	38
19	Huddersfield	31	9	10	12	-18	37
20	Sheffield Wed	31	10	6	15	-9	36
21	Wolves	32	9	8	15	-8	35
22	Barnsley	31	9	7	15	-11	34
23	Bristol City	32	9	4	19	-15	31
24	Peterborough	30	9	3	18	-12	30

CF
ELEVEN

THE OFFICIAL CARDIFF CITY FC MATCH PROGRAMME

CARDIFF CITY

•—VERSUS—•

DERBY COUNTY

TUE 5TH MAR 7:45PM

npower CHAMPIONSHIP   MATCH 35   £3

MATCH SPONSOR:
IAN WILLIAMS CARPENTRY LTD

MATCH BALL SPONSOR:
CIRCLE IT

Malaysia   **PUMA**   Player

17

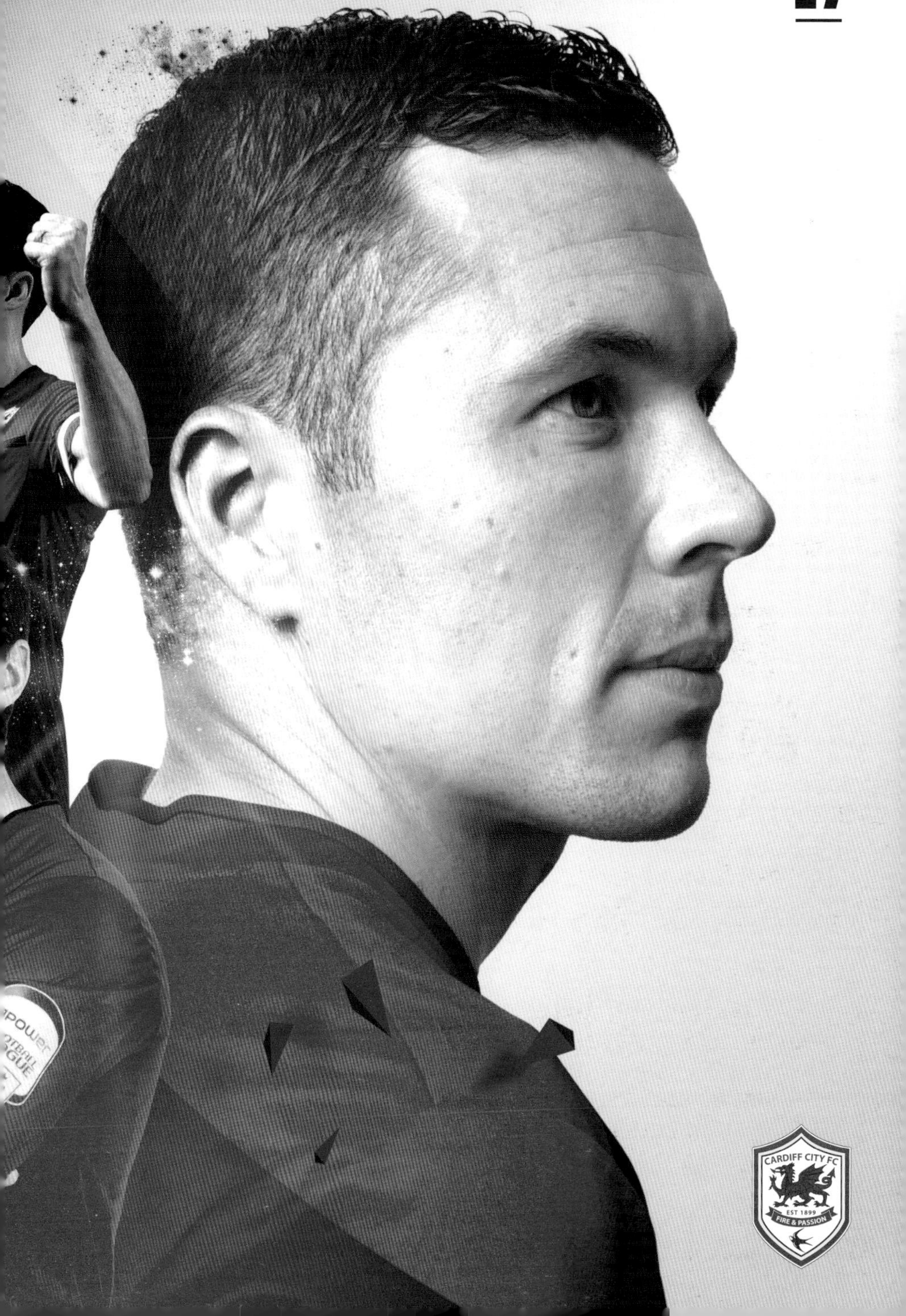

MALKY MACKAY
FOLLOW IT UP

Good evening and welcome back to Cardiff City Stadium for tonight's game with Derby County.

I'll start by extending that welcome to Nigel Clough, his staff, players and fans who have made the trip to South Wales from the Midlands tonight. I'm certain we'll have to be at our best today to take the points as Derby have some good players. They definitely gave us a very tough match up at Pride Park back in November when we had to really dig deep to take a point.

One of the (many!) beauties of the Championship is the quick turnaround in fixtures, so I'm really pleased that we've got the chance today to bounce back so quickly from Saturday's disappointment up at Middlesbrough. It was a mad ten minutes in the first half that ended up costing us the points and I was actually very pleased with the second half performance – plenty of fight and a fair amount of quality and on another day we would have claimed the point that I thought our overall efforts just about deserved.

However, it wasn't to be. Middlesbrough have some very good players and are fighting for their lives to get into the Play-Offs, so it was just the kind of game we know we'll be facing on a regular basis from now through to the end of the season in May. The important thing is to take on board the lessons to be learned from a loss and apply them in the next match. Thankfully that is something that we have largely done well this season. Most times we've managed to follow up a poor result or performance with a significantly better one, so I'll be looking for the same tonight.

Before the trip north, we had gone to Wolverhampton and came back with all three points last Sunday which was very pleasing. I felt our first half performance was as well as we have played all season and the only disappointment at half time was that our lead was 'only' 1-0.

Again, with the players they have we knew Wolves would come out fighting in the second half, but I thought we weathered the storm fairly comfortably and managed to get ourselves 2-0 up, only to concede almost immediately to make for a tense last twenty minutes.

It doesn't take a genius to see what Fraizer Campbell has brought to us since he signed in January – five goals in only four starts tells the story – and underlines how important it is to get your recruitment right both in the summer and in the January window. He was a player we had focused on almost as soon as we lost Nicky Maynard to injury, so I was very pleased that we managed to land him for such a favourable price. I am certain he will go on to prove a significant long-term asset to the club.

You will have seen in the press this week that TG has decided to step down as Chairman of the club after almost three years at the helm. I would like to place on record my huge thanks to TG who was been a great source of help and guidance since I joined the club in 2011.

We have always known that TG's extensive business commitments in Malaysia meant that this could happen and it is a tribute to him and his attitude to Cardiff City that he has decided to step down at this time as he didn't feel he could contribute enough of his time to do the job properly.

Any of you who have met TG since he started his association with the club will agree when I say he has been an absolute gentleman and a pleasure to deal with and a fine ambassador for Cardiff city Football Club in Malaysia. I wish him well for his future pursuit and he remains a firm friend of the club. I'm sure we'll still see him visiting the stadium whenever his schedule permits in the future.

Back to this evening – it's another big midweek night for us and, once again, we're counting on your fantastic support. It really does make a difference for the players to hear the noise generated from the stands so make sure you get behind them!

Enjoy the game.

"THE IMPORTANT THING IS TO TAKE ON BOARD THE LESSONS TO BE LEARNED FROM A LOSS AND APPLY THEM IN THE NEXT MATCH"

MALKY'S NOTES IN PROUD ASSOCIATION WITH

EDWARDS
COACH HOLIDAYS

CARDIFF CITY 0
BRIGHTON 2

Orlandi (43), Ulloa (90)

TUESDAY ▶ 19TH FEBRUARY ▶ 7.45PM Full Attendance **23,782**

🏠 **22,880**
🚌 **902**

City were unfortunate not to come away with something from a game that they dominated. Having gone close through Craig Noone and Craig Bellamy, Cardiff found Tomasz Kuszczak in inspired form. Peter Whittingham tested him with an exquisite effort from range, before Leonardo Ulloa brought the best out of David Marshall. However, the Seagulls proved clinical, and a low cross on the break from David López was converted by Andrea Orlandi on the stroke of half-time.

The second half brought new ideas with substitute Craig Conway in particular impressing, cutting in from the left twice to fire against the crossbar. Bellamy was denied a penalty on the hour mark, whilst Aron Gunnarsson and Fraizer Campbell each had efforts saved.

With time running out Cardiff were creating at will but couldn't find the finishing touch, and in the dying moments the game was put beyond doubt as Brighton punished on the break, Ulloa's deflected effort deceiving Marshall.

FANS SAY "This was definitely a game we could have won, but we're still in a good position for the rest of the season." *– Craig Brazel*

MALKY

"We ended up with twenty-two attempts on target compared to their two and I have to say that I think we started really well. Their goal in my opinion led a charmed life at times, but these things happen."

OATWAY

"We were fortunate to get Tomasz Kuszczak as I think he is a Premier League player. I think Cardiff will be untouchable though and they won't get caught, so the boys are delighted to have won here."

CONNOLLY

"I thought we had a couple of great chances. We're disappointed we didn't win but if we took those chances we would have won comfortably. In the second half it was wave after wave of attack."

REFEREE: K. Stroud

EST 1899		ALBION

12	⚑	1

58%	42%

POSSESSION

3	🟥	1

SHOTS
12 ON 4
7 OFF 2

st-match reaction from Malky Mackay,
arlie Oatway and
att Connolly on
rdiff City Player

CARDIFF CITY Player

rdiff City: Marshall, Taylor,
Hudson, Turner, Connolly,
hittingham, Noone (Conway),
nnarsson, Smith, Campbell
elguson), Bellamy.
bs not used: Lewis,
cNaughton, Cowie,
m Bo-Kyung,
ason.

**Brighton &
Hove Albion:**
Kuszczak, Bruno,
El-Abd, Upson, Bridge,
Hammond (Calderon), Orlandi
(Dicker), David Lopez, Bridcutt, Buckley
(Forster-Caskey), Ulloa.
Subs not used: Ankergren, Vicente,
LuaLua, Barker.

251

No way? Robert Kuszczak's heroic performance earns Brighton victory in Cardiff.

WOLVES 1

Sako (70)

CARDIFF CITY 2

Campbell (20, 67)

SUNDAY ▶ 24TH FEBRUARY ▶ 2.00PM Full Attendance 20,930

🏠 18,424

🚌 2,506

MALKY

"Parts of the first half were as good I think as we've played all season. I thought overall we were excellent in the way we controlled and kept the ball today, even in the six minutes of added on time."

SAUNDERS

"There were a lot of positives to take out of the game but we made two catastrophic mistake But we managed to reply straight away and then Sylvan misses an open goal for two-all."

Cardiff regained an eight point lead at the top of the Championship with a good performance against a Wolves side in free-fall. Whittingham – Wolves' tormentor in the reverse fixture with his sublime hat trick – had a low drive deflected early on, before an Aron Gunnarsson trademark long throw was flicked on by Turner, leaving Campbell to convert the simplest header.

The second half brought the same composure shown throughout the opening forty-five, with Bellamy finding the net after Ikeme spilled a Don Cowie effort, but the linesman's flag cutting celebrations short.

Once again though it was Fraizer's day, Bellamy providing a pinpoint cross from a dead ball that Campbell met emphatically, heading in his fifth goal in just five games. A nervous finale ensued when Sako converted a free kick minutes later and substitute Ebanks-Blake missed a golden opportunity from six yards, but Cardiff held on to take three points home.

CAMPBELL

"It was a tough game and we're delighted t have come away with three points. We've got to carry on the way we play, passing teams to death, and hopefully by the end of the season that wi be enough."

FANS SAY
"What a great lad and player Fraizer Campbell is! I cannot wait to let him loose on the Premier League – when he reaches full fitness he will be epic!" – *Richard Madley*

THE BREAKDOWN

REFEREE: S. Attwell

1 — 7

50% 50%

POSSESSION

1 — 1

SHOTS

2 ON 7

4 OFF 4

post-match reaction of this game from Malky
...kay, Dean Saunders
...Fraizer Campbell on
...iff City Player

CARDIFF CITY Player

...es: Ikeme, Johnson, Robinson,
...ss, Batth (Ebanks-Blake),
...herty (Foley), Henry,
..., Doumbia (Doyle),
...rdarson.
...s not used:
...ries, Ward,
...ards, Davis.

Cardiff City:
Marshall, Taylor,
Hudson (McNaughton),
Turner, Connolly,
Whittingham, Cowie (Kim Bo-
Kyung) Conway, Gunnarsson, Campbell
(Helguson), Bellamy.
Subs not used: Lewis, Noone, Mutch, Mason.

This one's for you kid. Bellamy makes a youngster's day after another win at Molineux.

MIDDLESBROUGH 2
Dyer (13), Ameobi (17)

CARDIFF CITY 1
Gunnarsson (67)

SATURDAY ▶ 2ND MARCH ▶ 3.00PM Full Attendance 15,440

🏠 14,829

🚌 611

MALKY

"We shot ourselves in the foot a bit and gave away two goals which we would normally never concede. But we put in a spirited second half and we had enough chances to have got the leveller."

MOWBRAY

"The character got us through today. Sometimes when you've been on a run like we have yo forget how to win football matches, but we battled to get through today."

Two quick-fire goals in the first twenty minutes gave Middlesbrough only their second win of 2013. Kieron Dyer scored from just a few yards out after Ismael Miller's pull back. Sammy Ameobi, who was making his debut for the Smoggies, added a second soon after. Ameobi showed some great footwork inside the area and curled home from ten yards out and Middlesbrough went into half-time deserved 2-0 leaders.

The second half saw a much-improved City performance though. Malky's men imposed constant pressure on the 'Boro back four and finally got their breakthrough on sixty-seven minutes when Aron Gunnarsson headed home from a Craig Bellamy corner.

The last five minutes saw Cardiff keeper David Marshall pushing forward to try and find an equaliser. Heidar Helguson and Fraizer Campbell came close in the dying minutes, but City ended with their first away loss in ten games.

WHITTINGHAM

"This is our first away defeat since November. We have bounced back before and need to against Derby. That' the time to put a few wrongs right."

FANS SAY "Disappointing to blemish our superb away record, but this side always responds and will again on Tuesday evening." – *Chris Matthews*

THE BREAKDOWN

REFEREE: M. Haywood

6 ⚑ **15**

50% **50%**

POSSESSION

0 **0**
2 **3**

SHOTS

5 ON 6

6 OFF 7

e post-match reaction of this game from
lky Mackay and
y Mowbray on
diff City Player

CARDIFF CITY Player ▶

ddlesbrough: Steele, Friend,
Manus, Leadbitter (c), Ameobi
desma), Bailey, Dyer (Emnes),
es, McEachran,
cDonald, Miller (Main).
s not used: Leutwiler,
liday, Williams,
allwood.

Cardiff City:
Marshall,
McNaughton
(Nugent), Taylor, Connolly,
Turner, Whittingham (c), Conway,
Smith (Helguson), Gunnarsson,
Campbell, Bellamy (Noone).
Subs not used: Lewis, Cowie, Kim, Mason.

259

All good things ... City's four month away record comes to an end at the Riverside.

THE CHAMPIONSHIP
KEEPING UP THE PRESSURE

The weekend of Championship fixtures kicked off on Saint David's Day with a welcome result from a **Cardiff City** perspective. Fellow promotion challengers **Watford** appeared to be in complete control over relegation-threatened **Wolves** on Friday night, passing the ball with the flair and fluidity instilled in them by their boss Gianfranco Zola – but then up stepped Wolves' Bakary Sako. His injury time equaliser was a strike that flattered Dean Saunder's faltering side, but the marauding French play-maker deserved it on individual performance alone.

While the Hornets were unable to close the gap at the top prior to our fixture at the Riverside, **Hull City** made no mistake. Spurred on by **Crystal Palace's** Friday night defeat of Derby County, the Tigers leapt into second place courtesy of an emphatic 5-2 win over **Birmingham City.** Braces from home débutant George Boyd and Egyptian international Gedo (who has now scored 5 in 6 during his loan spell from Al Ahly) helped Steve Bruce's men to close the gap to five points.

Of course, we still hold that game against **Leicester City** in hand, and the Foxes themselves lost some ground on the automatic places with a late defeat to **Ipswich Town** on Saturday. Mick McCarthy himself admitted that Leicester were the better side, but David McGoldrick's winner was all that mattered as the Tractor Boys continued their climb up the table.

Under McCarthy Ipswich have developed a solid 6 point gap between themselves and **Peterborough United,** who top the relegation zone. However, the Posh are showing signs of pulling away from Wolves, with whom they are level on points, having played a game fewer. Their 3-2 away victor over **Blackburn Rovers** was one of four weekend matches with five or more goals – all three of Peterborough's coming courtesy of Dwight Gayle.

The young striker was playing for Stansted in the ninth tie two seasons ago, but he made a flying start for the Posh o Saturday, completing a perfect hat-trick (left foot, right fo and header) within 16 first half minutes. That was enough to take the match beyond Rovers, who staged a late, but ultimately unsuccesful, comeback.

However, Gayle wasn't the only player of the afternoo to take a match ball home. Down on the south coast, **Brighton & Hove Albion's** Argentinean target man Leonardo Ulloa became the first ever player to net a hat-trick at the AMEX stadium. The Seagulls trounced 19th placed **Huddersfield Town** 4-1, leaving the Terriers one of a handfu of sides positioned precariously above the relegation zone. **Barnsley** and **Sheffield Wednesday** are two others, and they didn't help their causes this weekend, losing to **Bolton Wanderers** and **Nottingham Forest** respectively.

Further up into mid-table, **Leeds United** bea **Millwall** 1-0 by means of a penalty dispatche by January signing, and manager's namesake Stephen Warnock. Meanwhile **Burnley** also prevailed with a one goal margin as Charlie Austin's screamer (and first in five games) was enough to sea the points at **Charlton Athletic.**

Finally, **Blackpool** vs **Bristol City** proved to be the exception to an otherwise goal-filled afternoon. The spoils were shared in a 0-0 draw at Bloomfield Road thanks in no small part to Tom 'Bungle' Heaton's sensational save at the death. The former City man leave Paul Ince still waiting to oversee a goal as Blackpool bos

≫ LEADING SCORERS

1	2	3	4	5
69	61	56	56	54
≫ WATFORD	≫ CRYSTAL PALACE	≫ CARDIFF CITY	≫ LEICESTER	≫ MIDDLESBROUG

tatistical look at away form in the division

's defeat at the Riverside on Saturday would have come as quite a
prise to anyone who had studied the form books prior to the
ad's trip north-east. While **'Boro** were in dire form, with just one
from their previous nine outings, Malky's troops had been
eccable on the road, collecting 23 from a possible 27 points away
m South Wales.

s often the case in the Championship, the away form books throw
a few surprising statistics, as several clubs' performances on the
d of late have belied their league positions.

e of those sides is Dave Jones' **Sheffield Wednesday,** who haven't
away from home since **Craig Conway's** late strike condemned
m to defeat at CCS back on 2nd December! Since then, four wins
two draws have aided their ascent to their current position four
nts off the relegation zone.

club currently rooted to the bottom of the pile is **Bristol City**. And
despite earning a credible 0-0 draw at **Blackpool** on the
weekend, no one has fared worse on their recent
travels than the Robins. A run of five consecutive
away defeats preceded Saturday's result, making
the drop seem ever more likely for Sean
O'Driscoll's side.

Over the course of the whole season,
Charlton are the team whose home
and away form has shown the least
correlation. The Addicks have won
just 4 of their 19 Championship
fixtures at the Valley. However, if the
table were drawn up solely on away
results, **Chris Powell's** men would
be sitting in fourth place, having
racked up seven wins and four draws
from their 17 away matches.

So away form clearly doesn't count
for everything in this division. And
that's fortunate for **Crystal Palace,**
whose weekend victory was their
first win on the road since a 2-1
defeat of Peterborough on 10th
November!

ID YOU KNOW?

his evening's visitors **Derby County**
oked set to claim a point against
rystal Palace on Friday night as they
ere awarded an 88th minute penalty
t Pride Park. However, Eagles stopper
lian Speroni *(pictured)* kept out Connor Sammon's effort for
's second penalty save of the campaign. It was the sixth time
referee has pointed to the spot in the Rams' favour this
ason, and the first of those not to be converted. **Palace** are in
ct the top penalty earners in the league with twelve to their
ame (10 scored) while **City** have earned three, all at home,
d all dispatched by **Peter Whittingham.**

LATEST RESULTS

Friday, 1st March
Derby County 0–1 Crystal Palace
Wolves 1–1 Watford

Saturday, 2nd March
Leeds United 1–0 Millwall
Barnsley 2–3 Bolton Wanderers
Blackburn Rovers 2–3 Peterborough United
Blackpool 0–0 Bristol City
Brighton & Hove Albion 4–1 Huddersfield
Charlton Athletic 0–1 Burnley
Hull City 5–2 Birmingham City
Ipswich Town 1–0 Leicester City
Middlesbrough 2–1 Cardiff City
Sheffield Wednesday 0–1 Nottingham Forest

TONIGHT'S GAMES

(All games kick off at 7:45pm unless otherwise stated)
Birmingham City v Blackpool
Bolton v Blackburn Rovers (8:00pm)
Bristol City v Brighton & Hove Albion
Burnley v Barnsley
Cardiff City v Derby County
Crystal Palace v Hull City (8:00pm)
Huddersfield Town v Middlesbrough
Leicester City v Leeds United
Millwall v Wolves
Nottingham Forest v Ipswich Town
Peterborough United v Charlton Athletic
Watford v Sheffield Wednesday

2012/13 NPOWER CHAMPIONSHIP LEAGUE TABLE

Pos	Team	P	W	D	L	GD	Pts
1	**Cardiff City**	34	22	4	8	20	70
2	Hull City	35	20	5	10	12	65
3	Watford	35	19	6	10	25	63
4	Crystal Palace	35	17	10	8	19	61
5	Leicester City	34	17	6	11	27	57
6	Brighton	34	14	13	7	15	55
7	Middlesbrough	35	17	3	15	1	54
8	Nottm Forest	35	13	12	10	4	51
9	Leeds United	34	14	7	13	-4	49
10	Bolton	35	12	12	11	4	48
11	Burnley	35	13	8	14	0	47
12	Blackburn	35	11	12	12	-2	45
13	**Derby County**	35	11	11	13	1	44
14	Millwall	34	12	8	14	-6	44
15	Charlton	35	11	10	14	-5	43
16	Blackpool	35	10	12	13	1	42
17	Birmingham	35	10	12	13	-12	42
18	Ipswich Town	35	11	9	15	-19	42
19	Huddersfield	35	10	11	14	-25	41
20	Sheffield Wed	34	11	7	16	-9	40
21	Barnsley	34	10	7	17	-13	37
22	Peterborough	34	11	3	20	-10	36
23	Wolves	35	9	9	17	-10	36
24	Bristol City	35	10	5	20	-14	35

CF ELEVEN

THE OFFICIAL CARDIFF CITY FC MATCH PROGRAMME

CARDIFF CITY

•—VERSUS—•

LEICESTER CITY

TUE 12TH MAR 7:45PM

npower CHAMPIONSHIP   MATCH 36 £3

MATCH SPONSOR:
KENNY ROGERS ROASTERS

MATCH BALL SPONSOR:
THE VALE RESORT

Malaysia   **PUMA** Player

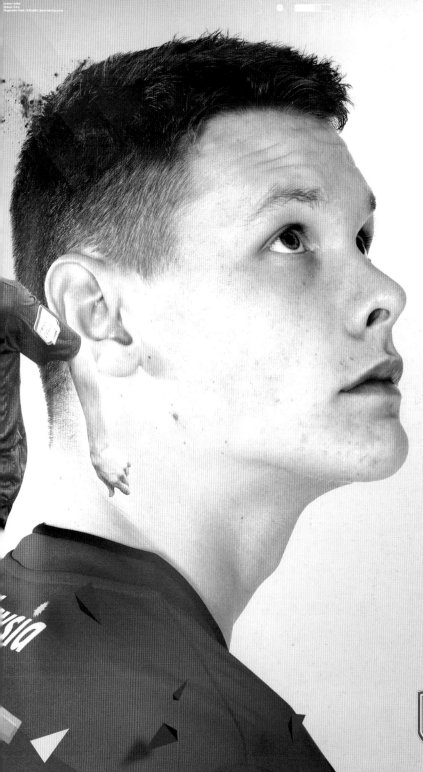
18

MALKY MACKAY

EVERYTHING COUNTS

Good evening and welcome to Cardiff City Stadium for tonight's game with Leicester City. I'll start in the usual way by welcoming Foxes' boss Nigel Pearson, his staff, players and everyone who has made the trip from the Midlands tonight.

We're in an unusual situation of coming into this game after a full week without a fixture – the Tuesday to Tuesday pattern is not one that I have encountered before, but it has given us a valuable opportunity to get the squad in order and get the right amount of rest as well as preparation for this important match.

One of the benefits of this week has been that I believe we are coming into this match with a fully fit squad (fingers crossed!) with the obvious exception of Nicky Maynard who has been missing since his third game with us. On that subject, Nicky continues to make great progress in his rehabilitation and is closely following the comeback schedule we expected. Sometimes periods of adversity are the moments when you get to know people better and Nicky's attitude and application after such a bad injury have shown us all that he is as good a man as he is a player.

There are always long and lonely hours or rehabilitation and some very hard work to do, but Nicky has been a fantastic professional throughout and has totally bought into the tasks our excellent medical staff have set him. His smiling face has continued to light up the training ground on a daily basis and he's been a pleasure to be around. It's also been a big week for him because he became a father for the second time when his fiancée gave birth to a little boy called Trent last Tuesday. Many congratulations to Nicky and Tara from everyone at the club.

Last week's game here against Derby was a frustrating one because we didn't really manage to get going and then gave away a silly goal to fall behind with not much time left on the clock. Many lesser teams would not have managed to come back after going a goal down with just fifteen minutes left to play, but it was testament to the spirit and belief in the squad that we responded so well, scored a nice equaliser and could have gone on to win it.

In the context of the season as a whole and the stage we are at, I very much saw the result as a point gained because we saw last Tuesday and again on Saturday how unpredictable this league is and how difficult it is for teams at the top to keep picking up wins.

Without taking anything for granted, we are in a very healthy position and one which we can significantly improve with a win tonight, but Leicester's recent blip will probably make that an even harder task as they'll be keen to get their push for promotion back on track as soon as possible. They have a squad packed full of talented players, some of whom have bags of Premier League experience, so we know it will be one of our toughest games of the season.

Our win up at the King Power stadium in December was particularly hard-fought and is a result I would mark down as one of our best this season because I've felt all along that whoever finishes above Leicester will probably end up winning promotion. Throughout the many twists and turns in the Championship this season, that feeling hasn't altered.

After today's game we will have ten league fixtures remaining, so we are coming towards the home straight. It goes without saying that we are really counting on your fantastic support to help us continue to build on the progress we have made this season and make it one to remember. Everything counts.

As I've said before, the only way for any football club to move forward is by having everyone – fans, players, staff, owners – pulling together in the same direction with a common purpose and I'm sure we will not be distracted from our goal over the next two months.

"THE ONLY WAY FOR ANY FOOTBALL CLUB TO MOVE FORWARD IS BY HAVING EVERYONE – FANS, PLAYERS, STAFF, OWNERS – PULLING TOGETHER IN THE SAME DIRECTION WITH A COMMON PURPOSE "

MALKY'S NOTES IN PROUD ASSOCIATION WITH

EDWARDS
COACH HOLIDAYS

CARDIFF CITY 1
Noone (82)

DERBY COUNTY 1
Sammon (75)

TUESDAY ▶ 5TH MARCH ▶ 7.45PM Full Attendance 21,554

🏠 **21,250**
🚌 **294**

MALKY

"To come back and get the goal showed the resilience in the last 15 minutes, and we nearly got the winner. It's another point towards where we would like to go."

GARNER

"To come to Cardiff and dictate for large parts of the game against the leaders is frightening. We are gutted that we haven't got the three points."

Cardiff came up against a well organised Derby side, but still came away with an important point thanks to substitute Craig Noone's unmarked headed effort minutes after Conor Sammon had put the visiting team ahead.

A stop-start game saw a tight first half with David Marshall saving well from Paul Coutts' long range effort and Fraizer Campbell going close from an Aron Gunnarsson long throw at the other end. Derby's Chris Martin found the net, but celebrations were cut short for the travelling fans thanks to an offside flag.

The second half saw an improvement in Cardiff's forward play, and it was against the grain when Craig Conway was dispossessed deep in City territory and Sammon stroked home following a Ben Davies cross.

A typical Cardiff response saw the hosts pull level seven minutes later though, Andrew Taylor finding Noone with a fantastic ball to the back post, the winger unable to miss. This could prove a point to savour with one game less to go and a healthy lead still intact at the summit.

TURNER

"Unfortunately we've lost and bounced back with a draw today. It isn't what we wanted but it's only a block four games and over the whole season we're confident we've got what it takes."

FANS SAY "This team has more spirit and determination than the last side in the DJ era. This game should be a warning though that we can't always rely on that same spirit." – *Matthew Davies*

THE BREAKDOWN

REFEREE: K. Johnson

5 | 6

55% | 45%

POSSESSION

12 | 2

SHOTS

ON 8 | 6

OFF 4 | 2

st-match reaction from Malky Mackay, dy Garner and n Turner on rdiff City Player

CARDIFF CITY Player

rdiff City: Marshall, Taylor, Nugent, rner, Connolly, Whittingham, Gunnarsson, Conway estede), Smith (Noone), mpbell, Helguson lason).

bs not used: Lewis, cNaughton, wie, Kim.

Derby County: Legzdins, Roberts, Buxton, Keogh, Gjokaj, Coutts, Hendrick, Davies, Forsyth (Jacobs), Martin, Sammon.

Subs not used: Fielding, Hoganson, Doyle, Bennett.

269

High Noone. Craig's back-post leap earns
City a point from the jaws of defeat.

THE CHAMPIONSHIP
A WELCOME DISTRACTION?

Tonight we finally take on **Leicester City** with the chance to convert one of our games in hand into vital points. The fixture was twice postponed as the Foxes reached the fourth round of the F.A. Cup, and forced a replay against **Huddersfield Town,** before eventually bowing out of the competition.

But even after today we won't have caught up completely with some of our promotion rivals, as **Barnsley's** cup exploits put Saturday's match on hold as well. The Tykes have gone a few stages further than this evening's visitors, reaching the dizzy heights of the quarter-finals. Could they possibly eclipse that Cup run of 2008? While such Cup exploits can prove to be the highlight of a season, the resulting distractions and fixture pile-ups can come as unwanted side-effects. But does success in the Cup really have a negative impact on a side's performance in the league?

Of course we've enjoyed the occasional Cup run ourselves at Cardiff City in recent years, most recently last season's trip to Wembley (for what was then the Carling Cup Final) which preceded a very respectable top six League finish. But back in 2008 – en route to the F.A. Cup Final – we managed just two wins in our final six games following our semi-final victory over Barnsley.

There are plenty of similar examples of Cup runs hindering the League form of Championship sides, be that in domestic Cup competitions or even the Europa League (**Birmingham City** played a total of sixty-two games last year as a result of their involvement that competition). However, it's not unheard of that a cup distraction actually has a positive influence.

The losing semi-finalists in football are rarely remembered, but **West Bromwich Albion** deserve a mention after falling at the penultimate hurdle the 2008 F.A. Cup. While we faced **Barnsley** in on semi-final, the Baggies were edged out by eventual champions **Portsmouth** in the other. well as their extra fixtures in the F.A. Cup, Tony Mowbray's side also battled through several rounds of League Cup action. Nevertheless, the Midlands side never took their eye off the ball in the League and finished the season as champions, proving that balancing the two is not impossible

It was a similar story for **Reading** tw years later – except at the opposite end of the table. Having failed in the Play-Offs the year before, they were sitting in 23rd place in mid-January having won jus 5 of their 26 Championship matches. But then their F.A. Cup run began.

They may only have reached the quarter-finals, but the **Royals** journey involved two replays an the defeat of three top flight sides, including a victory over Liverpool at Anfield. Such a run could have taken a lot out of a relegation-threatened side, but Brian McDermott's m were able to carry their cup form across to the League. In the end, it was widely credited for a dramatic ascent up the division in which they lost just 4 of their remaining 20, finishing up in a lofty 9th place.

>> BOOK 'IM REF! - CHAMPIONSHIP YELLOWS

1	2	3	4	5
12	10	9	9	9
> SHANE LOWRY	> LIAM BRIDCUTT	> ADAM EL-ABD	> GREG HALFORD	> DAVID MEYLER

YOUNG AT HEART

statistical look at the Championship's seasoned pros

...is time last week, José Mourinho said that the whole world would ...ne in to watch his Real Madrid side's Champions League blockbuster ...ainst Manchester United.

...ut while **Ryan Giggs'** 1000th career appearance took up plenty of ...lumn inches prior to the match, it was another 39-year-old who ...ble the evening's headlines in the Championship – **Kevin Phillips.** ...e well-travelled striker netted a hat-trick in Palace's top of the table ...ash with **Hull City,** and he's one of several Championship forwards ...fusing to hang up their shooting boots.

...fact, we have a few experienced front men of our own here in the ...pital as Phillips' hat-trick drew him level on league goals with **Heidar** ...elguson on the night. And just a few years behind the Iceman are ...aig Bellamy and **Tommy Smith,** who have added vital experience to ...our front line this year – both exemplary models for the younger members of Malky's squad.

While the likes of Phillips and Helguson have set the standard for seasoned forwards in the division, they aren't the only ones to have retained their scoring touch.

Having joined on a free transfer from **Ipswich Town,** Trinidad & Tobagonian international **Jason Scotland** netted 4 times in his 5 five appearances for **Barnsley** either side of his 34th birthday this season.

Meanwhile, 79-cap Portuguese international **Nuno Gomes** surprised many a Championship fan in signing for **Blackburn Rovers** in the summer. However, the 36-year-old made an equally impressive early contribution for Rovers, scoring in 4 consecutive games in the opening month of the campaign.

Finally, **City** fell victim to an experienced player in their recent trip to the Riverside as **Kieron Dyer** netted his 1st league goal in 6 years. The former England international was 28 when he last notched a goal. That strike came for **Newcastle** in a 1-1 draw with a **Watford** side that still had **Malky Mackay** on their playing staff!

DID YOU KNOW?

...Last week saw a quirk of the Championship fixture list as all ...eight Championship clubs beginning with the letter 'B' faced each other on the same night. **Chris Eagles'** 93rd minute strike for **Bolton** against **Blackburn** was the only winner in the four matches, as the spoils were shared in **Birmingham v Blackpool, Bristol City v Brighton** and **Burnley v Barnsley!** One man who has enjoyed these fixtures over the course of the season is Birmingham City's **Curtis Davies** (pictured). Amazingly the centre-half has scored 6 goals against the other 'B' sides this season, with two each against **Blackpool, Blackburn** and **Burnley.** Bizarre!

WEEKEND RESULTS
Tuesday 5th March
Bolton Wanderers 1–0 Blackburn Rovers
Birmingham City 1–1 Blackpool
Bristol City 0–0 Brighton & Hove Albion
Burnley 1–1 Barnsley
Cardiff City 1–1 Derby County
Crystal Palace 4–2 Hull City
Huddersfield Town 2–1 Middlesbrough
Leicester City 1–1 Leeds United
Millwall 0–2 Wolves
Nottingham Forest 1–0 Ipswich Town
Peterborough United 2–2 Charlton Athletic
Watford 2–1 Sheffield Wednesday

MID-WEEK GAMES
(All fixtures kick-off at 7:45pm)
Burnley 0–1 Hull City (Monday)
Barnsley v Brighton & Hove Albion
Cardiff City v Leicester City
Leeds United v Peterborough

NEXT WEEKEND
Saturday 16th March
(All games kick off at 3:00pm unless otherwise stated)
Barnsley v Watford
Blackpool v Peterborough United
Derby County v Leicester City (8.00pm)
Hull City v Nottingham Forest
Ipswich Town v Bolton Wanderers
Middlesbrough v Birmingham City
Sheffield Wednesday v Cardiff City
Wolves v Bristol City

Sunday 17th March
Brighton & Hove Albion v Crystal Palace (12.00pm)
Blackburn Rovers v Burnley (12.30pm)

2012/13 NPOWER CHAMPIONSHIP LEAGUE TABLE

Pos	Team	P	W	D	L	GD	Pts
1	**Cardiff City**	35	22	5	8	20	71
2	Hull City	37	21	5	11	11	68
3	Watford	37	20	6	11	25	66
4	Crystal Palace	37	18	11	8	21	65
5	**Leicester City**	36	17	7	12	26	58
6	Nottm Forest	37	15	12	10	7	57
7	Brighton	36	14	14	8	14	56
8	Bolton	37	14	12	11	6	54
9	Middlesbrough	37	13	3	17	-2	54
10	Leeds United	36	14	9	13	-4	51
11	Burnley	37	13	9	15	-1	48
12	Charlton	37	12	11	14	-4	47
13	Blackpool	37	11	13	13	2	46
14	Birmingham	37	11	13	13	-10	46
15	Derby County	37	11	12	14	-1	45
16	Blackburn	36	11	12	13	-3	45
17	Millwall	35	12	8	15	-8	44
18	Huddersfield	37	11	11	15	-25	44
19	Sheffield Wed	36	12	7	17	-9	43
20	Ipswich Town	37	11	10	16	-20	43
21	Wolves	37	10	9	18	-10	39
22	Bristol City	37	11	6	20	-12	39
23	Peterborough	36	11	5	20	-10	38
24	Barnsley	35	10	8	17	-13	38

CF ELEVEN

THE OFFICIAL CARDIFF CITY FC MATCH PROGRAMME

CARDIFF CITY

• VERSUS •

BLACKBURN ROVERS

MON 1ST APR 3:00PM

npower CHAMPIONSHIP   MATCH 39   £3

2013 FOOTBALL LEAGUE FAMILY CLUB OF THE YEAR

MATCH SPONSOR:
EDWARDS COACHES

MATCH BALL SPONSOR:
SPORTFIVE

Malaysia   **PUMA®**   Player ▶

19

EVERYTHING TO PLAY FOR

Good afternoon and welcome back to Cardiff City Stadium for our Bank Holiday Monday game with Blackburn Rovers. I'll start by wishing everyone a very happy Easter, hoping you all had some nice family time together yesterday and have come to the match today in good form. This time of the season has long been considered a vital one and this year is no different with everything to play for over the next few weeks.

We've had three games since my last set of notes and they have brought us another four points in our quest at the top of the league. First of all there was the draw here with Leicester City, which is something that we may look back on as a vital point gained. It was the kind of game where there was a lot at stake and both teams looked like they had a fear of losing which made things tight on the pitch. I was particularly pleased that we managed to come back and take the point after having fallen behind with only about fifteen minutes left on the clock.

It's been a big few weeks for Rudy Gestede who got the equaliser on the night and then followed that up with his first international cap, and goal, for Benin in their World Cup Qualifier during the recent international break. As I've said before, I'm a big believer in international football as it marked the proudest moment of my career when I was selected to represent Scotland. Although, in light of my country's recent result against Wales, perhaps it's a subject that I'd rather not discuss at the moment!

We followed up the point against Leicester with a very solid and important win at Sheffield Wednesday. We went to Hillsborough knowing that it was going to be a physically demanding match. They play in a direct style and we had to combat that because I knew that once we had done so, our superior quality would be the ultimate difference in the match. It was also pleasing to see Don Cowie and Matthew Connolly on the scoresheet – they are both players who I would count amongst our many unsung heroes this season who have always uncomplainingly done whatever job has been asked of them for the good of the team.

Saturday's match at Peterborough was a disappointing way to get back into action after two weeks off. We started the match well and I thought were much the better team in the first half. Our lead was a just reward for the way we were playing, however, the game changed on a refereeing decision which was plainly wrong. What I thought at the time was then proven right when I watched the replays afterwards – Don Cowie clearly played the ball and the Peterborough guy then tripped over Don's outstretched leg.

Some incidents are vital, particularly in such a big game against a team who are really fighting for their lives at the wrong end of the table, so I was frustrated that we didn't manage to get back on top and take something from the game, especially as it would have been just reward for our two thousand plus travelling fans, who were once again outstanding.

I'd like to welcome Rovers boss Gary Bowyer, his staff, players and the Blackburn fans here today. It's fair to say that it's been an eventful season at Ewood Park, but they have a squad packed full of Premier League players, so we know today will be a very tough game for us. As ever, we are counting on your fantastic support to help us to another huge win.

I'd like to end my notes today by putting a shout out to the Clydebank Bluebirds. I know that Paul Cummings up in my old home town organises trips to our games whenever he can and we're always really grateful of any support from all corners of the UK!

Enjoy the game.

"THIS TIME OF THE SEASON
HAS LONG BEEN
CONSIDERED A
VITAL ONE AND
THIS YEAR IS
NO DIFFERENT "

MALKY'S NOTES IN PROUD ASSOCIATION WITH

EDWARDS
COACH HOLIDAYS

CARDIFF CITY 1
Gestede (90+3)

LEICESTER CITY 1
Keane (72)

TUESDAY ▶ 12TH MARCH ▶ 7.45PM | Full Attendance 23,231

🏠 222,55
🚌 976

Cardiff continued their march with another point against contenders Leicester thanks to a late Rudy Gestede header that cancelled out Michael Keane's seventy-second minute opener.

The Bluebirds were settled in the first half and David Marshall did well to keep out a long range Chris Wood effort, Gunnarsson blocking the follow up from Dyer. At the other end the best chance fell to Craig Noone who volleyed over from close range, Campbell waiting just behind.

The break saw injured captain Mark Hudson removed from the field of play. Campbell was inches from meeting Tommy Smith's cross with a diving header and Chris Wood was denied brilliantly by Marshall after breaking through.

On loan Manchester United centre back Michael Keane then fired a header against the post and made no mistake second time round when St. Ledger put the ball back in from the opposite side. Cardiff responded resiliently with Taylor arching a cross toward Gestede, who secured a point with his headed effort deep into injury time.

MALKY

"It shows a great fighting spirit to press and keep pressing and keep knocking the door. To get the actual goal in the end is a hard-earned rewar for that team tonight."

PEARSON

"It was a bit cruel o the players bearing in mind how late it was. This is never a easy place to come to and a bit of confidence has been lacking. But I thought we played very well."

GESTEDE

"We've been top of the league for a long time. We know wha we can do, we know our strengths. We just need to play like we know we can. I trust in my team."

FANS SAY
"This wasn't the best game or result from a Cardiff City point of view, but I'm glad Rudy came on and scored at the end." – *Nicola Bartlett*

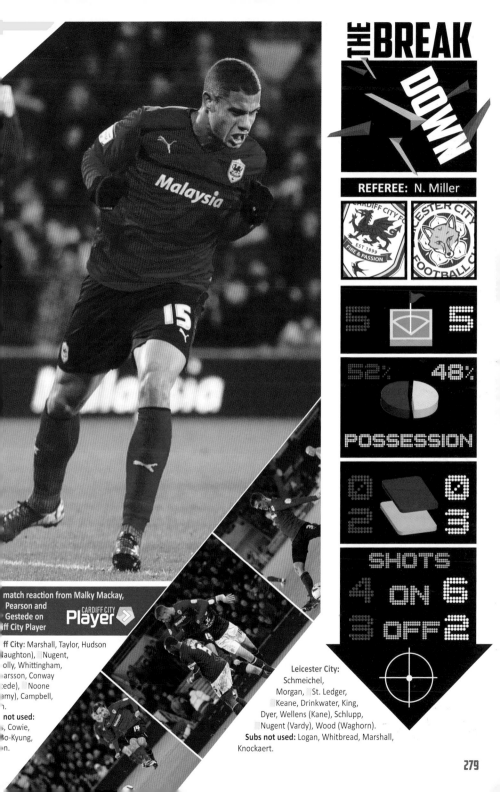

THE BREAKDOWN

REFEREE: N. Miller

5

52% 48%

POSSESSION

0 3

SHOTS

ON 6

OFF 2

match reaction from Malky Mackay, Pearson and Gestede on iff City Player

CARDIFF CITY Player

ff City: Marshall, Taylor, Hudson
laughton), Nugent,
olly, Whittingham,
arsson, Conway
ede), Noone
my), Campbell,
.

not used:
, Cowie,
o-Kyung,
n.

Leicester City:
Schmeichel,
Morgan, St. Ledger,
Keane, Drinkwater, King,
Dyer, Wellens (Kane), Schlupp,
Nugent (Vardy), Wood (Waghorn).
Subs not used: Logan, Whitbread, Marshall,
Knockaert.

279

Down with a thud. The Foxes' fall from grace continued in CF11.

SHEFFIELD WED 0
CARDIFF CITY 2

Cowie (45), Connolly (65)

SATURDAY ▶ 16TH MARCH ▶ 3.00PM Full Attendance 24,171

🏠 22,805
🚌 1,366

Malaysia

MALKY

"We've kept seven clean sheets away from home this season, which is huge. And that was our fourteenth clean sheet of the season on a day where we've dealt with their aerial threat."

JONES

"We've switched off at key times and that's disappointing. We've shown a little bit of naivety when maybe they've got that edge of experience over us

Cardiff picked up all three points on a day that saw promotion rivals Hull and Watford both lose. The first half produced very little in terms of chances for either side. However, the deadlock was broken right on the stroke of half-time.

A Craig Bellamy delivery caused problems for the Wednesday defence, who could only clear the ball the edge of their area; Don Cowie then struck a low driven shot, through a forest of legs into Chris Kirkland's net.

A swinging Peter Whittingham free kick allowed Matt Connolly to pick up his fifth goal of the campaign just after the hour mark. Connolly doubled City's lead, heading home after finding himself unmarked on the back post.

A seventieth minute free kick from Miguel Llera was the Owls' best chance, in a game where they created little to trouble Malky's men. The win meant that Cardiff stretched their lead at the top of the table to seven points, nine clear of third and with a game in hand over both immediate rivals.

BARNETT

"The win has put a smile on my face and I have two weeks to train with the squad before our next match. The international break gives me time to settle in Cardiff."

FANS SAY "A fantastic day out to Sheffield and a fantastic performance by the lads. Well done you Bluebirds!" – *Christian Burns*

THE BREAKDOWN

REFEREE: J. Linington

SWFC *Est.* 1867

CARDIFF CITY — EST 1899 — FIRE & PASSION

3

45%   54%

POSSESSION

3

SHOTS
3 ON
3 OFF

e post-match reaction of this game from
alky Mackay, Dave
nes and Leon Barnett
Cardiff City Player

CARDIFF CITY Player ➤

effield Wednesday: Kirkland,
uxton, R Johnson, ▢ Gardner,
era, Antonio (Maguire),
élan (▢ J Johnson), Pugh
Madine), ▢ Prutton,
e, Lita.
ubs not used:
ywater, Taylor,
emedo,
cCabe.

Cardiff City:
Marshall, Connolly,
Nugent, Barnett, Taylor,
Whittingham, Cowie,
Gunnarsson, ▢ Helguson
(Gestede), Campbell, ▢ Bellamy (Smith).
Subs not used: Lewis, McNaughton,
Conway, Kim, Mutch.

283

Happier times. Ghosts of 2009 are vanquished for Kev and co. at Hillsborough.

NPOWER CHAMPIONSHIP

PETERBOROUGH UTD 2
McCann (Pen 72, Pen 79)

CARDIFF CITY 1
Gunnarsson (23)

SATURDAY ▶ 30TH MARCH ▶ 3.00PM Full Attendance 9,236

🏠 **7,062**

🚌 **2,174**

MALKY

"We're disappointed in our own defending round about both of the penalties, because we caused our own problems to allow the referee the chance to give them."

FERGUSON

"We have beaten a team that is bound for the Premier League twice – and we have done it on merit on both occasions. Hopefully it turns out to be a big win for us."

The Bluebirds' first of two games in three days ended in defeat at a ground that Cardiff have historically struggled at, Peterborough once again defining the strength of the league with a win that pulls them back out of the relegation zone. Posh started proceedings with an effort from Gayle, saved well by Marshall before Cowie whipped the ball into the area from a corner that Turner flicked toward the back stick. Gunnarsson tucked the ball home to take the lead, the latter of the half being played out routinely.

Posh came out of the blocks quicker than the Bluebirds after the interval, the Cardiff defence holding before Whittingham was unlucky to see his effort fall wide. However, Cowie was then adjudged to have brought down Mendez-Laing inside the Cardiff box to hand Peterborough a way in.

Substitute McCann converted, and just seven minutes later the reversal was complete, McCann again slotting away from the spot after Connolly appeared to bring down Gayle inside the area. Gestede had two late chances, but there would be no joy from this one for City.

FANS SAY
"We can't get too downbeat when we lose – we're still in a really strong position. Today wasn't great, but we've got eight games to secure the goal now." – *James Morton*

GESTEDE

"We're disappointed not to win today, especially in front of the travelling Cardiff fans who were amazing as usual. We'll keep our heads up now and focus on Blackburn."

THE BREAKDOWN

REFEREE: E. Ilderton

9 ⚑ **3**

47% **53%**
POSSESSION

SHOTS
7 ON **5**
6 OFF **7**

post-match reaction of this game from
...ky Mackay and
...en Ferguson
...ardiff City **Player** ▶

CARDIFF CITY Player ▶

...rborough United: Olejnik,
...ck, Zakuani, Little, Rowe,
...ell (Mendez-Laing),
...linand (McCann), Knight-
...ival, Payne, Tomlin
...nett), Gayle.
s not used: Day,
...ey, Swanson,
...elier.

Cardiff City:
Marshall, Taylor,
Turner, Connolly,
Barnett, Whittingham
(Conway), Cowie, Gunnarsson,
Smith, Helguson (Mason),
Campbell (Gestede).
Subs not used: Lewis, McNaughton,
Kim Bo-Kyung, Mutch.

287

Incoming! Goals, talent and drive eclipsed Gunnar's monstrous throwing ability during 2012/13.

THE CHAMPIONSHIP

TRADING PLACES

By 5pm on Saturday afternoon, results from elsewhere in the Championship seemed as good as we could have hoped from a Cardiff City perspective, providing one positive after our slip-up at London Road.

Unfortunately, **Hull City** went on to beat **Huddersfield Town** in the evening kick off through George Boyd's fine strike. But still, that made them the only side in the top nine to taste victory on the Easter weekend.

Late season jitters can play a vital role as the pressure mounts in this final stretch of the season, but of course that doesn't apply to those who have nothing left to play for. **Birmingham City** were a prime example of a mid-table side playing with no fear, as a four goal haul at Selhurst Park came courtesy of youngsters Nathan Redmond (pictured), Ravel Morrison and Shane Ferguson, aged 19, 20 and 21 respectively. The emphatic result denied Ian Holloway *(pictured)* and **Crystal Palace** the chance to momentarily overtake Hull into second place.

Despite losing two successive matches prior to the international break, **Watford** also took to the pitch against **Burnley** on Friday with an opportunity to break into those automatic places. Having twice cancelled out first half Charlie Austin strikes, Gianfranco Zola's men appeared to be heading for victory through Forestieri's second classy finish. However, 25-cap Wales international Sam Vokes did a favour for the other promotion challengers, slotting home an injury time equaliser for the Clarets.

Elsewhere in the top third the trend was continued as points were dropped left, right and centre. In the only top 6 clash of the weekend, the spoils were shared between **Brighton** and **Nottingham Forest,** who are unbeaten in seven matches under Billy Davies. Argentinean goal machine Leonardo Ulloa took first blood with his eighth in as many games, but 3 goals in a frenetic final 10 minutes, left the final score at 2-2.

Leicester City were at an instant disadvantage against **Millwall** as Wes Morgan was sent off just 3 minutes in. But it took until three minutes from time for the Lions to take advantage, as Alan Dunne eventually slotted past the ever impressive Kasper Schmeichel. The final faltering top nine side was **Middlesbrough,** who fell victim to a resurgent **Wolves** in one of several goal-fests. But despite their 3-2 win Dean Saunders team remain in the drop zone with just seven games remaining to secure survival.

The goals were flowing in equal measure among the mid-table sides as **Ipswich Town** trounced **Leeds United** 3-0, aided by Tom Lees' early dismissal for a reckless challenge. Elsewhere, **Charlton Athletic** came back from two goals down to beat fellow mid-table outfit **Bolton Wanderers** at the Valley – Yann Kermorgant completing the turnaround from the spot (we'd imagine with a more polished technique!). Meanwhile **Blackpool** and today's visitors **Blackburn Rovers,** both struggling for wins, played out a 1-1 draw in the Lancashire derby.

At the bottom, **Bristol City's** chances of survival are looking grim as a 3-0 defeat to **Derby County** left them six points adrift at the foot of the table. And finally, **Sheffield Wednesday** won their relegation scrap against **Barnsley,** leaving 3 places, and just a 2 point gap, between the two South Yorkshire sides.

⟫ LEADING SCORERS

1	2	3	4	5
75	67	61	59	50
⟫ WATFORD	⟫ CRYSTAL PALACE	⟫ CARDIFF CITY	⟫ LEICESTER	⟫ NOTTM FOREST

CRICKET SCORES

statistical look at this season's most convincing victories

rmingham's 4-0 rout at Selhurst Park reversed the usual trend for e Clarke's side, who have been on the other end of a few mprehensive defeats this year. In fact, the Blues are the only side in e division to have been beaten by a two, three, four and five goal argin in this campaign.

day's win was the first time that they have won by more than two als all season. They now leave **Huddersfield, Leeds United** and arlton as the only other sides yet to do the same.

icester and Watford have dished out the most rashings so far this season, as they are the only ams in the league to have won by two, three, ur and five goals this term. The Hornets' cord being even more impressive as they've on by three goals on three separate casions – and by four goals twice!

far this season, only **Leicester** and ackpool have hit a side for six. th of those victories were 6-0 aulings of then ugglers **Ipswich** wn, before Mick cCarthy had overseen their later rise up e table.

y's 4-0 home win over **Burnley** back in tober remains our biggest win of the ampionship campaign. But we are far from ne in that sense, as our closest challengers ll City haven't won by more than 3 goals all ason.

course the knack for grinding out results, of th us and Hull, has more than made up for at. 17 of our 23 Championship victories have en by just a one goal margin, a record that ly the Tigers are close to. While they've d 16 wins decided by one goal, **Leeds** ited and **Crystal Palace** are the next arest contenders with just eleven.

DID YOU KNOW?

Following **Rudy Gestede's** call up (and début goal) for Benin, City players have now been capped for countries in Africa, Asia, Europe, Australia and North America whilst playing for the Bluebirds – with South America the only footballing continent not represented. unichi Inamoto notched some of his 82 international caps for Japan during his spell in Cardiff, while the incomparable **Eddie Johnson** *(pictured)* played for the USA national side whilst on loan to us from Fulham. Finally, **Tony Vidmar** represented Australia (for whom he is now assistant manager of the U17s) throughout his career in South Wales, and scored one of his 3 goals in 76 caps against the Solomon Islands in 2004.

npower
FOOTBALL LEAGUE

LATEST RESULTS

29th/30th March

Blackburn Rovers 1–1 Blackpool
Watford 3–3 Burnley
Crystal Palace 0–4 Birmingham
Derby County 3–0 Bristol City
Leicester City 0–1 Millwall
Charlton Athletic 3–2 Bolton Wanderers
Ipswich Town 3–0 Leeds United
Nottingham Forest 2–2 Brighton & Hove Albion
Peterborough United 2–1 Cardiff City
Sheffield Wednesday 2–1 Barnsley
Wolves 3–2 Middlesbrough
Huddersfield Town 0–1 Hull City

TODAY'S GAMES

(All games kick off at 3:00pm unless otherwise stated)

Barnsley v Leicester City
Birmingham City v Wolves
Blackpool v Crystal Palace
Bristol City v Sheffield Wednesday
Burnley v Nottingham Forest
Cardiff City v Blackburn Rovers
Leeds United v Derby County (5:05pm)
Millwall v Ipswich Town

TOMORROW'S GAMES

Bolton Wanderers v Huddersfield Town (8.00pm)
Brighton & Hove Albion v Charlton Athletic
Hull City v Watford
Middlesbrough v Peterborough United

2012/13 NPOWER CHAMPIONSHIP LEAGUE TABLE

Pos	Team	P	W	D	L	GD	Pts
1	**Cardiff City**	38	23	6	9	21	75
2	Hull City	39	22	5	12	11	71
3	Watford	39	20	7	12	24	67
4	Crystal Palace	39	18	11	10	14	65
5	Nottm Forest	39	16	13	10	8	61
6	Brighton	39	15	15	9	16	60
7	Leicester City	39	17	8	14	24	59
8	Bolton	39	14	12	13	4	54
9	Middlesbrough	39	17	3	19	-4	54
10	Birmingham	39	13	13	13	-5	52
11	Leeds United	39	14	10	15	-8	52
12	Derby County	39	13	12	14	3	51
13	Burnley	39	13	11	15	-1	50
14	Charlton	39	13	11	15	-5	50
15	Millwall	37	14	8	15	-5	50
16	Ipswich Town	39	13	10	16	-16	49
17	Blackpool	39	11	14	14	1	47
18	**Blackburn**	38	11	14	13	-3	47
19	Huddersfield	39	12	11	16	-25	47
20	Sheffield Wed	38	13	7	18	-10	46
21	Peterborough	39	13	6	20	-8	45
22	Wolves	39	12	9	18	-8	45
23	Barnsley	38	12	8	18	-12	44
24	Bristol City	39	11	6	22	-16	39

CF ELEVEN

THE OFFICIAL CARDIFF CITY FC MATCH PROGRAMME

CARDIFF CITY

— VERSUS —

BARNSLEY

TUE 9TH APR 7:45PM

npower CHAMPIONSHIP   MATCH 41 £3

2013 FOOTBALL LEAGUE FAMILY CLUB OF THE YEAR

MATCH SPONSOR:
THE VALE RESORT

MATCH BALL SPONSOR:
BRECON CARREG

TEAM SPONSOR:
ARUP

Malaysia   PUMA   Player

MALKY MACKAY

TACTICAL DISCIPLINE

Good evening and welcome back to Cardiff City Stadium for tonight's game with Barnsley.

I'd like to welcome David Flitcroft, his staff, players and everyone who has travelled from Yorkshire for this evening's match. David has done a fantastic job since taking over as Barnsley boss earlier this season, so we know we'll have to be at our best to pick up a result tonight.

It's always good to see young, British managers given their chance at this level and David has certainly taken his opportunity impressively as he has led Barnsley away from the danger zone in just a few months in charge. However, much like ourselves, they still have work to do, so it will be a tight, tough match here today, I'm sure.

I was really pleased with the tactical discipline we showed in Saturday's game at Watford. Right from the beginning we managed to impose ourselves well on the game – something that is not always easy when you are playing away from home against a very good team – and we had much the better of the first half.

We also knew that the onus was on Watford to win the game, so we were expecting them to put us under more pressure after the break. Of course they did just that, but we held firm and didn't really allow them to create any chances to speak of whilst remaining lively on the break ourselves.

Under those circumstances, a point was a positive result and takes us another small step closer to achieving our objective of the season. The way we played was particularly pleasing if you consider that Watford are comfortably the league's top scorers this season with an abundance of attacking talent in

Of course it meant two clean sheets in a week, coming on the back of the comprehensive victory over Blackburn Rovers here on Easter Monday. In beating Rovers I felt we produced one of our most complete performances of the season, totally dominating the match from the first whistle. We played with a tempo and aggression which Blackburn simply couldn't live with and once Fraize Campbell got the first goal I felt it was just a question of how many we would win by.

As you will have seen, we brought in Leon Barnett on loan from Norwich City last month and he has had a very positive start to his career in a Cardiff shirt with three clean sheets in his first four matches. He is an experienced, calm campaigner and has slotted straight into the squad with no fus at all. We're hoping he'll be with us through to the end of the season.

There was a fantastic crowd here for the Blackburn game last week and the travelling support at Vicarage Road on Saturday was magnificent – mor than 2,000 Bluebirds fans amassed behind the goa was a very impressive sight and definitely played a role in keeping the lads going. I'll expect more of the same here tonight because to keep moving forward we need everyone associated with the clu – players, staff, fans – pushing hard in the same direction.

As the season nears its end, it becomes ever more important to simply focus on the challenge immediately in front of us – Barnsley here tonight and only then switch attention to the next game once we have overcome this hurdle.

So please get behind the team tonight, because

"THE WAY WE PLAYED WAS PARTICULARLY PLEASING IF YOU CONSIDER THAT WATFORD ARE COMFORTABLY THE LEAGUE'S TOP SCORERS THIS SEASON"

CARDIFF CITY 3

Campbell (40), Mason (86), Whittingham (Pen 90)

BLACKBURN 0

MONDAY ▶ **1ST APRIL** ▶ **3.00PM** | Full Attendance **24,327**

🏠 **23,928**
🚌 **399**

MALKY

"We got our 15th clean sheet of the season which is something I am really pleased with - but I am delighted with the whole team performance today. We dominated from start to finish."

BOWYER

"We came under a lot of pressure from Cardiff today. They are top of the league for a reason and I thought they played particularly well. We weren't at the level we can be."

Cardiff City showed their promotion credentials with an emphatic 3-0 victory over Blackburn Rovers on Easter Monday. The first half was largely a frustrating one for the home side.

City had penalties turned down, shots hitting the woodwork and efforts cleared off the line before Fraizer Campbell ended the frustration five minutes before the break. Campbell found himself in acres of space and nodded a simple header in at the back post from a well drilled Bellamy corner.

Malky's men maintained their dominant performance in the second half and Blackburn showed very little threat throughout the ninety minutes, failing to get a single shot on target. Despite this it took Cardiff until the 86th minute to double their lead. Substitute Joe Mason jinked inside the box, found himself some space and struck the ball sweetly through the keeper's legs after a fine Gunnarsson through-ball. Peter Whittingham then put the game well and truly to bed, converting an injury time spot kick after Mason was brought down in the box by Scott Dann.

TAYLOR

"It is important to make changes when you're playing two games in three days. That's why we've got such a big squad. A lot of the lads who came in took their chance well."

FANS SAY "Superb performance by the boys today. Man of the Match was Kim or Mutch, and Conway and Bellamy worked so hard. Couldn't fault any player." – *John Coleman*

REFEREE: C. Pawson

57% **43%**

POSSESSION

SHOTS

ON 2
OFF 2

Malaysia

20

t-match reaction from Malky Mackay,
y Bowyer and
rew Taylor on
diff City Player

CARDIFF CITY Player

diff City: Marshall, Taylor, Turner,
nett, Connolly, Kim,
narsson, Mutch
hittingham), Conway,
amy (Gestede),
npbell (Mason).
s not used: Lewis,
vie, Noone,
oin.

**Blackburn
Rovers:** Kean
(Sandomierski), Dann,
Kane, Hanley, Pedersen,
Murphy (Rhodes), Morris, Bentley
(Dunn), Jones, Best, Kazim-Richards.
Subs not used: Givet, Rekik, Stewart,
Goodwillie.

297

Running the show. Kim Bo-Kyung's sublime season run-in begins with a masterful showing against Blackburn.

WATFORD

CARDIFF CITY

SATURDAY ▸ 6TH APRIL ▸ 5.20PM

Full Attendance 15,500

🏠 13,371

🚌 2,129

MALKY

"Our back four as a whole blocked crosses, they blocked shots. The midfield in front of them, the wingers, the forwards – I can't really pick anybody out because I thought overall it was a real intelligent game plan and an intelligent team performance."

ZOLA

"I believe we tried everything we could to win the game. The reason why we didn't win was because they are a tough team to beat. It is no coincidence they are in the position they are in."

MARSHALL

"It was a good point and it keeps everyone behind us. Watford is a difficult place to go as they score a lot of goals, but we have been hard to beat this season and we stuck to our task. The back four were brilliant."

A hard fought point was earned at Vicarage Road, seeing near 2,200 travelling fans enjoy the rare scenario of celebrating a goalless draw. There was very little to choose between the two teams in a very nervy first half. Cardiff's best opportunity came after eighteen minutes when Kim Bo Kyung fired the ball across goal.

The deflected shot hit Manuel Almunia, who had spread his body well. Deeney had the best chance at the other end of the field when Matej Vydra set him up with his knock down, but the striker failed to add to his sixteen goal tally.

In the second half, City's best chance fell to Joe Mason. He broke clear of defender Joel Ekstrand and found himself with the Watford keeper to beat, but again Almunia saved well.

Watford then may have thought they had got the winner after fifty-five minutes when Deeney produced a great glancing header, denied by David Marshall who kept up his brilliant form, saving low to his right. Cardiff kept a well deserved clean sheet and prevented the Hornets closing the gap at top of the Championship.

FANS SAY

"A class performance! Midfield were strong, KimBo is outstanding, defence was unrelenting and City are heading for the Promised Land .... C'mon Bluebirds!" – *Paul Wilkins*

THE BREAK DOWN

REFEREE: M. Halsey

6

48% **52%**
POSSESSION

0 **1**

SHOTS

5 ON **7**

5 OFF **3**

e post-match reaction of this game from
alky Mackay and
anfranco Zola on
rdiff City Player

CARDIFF CITY Player ➤

atford: Almunia, Doyley, Briggs,
Cassetti, Chalobah, Ekstrand,
ya, Abdi, Battocchio (Hogg),
eney, Vydra (Forestieri).
bs not used: Bond,
dil, Thompson,
ates, Geijio.

Cardiff City:
Marshall, Taylor,
Turner, Barnett,
Connolly (McNaughton),
Conway (Smith), Kim,
Gunnarsson, Mutch, Mason
(Gestede), Bellamy.
Subs not used: Lewis, Whittingham,
Cowie, Helguson.

301

Cheers Leon. Barnett's defensive performances in the absence of skipper Hudson played a huge part in the season's closing weeks.

THE CHAMPIONSHIP

SHARED SPOILS & LATE DRAMA

Before Cardiff City's well-earned and welcomed point at Vicarage Road, numerous other deadlocks took place over the weekend. The spoils were shared in six different Saturday fixtures in total, including one for visitors **Barnsley** at **Crystal Palace** – the Tykes forced to wear the Eagles away colours by the referee due to too close a colour clash. **Birmingham** and **Millwall** also played out a 1-1 draw in a mid-table affair that was not without controversy. The Lions thought they had taken the lead when Chris Taylor's goal-bound strike was prodded in by Southampton loanee Richard Chaplow, but for the dreaded raised linesman's flag. However, after conferring with his assistant, referee Keith Hill decided to overrule the offside decision and give the goal. But it wasn't over there, as the fourth official then chipped in to add to the confusion, and recommend (correctly) that the goal should not be awarded.

Elsewhere Lewis McGugan scored for the sixth consecutive game to salvage a point for **Nottingham Forest** against ten-man **Blackpool.** Saturday's visitors Forest have made a late surge into the top six under Billy Davies, and a crucial play-off six-pointer between the two teams directly below them took place on the weekend as

well. Yet another draw was the result between **Brighton** and **Leicester City,** leaving that particular race as difficult to call as ever. Kazenga LuaLua's 88th minute equaliser kept them in sixth and seventh place respectively and was also part of another weekend trend of crucial late strikes.

None came later than *(pictured)* Jonathan Obika's 96th minute headed winner for **Charlton** against managerless **Leeds United** at the Valley. But it was a similar story at Pride Park where Mick McCarthy claimed he could hear the police sirens after his **Ipswich** side 'stole' the three points off **Derby County,** courtesy of Carlos Edwards' 93rd minute long-range strike. The Rams had earlier missed their fourth penalty in a row, leaving their boss Nigel Clough looking fo a new spot-kick volunteer.

Rounding off the sequence of lat goals, Dwight Gayle's header in the 86th minute secured an important point for **Peterborough** in their relegation scuffle with **Huddersfield Town.** The Terrier may have thought they had won it through Murray Wallace's goa but the draw leaves them just one point above the drop zone, and the Posh who are lying in wait.

>> LEADING SCORERS

1	2	3	4	5
76	67	64	60	60
> WATFORD	> CRYSTAL PALACE	> CARDIFF CITY	> NOTTM FOREST	> LEICESTER

DOWN TO THE WIRE

statistical look at the relegation battle

While many Championship fans would have had their eyes firmly fixed upon Vicarage Road this weekend for our top of the table clash with Watford, the battle at the other end of the table remains every bit as intriguing.

In fact, while the point that we earned in Hertfordshire kept the gap between us and the Hornets at eight points, the same margin separates 23rd placed **Peterborough** from **Middlesbrough** who are currently ninth in the table. It's particularly tight either side of the dotted line at the foot of the table where a band of clubs are closely grouped together. Just one point separates five teams from **Wolves** in 19th to the second-bottom Posh.

Evidently this has been a particularly close and hard-fought campaign, and that has been proved by the fact that Darren Ferguson's *(pictured)* side are currently on 47 points – a tally which would have kept them comfortably clear of relegation last season. Last time out **Doncaster Rovers** finished bottom of the league with 36 points, while **Coventry** and **Portsmouth** took up the other two relegation places with only 40 points on the board – eight adrift from their nearest rival.

Of course, a ten point deduction did not help Pompey's cause that year. But the 'magic number' for Championship survival has been less than or equal to **Huddersfield's** current tally of 48 in each of the past five seasons. The last time it was as close as this was 2007/08, when **Leicester** were relegated to League 1 on the last day of the season with a final haul of 52 points.

Such a competitive relegation scrap makes for exciting viewing for the neutral, but it leaves a throng of clubs concerned that they could become embroiled in the battle in the remaining few games. One thing's for sure though – it'll go down to the wire once again.

DID YOU KNOW?

Saturday's goalless draw against promotion challengers Watford was Cardiff City's sixteenth clean sheet of the current campaign, seeing the Bluebirds as league leaders for being the meanest defence in the Championship. Credit in large part goes to the sterling efforts of City stalwart **David Marshall** with some magnificent saves, though as rightly said by Malky Mackay, the onus on defending falls on all shoulders in the squad. The team with fewest clean sheets comes as no surprise in the form of **Bristol City** with a total of five – a number which could certainly have been worse if not for the contribution, including some penalty saves of former Cardiff 'keeper **Tom Heaton**.

LATEST RESULTS
6th April

Birmingham City 1–1 Millwall
Bolton Wanderers 2–0 Wolves
Brighton & Hove Albion 1–1 Leicester City
Burnley 3–1 Bristol City
Charlton Athletic 2–1 Leeds Utd
Crystal Palace 0–0 Barnsley
Derby County 0–1 Ipswich Town
Huddersfield Town 2–2 Peterborough Utd
Hull City 1–0 Middlesbrough
Nottingham Forest 1–1 Blackpool
Sheffield Weds 3–2 Blackburn Rovers
Watford 0–0 Cardiff City

TONIGHT'S GAMES
(Both fixtures kick-off at 7:45pm)

Cardiff City v Barnsley
Millwall v Sheffield Wednesday

2012/13 NPOWER CHAMPIONSHIP LEAGUE TABLE

Pos	Team	P	W	D	L	GD	Pts
1	**Cardiff City**	**40**	**24**	**7**	**9**	**24**	**79**
2	Hull City	41	23	5	13	11	74
3	Watford	41	21	8	12	25	71
4	Crystal Palace	41	18	12	11	13	66
5	Nottm Forest	41	16	15	10	8	63
6	Brighton	41	15	17	9	16	62
7	Leicester City	41	17	9	15	22	60
8	Bolton	41	16	12	13	7	60
9	Middlesbrough	41	17	4	20	-5	55
10	Derby County	41	14	12	15	3	54
11	Burnley	41	14	12	15	1	54
12	Charlton	41	14	12	15	-4	54
13	Birmingham	41	13	14	14	-6	53
14	Ipswich Town	41	14	11	16	-15	53
15	Millwall	39	14	10	15	-5	52
16	Leeds United	41	14	10	17	-10	52
17	Blackpool	41	12	15	14	2	51
18	Sheffield Wed	40	14	8	18	-9	50
19	Wolves	41	13	9	19	-9	48
20	**Barnsley**	**40**	**13**	**9**	**18**	**-10**	**48**
21	Huddersfield	41	12	12	17	-26	48
22	Blackburn	40	11	14	15	-7	47
23	Peterborough	41	13	8	20	-8	47
24	Bristol City	41	11	7	23	-18	40

CF ELEVEN

THE OFFICIAL CARDIFF CITY FC MATCH PROGRAMME

CARDIFF CITY

•VERSUS•

NOTTINGHAM FOREST

SAT 13TH APR 3:00PM

npower CHAMPIONSHIP MATCH 42 £3

2013 FOOTBALL LEAGUE FAMILY CLUB OF THE YEAR

MATCH SPONSOR:
TWL VOICE & DATA

MATCH BALL SPONSOR:
IAN WILLIAMS CARPENTRY

TEAM SPONSOR:
CONCRETE CANVAS

Malaysia **PUMA**® Player

21

BRING THE NOISE

Good afternoon and welcome to Cardiff City Stadium for today's game against Nottingham Forest. Welcome also to Forest manager Billy Davies, his staff, players and all those who have travelled down from the East Midlands for the match. I'm sure there will be a big crowd here today, so I am expecting a great atmosphere, which can only be a help to the players.

In starting my notes I'm pleased to confirm that thanks to the support of Chris Hughton and Norwich City, Leon Barnett will be staying with us until the end of the season. We are very grateful to Norwich for their help and look forward to Leon continuing his impressive form in a Cardiff City shirt for our remaining games.

Tuesday night's game against Barnsley was an evening of huge frustration, but it's important to continue focusing on the positives – we added another point to our total and are now in a very healthy position with just five league matches to go. Obviously, the manner of conceding so late in the game made it feel like a loss, but I felt we had played well and deserved to be further in front. Had we taken some of the chances we created, it would have given us some breathing space because at 1-0 you are always susceptible to a random late goal.

But, as I said, it's important to keep looking at the many positives and I felt that the overall performance was good. If we continue playing to that level over the remaining games, I'm sure we will reap the rewards we all seek. Ben Turner became the eighteenth different City player to get onto the score-sheet this season, which underlines how much of a team effort it has been.

It has been a positive week for the club with the Development Squad completing their league campaign with a 3-1 win at Barnet on Wednesday

which means that they are guaranteed a place in the end of season play-offs. It is not yet certain who they will be playing as there are still some fixtures to be played, but I would like to take this opportunity to congratulate coach Kevin Cooper and the lads in the squad who have performed so well.

This is the first season of the Development Under 21 League, which was introduced under the auspices of the much-discussed EPPP plan for reorganising youth football and it was unclear how things would settle down because the plan was finalised so late in the pre-season. However, bearing that in mind, I think our Under 21 team has been a very positive development for the club, giving players like Deji Oshilaja, Luke Coulson, Tommy O'Sullivan, Declan John and Kadeem Harris a decent platform to learn and continue their footballing education. It has also worked well in giving Rhys Healey exposure to a proper professional league after having joined us from Connah's Quay in the Welsh League in the January transfer window. Rhys has scored five goals in five starts for the u21s, so we have been really impressed with how he has acquitted himself.

It'll be worth looking out for the play-off schedule once it is announced because I know everyone at the club would be grateful for your continued support.

I really expect the stadium to be rocking today – no doubt Forest will bring a large and loud travelling support with them – and I am expecting a real sea of noise. There is no doubt that the atmosphere generated from the stands does have a real impact on the men on the pitch, so we are counting on hearing you all in fine voice again today.

Enjoy the game.

"IF WE CONTINUE PLAYING TO THAT LEVEL OVER THE REMAINING GAMES, I'M SURE WE WILL REAP THE REWARDS WE ALL SEEK"

MALKY'S NOTES IN PROUD ASSOCIATION WITH

EDWARDS
COACH HOLIDAYS

CARDIFF CITY 1
Turner (59)

BARNSLEY 1
Foster (90+5)

TUESDAY ⏵ **9TH APRIL** ⏵ **7.45PM** | Full Attendance **22,584**

🏠 **22,341**
🚌 **243**

MALKY

"I was delighted with how we played; we were playing a team fighting for their lives. We dominated and had chances, but we could have been more clinical and finished the game off."

FLITCROFT

"To fit this game into our programme after the game against Palace and Easter week was asking a lot of this group. But you cannot ask for more than going 97 minutes against the champions-elect."

MUTCH

"They didn't have a shot on goal in the first half and I thought that we limited them well in the second half. When you look back at the match we had chances to make it easier on ourselves

Cardiff took another step toward promotion in a game that should have been a leap but for a last minute heart-breaking equaliser at Cardiff City Stadium. The Bluebirds dominated from start to finish in one of the most one sided affairs at home this year, but couldn't punish the visitors' willingness to sit deep.

Craig Bellamy's shot on the turn was pushed onto the bar in the first half, with Aron Gunnarsson, Tommy Smith and Jordon Mutch all trying their luck only to find Tykes stopper Steele was in good form.

Barnsley struggled to get out of their own half, Cardiff's pressing was forcing possession turnover all over the pitch, and it seemed three points were sealed when Ben Turner volleyed home from the exceptional Kim Bo-Kyung's 59th minute corner.

Heidar Helguson then spurned a glorious one-on-one before Barnsley capitalised in injury time, Stephen Foster's deflected effort from outside the area deceiving David Marshall and creeping inside the opposite post.

FANS SAY
"It's hard to criticise the lads after such a positive and ambitious display. Things just went against us with the freak goal at the end." – *Owen James.*

310

THE BREAK DOWN

8 ⊘ 2

47% 53%

POSSESSION

2 ⊘ 1

SHOTS

14 ON 5

5 OFF 4

st-match reaction from Malky Mackay,
vid Flitcroft and
rdon Mutch on
rdiff City Player

CARDIFF CITY Player ➤

rdiff City: Marshall, McNaughton,
Barnett, Turner, Taylor,
Gunnarsson, Mutch, Kim Bo-
ung (Whittingham), Smith
onway), Bellamy, Mason
elguson).
bs not used: Lewis,
one, Nugent,
stede.

Barnsley:
Steele, Hassell,
Foster, Wiseman,
Kennedy, Dawson, O'Brien
(Cywka), Perkins, Mellis (Dagnall),
Harewood (Scotland), O'Grady.
Subs not used: Alnwick, Jones, Patterson, Rose.

Making it look easy. Mutchy's calibre shone following his return from a frustrating injury.

THE CHAMPIONSHIP

THAT'S GOT TO BE IT?!

Tuesday night saw dramatic injury-time action all round, reminding us of how late strikes in football can trigger frustration and delight in equal measures.

Only a couple of Championship fixtures took place as two of the sides involved in cup exploits this season finally caught up on some league action. F.A. Cup quarter-finalists **Barnsley,** who were resoundingly beaten 5-0 by Manchester City, travelled to South Wales, while relegation threatened **Sheffield Wednesday** were hosted by **Millwall,** who play their semi-final against **Wigan Athletic** today having gone one step further than the Tykes.

Both games seemed to follow the precedent set in what was a remarkable night for late drama in the Champions League. Borussia Dortmund looked certain to be eliminated from the competition, as they still needed two goals to overcome Málaga at the Westfalenstadion when the fourth official raised his board. They found the strength from somewhere though, as Marco Reus and Felipe Santana both netted in one of the most remarkable injury-time periods in recent memory.

From the Champions League to the Championship and a late strike at the New Den was every bit as important in the skirmish for survival at the bottom, as **Chris Maguire's** poached effort in the 92nd minute earned three vital points for a resurgent **Sheffield Wednesday.** Comoros international **Jimmy Abdou's**

first minute goal had given Millwall an early advantage before a free kick courtesy of scrum cap wielding Spanish centre-back **Miguel Llera** set the tie up for its dramatic finale.

The Owls are doing well of late. Our recent win at Hillsborough was their only defeat in their last six games – a run which has seen them rise up the tabl to 14th position. The division is still so tight that jus six points separate them from the drop zone but it looks like Dave Jones' men, buoyed by the loan acquisitions of **Stuart Holden** and former Bluebird **Seyi Olofinjana,** may just have don enough to secure survival.

Of course, the latest goal of the evening came at Cardiff City Stadium where **Stephe Foster's** 97th minute equaliser cancelled o **Ben Turner's** earlier effort to leave a bitter taste in the mouth at the final whistle. Fortunately, it's one that **Cardiff City** fans have not had to experience too often this season. In fact, we've been on the other end of late drama far more frequently throughout this campaign and as Malky sai post-match on Tuesday: "We're a point closer."

Indeed, Foster's strike four days ago was ju the fifth goal that we've conceded in the la ten minutes of matches this season, while we've scored during that period a total of 1 times – only **Blackpool** can better that, with 17 late strikes to their name. At the other en of the spectrum, just think of the fans of **Leec United** who have had to witness their team concede a whopping sixteen goals in the final ten minutes of matches this term!

⟩⟩ NET SHY

1	2	3	4	5
40	42	48	49	4
⟩ IPSWICH TOWN	⟩ HUDDERSFIELD	⟩ BLACKBURN	⟩ SHEFFIELD WED	⟩ MILLWALL

SAY, FOR INSTANCE...

A statistical look at the last 5 games

With five league matches remaining for most sides, now is the time that fans of all clubs start to analyse the run-ins of their rivals in order to predict the final standings.

Current form can provide the most reliable pointer as to how the division will look on May 4th, and today's visitors **Nottingham Forest** are one of the form teams in the league having avoided defeat in each of their last 10 games. Based upon recent performances, they have a projected points tally of 74 – a haul which would see them overtake faltering **Crystal Palace** into fourth place by the final day of the season.

If that were to happen, they would be likely to face another form side in the Play-Offs. **Bolton Wanderers** have won seven of their last ten games and will snatch sixth spot from the likes of **Brighton & Hove Albion** and **Leicester City** if their results continue in a similar manner. That would leave Watford, Nottingham Forest, Crystal Palace and Bolton making up the Play-Offs, in that order.

The relegation battle remains as hard to call as ever though, as just six points separate 13th position from 23rd. But **Blackburn Rovers,** who last weekend slipped into the drop zone for the first time this season, will stay there unless their poor current form improves. Defeat to **Sheffield Wednesday** last Saturday extended their winless run to 10 matches, and their projected points tally of just 49 would see the Lancashire side facing the prospect of a second successive relegation.

So, what about the top of the league? Well if the top three all continue in similar form for the remaining 5 games, we would end up with a minimum of 86 points, four points above **Hull City** and clear of third-placed **Watford** by seven. It's all hypothetical of course ... but come on City!!

DID YOU KNOW?

Cardiff City have shared the goals to such an extent in this campaign that we're still yet to see a player reach the ten league goals mark. Many would argue that it's better to split the goal-scoring duties rather than put the burden on one man's shoulders – and we're certainly in good company in that respect.

While each club in the bottom three has a player in double figures (including Blackburn's **Jordon Rhodes** on 24), neither of the top-two sides do. Second-placed **Hull City's** top scorers, **Sone Aluko** and **Robert Koren,** have just eight goals apiece – the same tally as **Peter Whittingham** and **Aron Gunnarsson** (pictured) for us.

LATEST RESULTS

Tuesday 9th April
Cardiff City 1–1 Barnsley
Millwall 1–2 Sheffield Wed

WEEKEND FIXTURES

Friday 12th / Saturday 13 April
(All games kick off at 3pm unless otherwise stated)
Barnsley v Charlton Athletic
Blackburn Rovers v Derby County
Blackpool v Burnley
Bristol City v Bolton Wanderers
Cardiff City v Nottingham Forest
Ipswich Town v Sheffield Wed
Leeds United v Sheffield Wed (12:30pm)
Leicester City v Birmingham City (Friday 7.45pm)
Middlesbrough v Brighton & Hove Albion
Peterborough Utd v Watford
Wolves v Huddersfield Town

MIDWEEK FIXTURES

Tuesday 16th April
(All fixtures kick-off at 7.45pm unless otherwise stated)
Barnsley v Derby County
Blackburn Rovers v Huddersfield Town
Blackpool v Sheffield Wed (8.00pm)
Bristol City v Birmingham City
Cardiff City v Charlton Athletic
Ipswich Town v Crystal Palace
Leeds United v Burnley
Leicester City v Bolton Wanderers
Middlesbrough v Nottingham Forest
Millwall v Watford
Peterborough Utd v Brighton & Hove Albion
Wolves v Hull

2012/13 NPOWER CHAMPIONSHIP LEAGUE TABLE

Pos	Team	P	W	D	L	GD	Pts
1	**Cardiff City**	41	24	8	9	24	80
2	Hull City	41	23	5	13	11	74
3	Watford	41	21	8	12	25	71
4	Crystal Palace	41	18	12	11	13	66
5	**Nottm Forest**	41	16	15	10	8	63
6	Brighton	41	15	17	9	16	62
7	Leicester City	41	17	9	15	22	60
8	Bolton	41	16	12	13	7	60
9	Middlesbrough	41	17	4	20	-5	55
10	Derby County	41	14	12	15	3	54
11	Burnley	41	14	12	15	1	54
12	Charlton	41	14	12	15	-4	54
13	Birmingham	41	13	14	14	-6	53
14	Sheffield Wed	41	15	8	18	-8	53
15	Ipswich Town	41	14	11	16	-15	53
16	Millwall	40	14	10	16	-6	52
17	Leeds United	41	14	10	17	-10	52
18	Blackpool	41	12	15	14	2	51
19	Barnsley	41	13	10	18	-10	49
20	Wolves	41	13	9	19	-9	48
21	Huddersfield	41	12	12	17	-26	48
22	Blackburn	40	11	14	15	-7	47
23	Peterborough	41	13	8	20	-8	47
24	Bristol City	41	11	7	23	-18	40

DETAILS PRIOR TO THIS WEEKEND'S GAMES

315

CF ELEVEN

THE OFFICIAL CARDIFF CITY FC MATCH PROGRAMME

CARDIFF CITY

VERSUS

CHARLTON ATHLETIC

TUE 16TH APR 7:45PM

npower CHAMPIONSHIP MATCH 43 £3

2013 FOOTBALL LEAGUE FAMILY CLUB OF THE YEAR

MATCH SPONSOR:
THE VALE RESORT

MATCH BALL SPONSOR:
EGAN WASTE

TEAM SPONSOR:
DVS LTD

Malaysia **PUMA** Player >

22

MALKY MACKAY

PLAY THE GAME

Good evening and welcome back after only a short few days for tonight's game with Charlton Athletic.

I'll start by extending that warm welcome to Addicks manager and my old friend Chris Powell who brings his team to Wales this evening in fine shape. I'm sure they will have a spring in their step after their impressive win at Barnsley on Saturday and it looks like they are going to end their season on a very positive note.

Indeed, Charlton's recent good run has put them within touching distance of the play-offs with just four matches left to play and so Chris, his players and staff deserve enormous credit for doing so well in their first season back in the Championship. Chris has been a good friend of mine since we played together at West Ham and were then team mates again at Watford and he has always been one of football's undoubted good guys who tries to do things in the proper way. He was also a very distinguished Chairman of the PFA at the tail end of his playing career, so he has much to be proud of.

It is always good to see people who have worked hard at their careers and treated people with respect then go on to achieve success so to see Charlton win promotion last season, ahead of clubs with considerably larger budgets, and then to perform so well at this level in this season reflects very well on Chris and everyone at the club. Having said all that, I obviously hope that they don't have any success here tonight as we have our own, well-publicised agenda to pursue!

Saturday's win over Nottingham Forest was another very good performance and underlined a point I made after the Barnsley game last week. If you analyse the two games, I felt that there was not a great deal to choose between the way we played, yet the first game resulted in a home draw with a struggling side and the second ended up in a resounding win against a team making a serious push for promotion.

Success on the pitch is often a question of inches and where against Barnsley we got frustrated because things didn't go our way, on Saturday we were 2-0 up soon after half time and then went on to produce some of the best football seen at this ground this season. Without wishing to sound selfish, the only disappointment I felt after the game was that we had not gone on to win even more decisively than the final 3-0 scoreline.

I was also delighted to see Heidar and Rudy on the score sheet. Heidar has been an absolute warrior for us this season and the amount of work he puts in every time he takes to the pitch is incredible. Across my career I don't think I have worked with a better professional – someone who instinctively understands what it takes to win matches at this level and will put his personal well-being on the line in the name of the team – so his goal gave me particular pleasure.

Similarly, Rudy has had to bide his time this season and may not have played as much as he would have liked but once we lost Heidar to injury, Rudy filled his boots admirably and scored two text book powerful headers in a way that few players in the Championship can. His first goal was a real throwback – it almost looked like it was Jimmy Johnstone crossing and Joe McBride Senior heading rather than Andrew Taylor and Rudy in action!

Needless to say we are expecting another big crowd here tonight and I thought the atmosphere here on Saturday was excellent so we are hoping for more of the same this evening. As ever your support is vital and very much appreciated by all of us. Enjoy the game.

"AS EVER YOUR SUPPORT IS VITAL AND IS VERY MUCH APPRECIATED"

MALKY'S NOTES IN PROUD ASSOCIATION WITH

EDWARDS
COACH HOLIDAYS

CARDIFF CITY 3

Helguson (26), Gestede (60, 66)

NOTTM FOREST 0

SATURDAY ▶ 13TH APRIL ▶ 3.00PM | Full Attendance 26,588

🏠 24,542

🚌 2,046

MALKY

"We had to go toe to toe from the first minute and we did that. We got the goal and, although it can be difficult to play against 10 men, we were absolutely on the money."

DAVIES

"We talked about players from Cardiff they've scored abou thirty goals from set plays this season. As it happened, against a Premier League squad, it was always going to be very difficult."

Cardiff's emphatic victory against a Forest side unbeaten in ten put the team within a point of promotion with four games remaining. The record crowd had to wait just twenty-six minutes for Heidar Helguson to open the scoring from a Craig Bellamy free kick, nodding home at the far post. Marshall came to the rescue diving on a loose ball inside the Cardiff six yard box, but Forest's day took a turn for the worse when Henderson was dismissed for an elbow on Helguson.

Cardiff were in no mood to take their foot off the gas, aided by a man advantage moving the ball increasingly freely in midfield. Taylor picked up the ball from a Bellamy free kick that ricocheted off the post and delivered a killer ball to Gestede, who made no mistake at the back post.

Kim was instrumental, his guile on the ball creating a host of chances throughout including a twenty yard effort for the South Korean on the turn. It was the play maker that delivered six minutes later from a corner to find Gestede, the striker dominating in the air to secure his brace.

GESTEDE

"It was my first double for the club and it was a good win this afternoon, but we have a big game on Tuesday night. It has been two brilliant years fo me at Cardiff City."

FANS SAY

"This was a great performance and result for us against Nottingham Forest. Now let's make sure we fill Cardiff City Stadium against Charlton and Bolton!" – *Terry Walters*

320

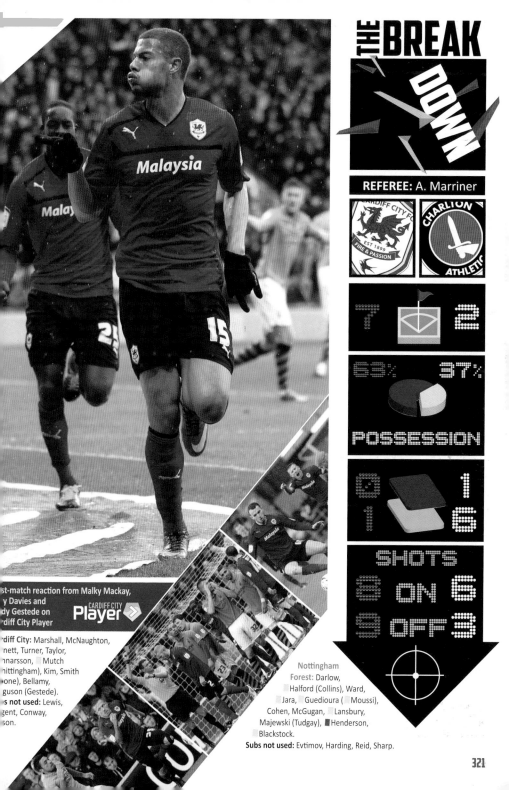

REFEREE: A. Marriner

7 ⚑ 2

63% 37%

POSSESSION

1 ☐ 1
1 ☐ 6

SHOTS

8 ON 6

9 OFF 3

Post-match reaction from Malky Mackay, Kevin Davies and Rudy Gestede on
Cardiff City **Player** ➤

Cardiff City: Marshall, McNaughton, Bennett, Turner, Taylor, Gunnarsson, Mutch (Whittingham), Kim, Smith (Noone), Bellamy, Ferguson (Gestede).
Subs not used: Lewis, Nugent, Conway, Mason.

Nottingham Forest: Darlow, Halford (Collins), Ward, Jara, Guedioura (Moussi), Cohen, McGugan, Lansbury, Majewski (Tudgay), Henderson, Blackstock.
Subs not used: Evtimov, Harding, Reid, Sharp.

Nearly there. Rudy rules over Forest as promotion edges ever nearer.

THE CHAMPIONSHIP

QUICK-FIRE DOUBLES

The weekend saw another action-packed round of Championship fixtures as two thirds of Saturday afternoon's goals came after the interval – several matches being decided by quick-fire second half strikes.

Of course, **Rudy Gestede's** second half double of headers secured a vital win against **Nottingham Forest** in the capital, ending the visitors' ten match unbeaten run. Rudy nodded home both of his goals between the 60th and 70th minutes – and it was during that ten minute spell that crucial goals flew in up and down the country, deciding the outcomes of numerous matches.

That was certainly the case at London Road as **Watford** were the latest victims of **Peterborough United,** who haven't lost in nine league matches. Strikes from **Dwight Gayle** and **Lee Tomlin,** in the 61st and 67th minute respectively, sandwiched a red card for **Marco Cassetti** in a frenetic period of play. The Italian international was dismissed for scything down former Stansted striker Gayle, who has now scored 13 goals in 24 games for the Posh.

It was the same story in the relegation six-pointer between **Wolves** and **Huddersfield Town,** as another quick double decided the outcome of the match in similar fashion. With the score at 1-1 in the 65th minute Roger Johnson missed a gilt-edged chance to put Wolves in the lead. And they were certainly made to pay for it as the Terriers brought on **Jermaine Beckford** who struck twice before the clock hit 70. That result thrust **Dean Saunders'** *(pictured)* men back into the bottom three, with Huddersfield three points above them in 19th position.

Just one minute separated the two goals from Beckford, who managed to fit in a booking for his overzealous celebrations in between. But at almost the exact same time **Luke Varney** was the protagonist in another relegation scrap, as his speedy brace for **Leeds United** left **Sheffield Wednesday** in the drop zone. With the Owls in the lead courtesy of **Jermain Johnson's** first half effort, two excellent Varney headers in the 63rd and 69th minutes gave Leeds the points in Brian McDermott's first match at the helm.

However, the most remarkable result of the afternoon broke that particular pattern as this evening's visitors smashed **Barnsley** 6-0 at Oakwell. Only **Hull, Watford** and ourselves have more away wins than the **Addicks,** who spread the goals around the team and throughout the match – with just over ten minutes separating each goal.

Elsewhere **Bolton Wanderers,** one of the form sides of the division, benefited from an early goal away to **Bristol City** as Liam Fontaine turned the ball into his own net inside the first three minutes. After **Steven Davies** equalised for the Robins his namesake Craig restored the Trotters' lead from the spot as they overtook **Nottingham Forest** into sixth place.

Bolton are now just two points behind **Brighton & Hove Albion,** who stepped into fifth place thanks to goals from their Spanish contingent **Andrea Orlandi** and **David Lopez.** Meanwhile, in the race for the automatic places **Hull City** took advantage of Watford's slip-up to earn a nine point cushion in second place. **Robert Koren** came off the bench to head home a late winner for the Tigers who have now won successive games for the first time since February. We've witnessed quite a weekend!

➤➤ CLEAN SHEETS

1	2	3	4	5
17	15	15	14	14
➤ CARDIFF CITY	➤ BRIGHTON	➤ HULL CITY	➤ IPSWICH	➤ LEICESTER

"PUT IT ON ME 'EAD SON!"

statistical look at the assists charts

...ne of the main reasons for City's success in their convincing ...in over Nottingham Forest was undoubtedly the consistent quality ...their delivery into the box, both from the dead ball and in open ...ay.

...hile **Andrew Taylor's** immaculate whipped cross picked out the ...riving **Rudy Gestede** for our second goal, **Craig Bellamy's** *(pictured)* ...swinging delivery caused problems for the Forest defence all ...ternoon, resulting in both of the other two headers.

...deed, Bellamy took his total assists tally over the course of the ...ason to nine, meaning that he has directly contributed to (scored or ...sisted) a grand total of 19% of our goals this season.

...doing so, Craig overtook both **Peter Whittingham** and **Craig Noone** ...the assists charts. The two playmakers have seven set-ups apiece, ...d are particularly adept at picking out the heads of their centre-...lves. **Mark Hudson** is the leading recipient of Noone assists, while ...hittingham's left foot has created goals for ...atthew Connolly on three separate occasions.

...eidar Helguson sits just behind those two ...th six assists to his name, showing ...e important role that the Iceman ...ays in supplying, as well as ...coring, goals. Interestingly, half ...Heidar's assists have been ...t-ups for strike partner **Joe** ...ason – perhaps the classic big ...an, little man partnership lives ...!

...ris Eagles and **Thomas Ince** top the ...vision assists charts with 12 each, ...hile **Robbie Brady** and **Ross** ...cCormack are not far behind with 10 ...iece. Zimbabwean midfielder ...adley Pritchard has set up 9 of ...night's visitors' goals this season, 3 ...which were dispatched by a familiar ...me to City fans – **Yann Kermorgant.** ...t's hope we can stop that ...mbination this evening!

DID YOU KNOW?

Charlton Athletic hit nine-man **Barnsley** for six at Oakwell in their previous Championship outing. In doing so they became just the third side to win by six goals all season, and the first to do so away from home. **Ipswich Town** are unlucky enough to have been on the wrong end of both of those previous thrashings, at the hands of **Blackpool** and **Leicester City** respectively. However, the Addicks can also boast the fact that they had six different scorers in their match – a feat that both Leicester and Blackpool were unable to match.

LATEST RESULTS
Friday 12th / Saturday 13 April
Barnsley 0–6 Charlton Athletic
Blackburn Rovers 2–0 Derby County
Blackpool 1–0 Burnley
Bristol City 1–2 Bolton Wanderers
Cardiff City 3–0 Nottingham Forest
Ipswich Town 1–2 Hull City
Leeds United 2–1 Sheffield Wednesday
Leicester City 2–2 Birmingham City
Middlesbrough 0–2 Brighton & Hove Albion
Peterborough United 3–2 Watford
Wolves 1–3 Huddersfield Town

TONIGHT'S GAMES
(All fixtures kick-off at 7.45pm unless otherwise stated)
Barnsley v Derby County
Blackburn Rovers v Huddersfield Town
Blackpool v Sheffield Wednesday (8pm)
Bristol City v Birmingham City
Cardiff City v Charlton Athletic
Ipswich Town v Crystal Palace
Leeds United v Burnley
Leicester City v Bolton Wanderers
Middlesbrough v Nottingham Forest
Millwall v Watford
Peterborough United v Brighton & Hove Albion
Wolves v Hull City

WEEKEND GAMES
(All fixtures kick-off at 3.00pm unless otherwise stated)
Birmingham City v Leeds United
Bolton Wanderers v Middlesbrough
Brighton & Hove Albion v Blackpool
Burnley v Cardiff City (12.45pm)
Charlton Athletic v Wolves
Crystal Palace v Leicester City
Derby County v Peterborough United
Huddersfield Town v Millwall (12.30pm)
Hull City v Bristol City (Friday, 7.45pm)
Nottingham Forest v Barnsley
Sheffield Wednesday v Ipswich Town
Watford v Blackburn Rovers

2012/13 NPOWER CHAMPIONSHIP LEAGUE TABLE

Pos	Team	P	W	D	L	GD	Pts
1	**Cardiff City**	42	25	8	9	27	83
2	Hull City	42	24	5	13	12	77
3	Watford	42	21	8	13	24	71
4	Crystal Palace	41	18	12	11	13	66
5	Brighton	42	16	17	9	18	65
6	Bolton	42	17	12	13	8	63
7	Nottm Forest	42	16	15	11	5	63
8	Leicester City	42	17	10	15	22	61
9	**Charlton**	42	15	12	15	2	57
10	Middlesbrough	42	17	4	21	-7	55
11	Leeds United	42	15	10	17	-9	55
12	Blackpool	42	13	15	14	3	54
13	Derby County	42	14	12	16	1	54
14	Burnley	42	14	12	16	0	54
15	Birmingham	42	13	15	14	-6	54
16	Sheffield Wed	42	15	8	19	-9	53
17	Ipswich Town	42	14	11	17	-16	53
18	Millwall	40	14	10	16	-6	52
19	Huddersfield	42	13	12	17	-24	51
20	Blackburn	41	12	14	15	-5	50
21	Peterborough	42	14	8	20	-7	50
22	Barnsley	42	13	10	19	-16	49
23	Wolves	42	13	9	20	-11	48
24	Bristol City	42	11	7	24	-19	40

CF ELEVEN

THE OFFICIAL CARDIFF CITY FC MATCH PROGRAMME

CARDIFF CITY

VERSUS

BOLTON WANDERERS

SAT 27TH APR 3:00PM

 npower CHAMPIONSHIP   MATCH 45   £3

2012/13 FOOTBALL LEAGUE CHAMPIONS

MATCH SPONSOR: PYRAMID HYGIENE

MATCH BALL SPONSOR: GMB

TEAM SPONSOR: HEATWISE

23

MALKY MACKAY

FOR ALL OF US

Good afternoon and welcome to Cardiff City Stadium for the last time this season for today's game with Bolton Wanderers.

I'd like to start by thanking all of you for the enormous part you have played in making this season such a special one for the club and all of South Wales. Together we have all made history and led this club to only its third ever league title in 114 years of trying.

Obviously we are all thrilled with the success and I feel that the accolade of being named the best team in the division is just reward for the enormous amount of work that has gone on here since I first made the journey to Wales almost two years ago. Every week we all see the incredible dedication and fantastic work ethic of the playing squad out there on the pitch, but there's always so much work behind the scenes that often goes unnoticed to the outside observer – work put in by our excellent football staff and dedicated office staff.

A lot of people have worked at this club, and supported it, for many years and during that period have lived through some very tough times, so moments like winning promotion last week would have meant an awful lot to them. I was particularly pleased that the players kept focused after all the hullabaloo and celebrations of last Tuesday and managed to produce a very good display last Saturday at Burnley. We fully deserved our half-time lead and were only disappointed not to be further in front.

Burnley had a lot to play for with their survival in the Championship still not confirmed, so it was no surprise that they came on so strongly in the second half and I think they perhaps deserved their point, even though the goal came very late.

You will have seen lots of talk in the papers since our promotion about which players we may or may not be going to sign this summer in preparation for our debut Premier League campaign – I've seen plenty of names that have made me chuckle – so I'd like to take this opportunity to assure you that we have already put in a lot of preparation for this moment and whatever squad reinforcements we do make before next season will be the result of our usual hard work and following a carefully laid-out plan.

I'd like to take this opportunity to welcome Dougie Freedman and his Bolton players, staff and supporters to Wales today. The league table obviously shows that this game is another huge one with Bolton currently in a play-off position, so there is plenty to play for and it is important that we respect the integrity of the league and play to our maximum both today and next Saturday when the season comes to its end at Hull.

I'll sign off for the last time this season with a heartfelt thank you to everyone who has helped and supported us over the course of this arduous but successful season. I'll look forward to seeing our travelling fans at Hull next Saturday, before our victory parade next Sunday. After that it's only a matter of time before we're back here in August when we'll welcome our fist ever Premier League visitors for a league match.

Enjoy the game, enjoy your summer and thanks again.

"TOGETHER WE HAVE ALL MADE HISTORY AND LED THIS CLUB TO ONLY ITS THIRD EVER LEAGUE TITLE IN 114 YEARS OF TRYING "

MALKY'S NOTES IN PROUD ASSOCIATION WITH

EDWARDS
COACH HOLIDAYS

CARDIFF CITY ☒

CHARLTON ☒

TUESDAY ▶ **16TH APRIL** ▶ **7.45PM** | Full Attendance **26,338**

🏠 **25,718**
🚌 **620**

MALKY

"I'm very proud of the Football Club tonight. It's an occasion which the fans of this Football Club have waited a long time for. Hopefully tonight goes some way to repaying that faith."

POWELL

"I hope they make a real fist of it because Cardiff and Swansea in the Premier League is going to be something! We've taken four points off Cardiff so I'm very pleased with the display tonight."

MARSHALL

"I think Watford were losing and we heard a roar, but I thought that was just our fans trying to keep us going for the 0-0. We needed a point, we got it and it's brilliant."

Cardiff City clinched promotion on a historic night at Cardiff City Stadium, the crucial point propelling the Bluebirds to the top Division for the first time in fifty-one years. Ricardo Fuller, the most dangerous player for the visitors, opened the shooting contest from long range inside the fourth minute, but neither goalkeeper was truly tested throughout.

Johnnie Jackson's long range free kick crashed against the post for the visitors, while Kim Bo-Kyung, who has emerged as a key player of late, responded with his own whipped dead ball that went agonisingly wide.

Andrew Taylor and Leon Barnett both tested with driven shots from range after the break, whilst Fuller brought the best out of Marshall from just inside the area. Craig Noone then falsely raised the roof, converting a point-blank header that was subsequently deemed offside. But the celebrations were merely delayed, the final whistle ending a hard fought draw and earning Cardiff City promotion to the Premier League.

FANS SAY "I was two years old when we last played in the top division. The lows have been many and the highs very few. I'm proud of my Club and the way we got there." – *Andrew Thomas*

THE BREAKDOWN

REFEREE: S. Mathieson

5

59% **41%**
POSSESSION

0 **1**

SHOTS
ON 9
OFF 4

Post-match reaction from Malky Mackay, Chris Powell, Mark Hudson and Craig Bellamy on Cardiff City Player

CARDIFF CITY **Player**

Cardiff City: Marshall, McNaughton, Taylor, Turner, Barnett, Kim Bo-Kyung, Noone (Smith), Gunnarsson, Mutch, Gestede, Bellamy.
Subs not used: Lewis, Nugent, Whittingham, Cowie, Conway, Mason.

Charlton Athletic: Hamer, Morrison, Wiggins, Solly, Dervite, Hughes (Gower), Jackson, Pritchard (Green), Harriotts, Kermorgant, Fuller (Obika).
Subs not used: Button, Taylor, Wilson, Kerkar.

331

We've done it. Long time servants Whittingham and Hudson celebrate promotion to the top-flight.

BURNLEY 1
Edgar (90+1)

CARDIFF CITY 1
Conway (27)

SATURDAY ▶ 20TH APRIL ▶ 12.45PM | Full Attendance **13,264**

🏠 **11,629**

🚌 **1,635**

MALKY

"It was a tremendous feeling on Tuesday night, but for us to go and win the title is something that we spoke about within a day. We wanted to go and get the boys their medals."

DYCHE

"I knew Malky would go hard and their team wouldn' back off. They've got some real talen there. They've done a great job, it must be said – Malky, his troops, his staff, his players."

Craig Conway's first half strike was enough for City to secure a 1-1 draw at Burnley and clinch the Championship trophy in the process.

The only sour note of the first half for the Welsh side were two ugly arms thrown in Kim Bo-Kyung's direction by Burnley's Ross Wallace, the one-cap Scotland international incredibly lucky not to have taken an early shower.

Knowing what was at stake, the second half was mostly about keeping possession for the Bluebirds. It was a plan which frustrated their hosts to no end – that was until they did grab a late equaliser, David Edgar netting in injury time not long after a wonder save from David Marshall had denied Danny Ings.

But it did nothing to hamper the celebrations that would ensue in front of the away end at Turf Moor, as Malky Mackay's side ensured some Football League silverware would soon be heading across the Severn Bridge and into CF11.

McNAUGHTON

"We've come so close before. Taking that extra step feels fantastic. I'm just chuffed for the fans. They have been waiting so long for this moment."

FANS SAY "We've now achieved what so many people thought would be impossible for Cardiff City Football Club." – *Sharon Lewis*

THE BREAKDOWN

REFEREE: S. Attwell

2 ⚑ **3**

44% **56%**

POSSESSION

2 **1**

SHOTS

6 ON **3**

3 OFF **7**

ee post-match reaction of this game from
Malky Mackay and
ean Dyche on
ardiff City Player **CARDIFF CITY Player ▸**

urnley: Grant , ▮Trippier,
afferty, Shackell (c), Long,
1cCann, Wallace (Paterson),
▮ Marney (Treacy), Stanislas
Edgar), Vokes, Ings.
ubs not used: Jensen,
'Neill, Bartley,
tock.

Cardiff City:
Marshall,
McNaughton, Taylor (c),
Turner, Barnett, Conway,
▮ Kim, Noone (Bellamy),
Gunnarsson, Mutch (Cowie), Gestede.
Subs not used: Lewis, Nugent, Whittingham,
Lappin, Mason.

335

Flying high. Celebrations continue following the title-clincher at Turf Moor.

THE CHAMPIONSHIP

RELENTLESS CONSISTENCY

'Relentless' was the word that Malky Mackay used to describe his Cardiff City side's pursuit of the Championship title over the course of this campaign. Now that that's been accomplished, today is the day that the players, fans and staff alike can all revel in their achievements as the trophy will finally be held aloft in the Capital of Wales.

It's been a long time coming too. City have refused to let go of that top spot in the division since a 2-1 away win over **Barnsley** restored our position there back on 24th November 2012. In doing so, the squad have shown remarkable consistency – a trait which has become another buzz word in the capital. While all around us have faltered, our place at the top has been the only constant in an otherwise topsy-turvy division.

A quick glance at the table on the day that we seized hold of first place, over five months ago, provides a perfect illustration of our status as the anomaly of the division. While the Bluebirds have been immovable at the top, the fortunes of those below us have varied almost immeasurably since that day.

The side we overtook by one point at the time were **Crystal Palace,** who had just seen a fourteen match unbeaten run put to an end by **Leeds United.** Twenty-six games on, and we are now eighteen points above the Eagles whose Play-Off ambitions still lie in the balance with no wins in their last seven Championship games.

The two teams directly below them on that day were **Leicester City** and **Middlesbrough,** both of whom have also failed to continue their momentum for the entirety of the campaign. Leicester, then in third, were still in and around the top two until mid-February and were unanimously considered to be our main promotion rivals when we did battle at King Power Stadium just before Christmas. However, their draw at Selhurst Park last Saturday saw them drop out of the top six altogether – with a final day bout for the Play-Offs against East Midlands rivals Nottingham Forest looking on the cards.

But it's been even worse for Tony Mowbray's *(pictured)* **Middlesbrough** who took up fourth place, only a point behind the Foxes, when we seized top spot. They now sit twelfth – just a point above **Ipswich Town** – who were firmly seated in the drop-zone with less than half of Boro' points haul at the end of November.

So, consistency has been very hard to come by for almost every team in this league, but some have discovered the secret at just the right moment – and today's visitors **Bolton Wanderers** epitomise that. Dougie Freedman has cited the Trotters' hard work and commitment to the cause as they've recently staked a solid claim for a top six finish. There's no questioning the impact that Freedman has had on a side that were down in twentieth place as recently as February, as the Scotsman has instilled discipline, consistency and a winning attitude in his troops in a very similar manner to his opposite number today.

>> LEADING SCORERS

1	2	3	4	5
29	27	25	20	20
> GLENN MURRAY	> JORDAN RHODES	> CHARLIE AUSTIN	> MATĚJ VYDRA	> CHRIS WOOD

ONE MORE RECORD?

A statistical look at City's record points haul

From our ten match unbeaten home run at the beginning of the campaign, to the biggest ever CCS crowd that watched us beat Forest two weeks ago, City have set several personal bests in the process of winning the title this year. But with only two matches remaining, just two more points would see this side make more history.

This year's first place finish sees us continue a sequence in which we have earned promotion in every year ending in three going back to 1983! And it was in that particular year that the final target that we're striving for was set – our highest ever league points tally.

Eighty-six points were notched up that season under Len Ashurst, but even that wasn't enough to secure top spot as we finished second to **Portsmouth**, going up to the old Division 2 thanks in part to the twenty-six league and cup goals scored by **Jeff Hemmerman**.

A decade later and promotion was tasted again in the capital. In fact, our first place finish in 1992/93 was the last time that we lifted a league-winning trophy until this very day. Advancing to Division 2 once more, this time with the late **Eddie May** at the helm, our final tally was eighty-three points as we went up alongside **Wrexham, Barnet** and **York City.**

As for the 2002/03 campaign, despite managing to clinch promotion to the second tier where we would remain for the next ten years, we actually set a lower points tally than we had in the previous year. The lottery of the Play-Offs decided both seasons as defeat to Stoke City in the semi-finals in 2001/02 was made up for with victories over **Bristol City** and then **Queen's Park Rangers** at the Millennium Stadium the following year.

This season our Club has re-written the history books from start to finish, and beating that eighty-six points haul today would round off a record breaking year in South Wales in the most fitting of styles.

LATEST RESULTS
Staurday, 20th April
Birmingham City 1–0 Leeds Utd
Burnley 1–1 Cardiff City
Bolton Wanderers 2–1 Middlesbrough
Brighton & Hove Albion 6–1 Blackpool
Charlton Athletic 2–1 Wolves
Crystal Palace 2–2 Leicester City
Derby County 3–1 Peterborough Utd
Huddersfield Town 3–0 Millwall
Nottingham Forest 0–0 Barnsley
Sheffield Wed 1–1 Ipswich Town
Watford 4–0 Blackburn Rovers

WEEKEND FIXTURES
(All fixtures kick-off at 3.00pm unless otherwise stated)
Barnsley v Hull City
Blackburn Rovers v Crystal Palace
Blackpool v Derby County
Bristol City v Huddersfield Town
Cardiff City v Bolton Wanderers
Ipswich Town v Birmingham City
Leeds United v Brighton & Hove Albion
Leicester City v Watford (Friday)
Middlesbrough v Charlton Athletic
Millwall v Nottingham Forest
Peterborough Utd v Sheffield Wed (5.20pm)
Wolves v Burnley

FINAL DAY
Saturday, 4th May
(All fixtures kick-off at 12.45pm)
Birmingham City v Blackburn Rovers
Bolton Wanderers v Blackpool
Brighton & Hove Albion v Wolves
Burnley v Ipswich Town
Charlton Athletic v Bristol City
Crystal Palace v Peterborough Utd
Derby County v Millwall
Huddersfield Town v Barnsley
Hull City v Cardiff City
Nottingham Forest v Leicester City
Sheffield Wed v Middlesbrough
Watford v Leeds Utd

2012/13 NPOWER CHAMPIONSHIP LEAGUE TABLE

Pos	Team	P	W	D	L	GD	Pts
1	**Cardiff City**	44	25	10	9	27	85
2	Hull City	44	24	6	14	11	78
3	Watford	44	22	8	14	27	74
4	Brighton	44	17	18	9	23	69
5	Crystal Palace	43	18	13	12	10	67
6	**Bolton**	**44**	**18**	**12**	**14**	**8**	**66**
7	Leicester City	44	18	11	15	23	65
8	Nottm Forest	44	16	16	12	4	64
9	Charlton	44	16	13	15	3	61
10	Birmingham	44	15	15	14	-4	60
11	Derby County	44	15	13	16	3	58
12	Middlesbrough	44	18	4	22	-7	58
13	Leeds United	44	16	10	18	-9	58
14	Ipswich Town	44	15	12	17	-13	57
15	Blackburn	44	14	14	16	-7	56
16	Burnley	44	14	13	17	-1	55
17	Blackpool	44	13	16	15	-2	55
18	Millwall	43	15	10	18	-9	55
19	Sheffield Wed	44	15	10	19	-9	55
20	Huddersfield	44	14	12	18	-22	54
21	Peterborough	44	14	9	21	-9	51
22	Wolves	44	14	9	21	-11	51
23	Barnsley	44	13	12	19	-16	51
24	Bristol City	44	11	8	25	-20	41

DETAILS PRIOR TO THIS WEEKEND'S GAMES

CARDIFF CITY 1
Noone (68)

BOLTON 1
Eagles (18)

SATURDAY ▶ 27TH APRIL ▶ 3.00PM | Full Attendance 26,418

🏠 **24,734**
🚌 **1,684**

MALKY

"To win promotion against Charlton was fantastic. To win the title against Burnley last weekend was great, but to actually lift the trophy in front of 27,000 people is something that will live with me forever. 27,000 people came here today for a party, but I knew my team would not just lie down and let a pre-season calibre game happen."

FREEDMAN

"It was a great point for us. I do not think we did enough to win but we showed the quality in the first half to deserve to get something out of the game. Malky is a good man and he deserves everything he gets. He has done a great job taking the club into the Premier League and I am pleased for him."

TURNER

"It is something we have worked towards for a long time now and it is fantastic to finally have the trophy in our hands and medals around our necks. I have played Championship football for my entire career and it will be nice to get a shot at the Premier League next season."

It was party time inside Cardiff City Stadium as Malky Mackay's men finally got their hands on that coveted Championship trophy; but with Bolton Wanderers still playing for a Play-off place they were determined to put a dampener on the celebrations. After eighteen minutes it looked like they were going to do just that.

Former Swansea defender Sam Ricketts made a jinking run down the right flank and supplied a measured pass to Chris Eagles who fired a shot passed David Marshall to give the Trotters the advantage.

Into the second half and City were really piling the pressure on the visitors. Tommy Smith nearly equalised from six yards but Ádám Bogdán scrambled across his goal to produce a save out of the top draw. Craig Noone had been introduced at the expense of Craig Conway and that substitution proved to be an inspired one as his sweetly struck free-kick squeezed its way inside the near post.

The scores remained level, but the real story in the final home game of the season was the lifting of the Championship trophy to scenes of jubilation.

FANS SAY "These were scenes that I've longed for since my first game as a little nipper in 1977 with my dad lifting me on to his shoulders. So pleased to share the occasion with him yesterday." – *Darren Churchill*

THE BREAK DOWN

REFEREE: M. Naylor

7 | 2

53% | 47%

POSSESSION

0 | 3

SHOTS

8 ON 5

3 OFF 4

ee post-match reaction
f this game from
lalky Mackay on
ardiff City Player

CARDIFF CITY Player »

ardiff City: Marshall, McNaughton
lugent), Taylor, Turner, Connolly,
onway (Noone), Kim,
unnarsson, Mutch (Smith),
estede, Bellamy.
ubs not used: Lewis,
hittingham,
elikonja, Mason.

**Bolton
Wanderers:**
Bogdán, Alonso,
Knight, Dawson, Ricketts,
Eagles, Pratley, Vela (Holden), Lee,
Medo, Sordell (C Davies).
Subs not used: Lonergan, Ream, Wheater,
Hall, Eaves.

341

A fitting moment. Director Steve Borley joins Tan Sri Vincent Tan in unveiling the Championship trophy at CCS.

HULL CITY 2
Proschwitz (58), McShane (63)

CARDIFF CITY 2
Campbell (49), Maynard (Pen 90+5)

SATURDAY ▶ 4TH MAY ▶ 12.45PM Full Attendance 23,812

🏠 21,629
🚌 2,183

MALKY

"It wasn't easy to focus with the attention on the game, but I have got a gre group of professionals. Th season is about going out and playing forty-six game and seeing where the land lies after that. I thought yo saw that here where right until the end, both teams were trying to beat each other. That's the way it should work."

BRUCE

"I've been in the game a long, long time and I don't think I've ever witnessed anything like that. What did we have A ten or twelve minute wait to find out the outcome (at Watford)! We were in tunnels, in corridors, there were people hiding in toilets it was incredible."

MAYNARD

"It's been a long eight months for me. I've been o for so long and it's just gre to cap the end of the seaso off with a goal. To be hones I didn't know if we had a designated penalty taker; we usually have Peter Whittingham, obviously wasn't on the pitch. A few o the lads were saying: 'Let Nicky take it'."

It was a thrilling end to a Championship season, which ultimately saw Hull City join Cardiff City in the Premier League. This was a game where three points for the home side would be enough to guarantee top-flight football – anything less and their fate would be sealed by the result at Watford.

The first half ended goalless but the second started with a lot more action. After only being on the field four minutes, former Hull star Frazier Campbell gave Cardiff the lead after a pin point pass from Kim Bo-Kyung.

In a frantic five minutes the game was turned on its head. Nick Proschwitz fired home from a cross on fifty-eight minutes and just five minutes later Paul McShane prodded home. Andrew Taylor was given his marching orders after picking up a second yellow, before a foul by Ben Nugent allowed Hull an injury time penalty to seal the game.

Proschwitz's spot-kick was saved by Marshall, before Cardiff were awarded their own penalty following a handball by Abdoulaye Faye. Maynard despatched, it finished 2-2, but Watford's defeat at home to Leeds meant the Tigers were promoted.

FANS SAY "Well done to Fraizer Campbell on scoring our first goal of the afternoon in the second half and congratulations to the returning Nicky Maynard for a good penalty as well." – *Julian Riddiford*

THE BREAKDOWN

REFEREE: K. Stroud

6 [flag] **5**

52% **48%**

POSSESSION

0 2 **1**

SHOTS

12 ON 4

4 OFF

ee post-match reaction
f this game from
alky Mackay on
ardiff City Player

CARDIFF CITY Player

ull City: Stockdale, Rosenior,
hester, McShane, Faye,
Elmohamady, Quinn,
leyler, Simpson
Proschwitz), Brady
athi), Boyd.
ubs not used:
kupovic, Hobbs,
ruce, Evans,
ryatt.

Cardiff City:
Marshall,
McNaughton, ■ Taylor,
Turner, ■ Nugent, Conway,
Kim (Gestede), Noone (Maynard),
■ Gunnarsson, Mutch, Velikonja
(Campbell).
Subs not used: Lewis, Whittingham,
Lappin, Smith.

345

Unrivalled. Marshall signs off an exemplary season with a last minute penalty save at Hull.

2012/13 – A SEASON REVIEW

Monday, 7th May 2012 - West Ham United 3-0 Cardiff City. The Hammers had won 5-0 on aggregate and progressed to the Championship Play-Off Final where they would go on to beat Blackpool to secure promotion. For the third year in a row, we'd fallen at the last – but in May 2012 it felt different.

In losing at Wembley against Blackpool in 2010 and then again to Reading at the semi-final stage in 2011, there was a general feeling that, as favourites on each occasion, we'd blown it. Cardiff City had become synonymous with the Championship Play-Offs and for all the wrong reasons, though at Upton Park in 2012 there was pride infused with disappointment. Arguably, we'd over-achieved that season – and under Malky, there was a sense that we could genuinely push on.

The subsequent summer was rife with transfer rumour, much of it concerning the anticipated permanent return to South Wales of Craig Bellamy. When that day came, on the eve of our final pre-season fixture at home to Newcastle, it felt as if a significant statement of intent was being made by Tan Sri Vincent Tan and our Football Club. What's more, this time Craig's talent would be complemented by what would become our finest squad of players in recent memory. He was joining us to lead and inspire with his talent and experience, but that dependence on him which was palpable during 2010/11 was now to be shared around what looked like becoming the perfectly crafted and assembled squad.

Our Championship season kicked off on August 17th, with Huddersfield Town's arrival to CF11 that Friday night bringing about a tingle of anticipation that would resonate for the following eight and a half months. Mark Hudson's injury time winner secured three points from a game in which the opposition had tried to sit and stifle, hopeful of a goal on the counter. It's a tactic that we'd sometimes succumbed to in seasons past – but this opening night win would illustrate, albeit with hindsight, the determination and spirit not to accept such excuses in 2012/13.

By the time the summer transfer window had closed, Malky had added Tommy Smith, Craig Noone, Matt Connolly, Kim Bo-Kyung and Nicky Maynard to the City ranks. My word, we had a strong squad – and it was no surprise that we became the bookies' tip for automatic promotion. We faced Wolves at home on September 2nd with all the pieces of the jigsaw seemingly in place – and we smashed them 3-1. Peter Whittingham was immense that day.

Another game in September stands out for me – the 3-0 home win over Blackpool. Not only had we triumphed against a side that had been our perennial tormentors, but we'd played – and most significantly worked – them off the field. Craig Bellamy in particular was magnificent. There was a moment towards the start of the second half in which he chased a lost cause down the right hand touch line and forced an unwitting Blackpool defence into conceding a corner. Joe Mason and Heidar Helguson played their parts as supporting hounds. Matt Connolly scored directly from the subsequent corner to put us three goals ahead – a passage of play that perfectly encapsulated Malky Mackay's squad of 2012/13.

A 2-1 win over Birmingham City on October 2nd put us top of the npower Championship for the first time in the season. The month brought about a seemingly significant victory at Portman Road during which Heidar bagged two of his total season tally of eight, while home wins six and seven against Watford and Burnley highlighted that the lads were really rallying for each other in the absence of the injured Nicky Maynard. We had a difficult few days at the start of November as we tasted back to back defeats for the only time in the season at Bolton and Charlton; but as I sat at The Valley commentating on that 5-4 finish, watching Nooney and Gunnar grab our third and fourth in injury time, I saw that unwavering passion for the Cardiff City shirt. It was boundless and inherent, even in defeat.

On November 24th 2012 we won a scrappy game 2-1 at Barnsley. It saw us return to the top of the Championship table from where we would not slip – and it also brought about a nine match unbeaten run on the road that would last until March. Our tenth straight home win against Sheffield Wednesday kicked off December in fine style – a month of performances that, in retrospect, went a long way to us achieving our promotion goal in my opinion. We won five out of our six December fixtures – and had the January transfer window to look forward to.

Into 2013 we strode, with points aplenty at the summit and bags of confidence. The F.A. Cup dictated that we would only play three Championship fixtures over four weeks, which brought about wins at Birmingham and Blackpool and an unmemorable stalemate at home to Ipswich. Significantly though, the Club secured the signing of Fraizer Campbell from Sunderland; the England international would score five goals in five games the following month as he marched on towards securing the npower Championship's 'Player of the Month' award for February. Rarely has a new signing made such an immediate and significant impact at Cardiff City.

March was somewhat uneventful in respect of what would follow, but nonetheless made for an appropriate apéritif to an April that would come, pass and ultimately stand to remain ingrained in City folklore forever. On April Fools' Day we eased past Blackburn Rovers at Cardiff City Stadium to reach the seventy-eight point mark. Little did we know that we'd in fact secured promotion that afternoon with eventual third place finishers Watford completing their campaign on seventy-seven! Four games later and we were playing for mathematical assurance of our promotion, secured with a home point against Charlton Athletic. From the moment referee Scott Mathieson blew his whistle that evening until the final throws of our victory parade in Cardiff Bay in May, this Football Club and the Capital City of Wales was celebrating.

Each of us will have our own defining memories of 2012/13. Conway's strike on his return against Sheffield Wednesday, Bellamy's efforts at Blackburn and Leicester or Heidar's warrior-like, blood-spattered finishes at home to Burnley and at Derby are some of mine. There's some terrific footage of these moments and more, but perhaps nothing compares to the video and imagery captured after the games against Charlton, Burnley and Bolton at the end of the season that indelibly document our success.

McNaughton aloft the shoulders of the City faithful post-Charlton, Malky being thrown in the air post-Burnley and Hudson lifting the trophy at a sunny CCS post-Bolton – each of these shots will remain iconic and serve as a reminder that, in 2013, our Football Club created history. Through talent, work-ethic and togetherness, Malky's squad became our Champions.

Mark Denham
May 2013

THE CHAMPIONSHIP

Examining the intricacies of the League's second tier in 2012/13

2012/13 may well be considered as one of the most competitive Championship seasons in memory. Cardiff City's reign at the top from November 24th until final day would be one of the few anomalies in an otherwise wholly unpredictable division.

Indeed, the outcome of nearly all of the sub-plots in the division – aside from that of who would be crowned League Champions – went right down to the wire. Nine of the twelve final day fixtures still had something riding on them, while the 'magic number' for survival was the highest in Championship history at fifty-five. Here's a look back at a frenetic Championship campaign and some of the most interesting aspects of it.

JOINING THE PACK

Joining the fun in the second tier for 2012/13 were six teams who, on paper at least, were certainly not there just to make up the numbers. Each of **Bolton Wanderers, Blackburn Rovers** and **Wolves** kept the cores of their Premier League squads intact. Bolton in particular managed to retain the services of such star names as Lee Chung-Yong, Zat Knight and Stuart Holden

Blackburn and Wolves didn't get off quite so lightly – although their outgoing players certainly aided the clubs' bank balances. Wanderers earned over £20 million through the sales of Steven Fletcher and Matt Jarvis (how significant their departures would prove), while Rovers received £12 million for Christopher Samba alone. Both clubs seemed fairly well equipped for a season in the second tier, as Blackburn put some of that recouped money towards the acquisitions of Jordan Rhodes and Leon Best. The relatively unknown new Wolves boss Ståle Solbakken meanwhile, scoured the French Ligue 1 for the likes of Tongo Doumbia and Bakary Sako.

Joining the second tier from below were three Clubs no doubt eager to replicate the achievements of Southampton and Norwich in previous years. **Charlton Athletic** had finished League One eight points clear of **Sheffield Wednesday**, while **Huddersfield Town** finally made the jump up after flirting with promotion for several years, courtesy of a dramatic Play-Off final penalty-shootout win over Sheffield United. Some very astute summer business by all three meant that an unheralded push for a top six spot would have been within their sights. While none quite achieved that feat, all three secured a further season in the division alongside Blackburn and Bolton – but at the expense of Wolves.

≫ TOP FIVE GOAL-SCORERS

1	2	3	4	5
30	29	25	22	20
≫ GLENN MURRAY	≫ JORDAN RHODES	≫ CHARLIE AUSTIN	≫ MATĚJ VYDRA	≫ TROY DEENEY

every good manager will stress, the first few games of a season offer very little indication as to how any one team likely to fare over the following months. After the anticipation of opening day and a fresh new fixture list came and nt, September saw top spot shared among three of the eight 'Bs' competing this year – namely **Brighton & Hove bion, Blackpool** and **Blackburn Rovers.** These three would ultimately finish fourth, fifteenth and seventeenth spectively.

special mention should also go to **Huddersfield Town** for an explosive start in their début Championship term. An ury time strike from Mark Hudson saw the Terriers leave the capital empty-handed on the opening evening, but a n of six games unbeaten followed as they soon rose up to second place.

the time the ten-match marker came around, City had tasted top spot for the first time. Half-way towards breaking e first of a plethora of records during e season (five of their ten straight me wins had already been mpleted), the Bluebirds led a top comprising of Leicester City, olves, Crystal Palace, Brighton, d Huddersfield. Three of those e teams would finish the season in the ay-Off places – one would be relegated.

the opposite end of the table, terborough United endured a dire start the campaign as they gave an early dition for the role of Championship nipping boys. Darren Ferguson's men re still pointless with seven games down, ough the fact that they ended such a run th a 1-3 away win over eventual promotion nners Hull City tells you all you need to ow about the Posh's ultimately ill-fated 12/13. Remarkably, Peterborough re the only side to record a league uble over Cardiff City during the season.

ONSISTENTLY INCONSISTENT

hile **Hull City** maintained a position in the top six for the vast majority of the campaign, several of our fellow tomatic promotion contenders underwent dramatic declines at various stages.

icester City were one of the sides who looked set to push us to the wire before falling well short. In fact, they even mmeted out of the Play-Off places altogether with just one match to go, but regained some form at the vital time scrape back in.

wever, no club epitomised the second half slump more than **Middlesbrough**. Tony Mowbray's men were just two ints off the automatic promotion places as late as January, and were rated by many fans as one of the most pressive sides to visit CCS during 2012/13. However, they ended up just a handful of points clear of relegation, after een defeats in their final twenty-one matches saw them drop down the table towards a sixteenth place finish.

ere were, of course, those who did the opposite to Boro and Leicester, turning their seasons around after Christmas. lton Wanderers are a prime example, their work ethic under Dougie Freedman rewarded with a rise from twentieth (at one stage) sixth place in the space of just two months. But even that was not enough for the Trotters, as a uple of draws in their final games coincided with one last push from their Play-Off rivals that saw them drop to venth.

ton's remarkable but ultimately unsuccessful surge up the table was mirrored by **Peterborough United** at the other d of the league. In fact, the Posh went on a ten game unbeaten run throughout March and April helping them on eir way to fifty-four points – a final tally which would have seen them fourteen points clear of the drop zone last ar, but this time, wasn't enough. You had to feel for Darren Ferguson's valiant troops.

WINDOW SHOPPERS

Dealing in the January window can be frustrating business, as inflated transfer fees and limited availability can make delving in to the market hazardous. That being said, there's no doubt that Cardiff City picked out a diamond deal in the form of **Fraizer Campbell**. The England international stepped up two minutes into his debut to deliver another Cardiff victory at Elland Road before going on to score seven goals in twelve appearances.

But City were not the only side to recruit some extra firepower after Christmas. **Chris Wood** *(pictured)* helped to spur on Leicester's season by scoring nine goals in as many games, after the Foxes pinched the Kiwi from under the nose of Millwall. Meanwhile Brighton plumped for Argentinean target man **Leonardo Ulloa** – another to get off to a flying start after scoring on his début before earning the accolade of being the first ever player to net a hat-trick at the AMEX Stadium.

Looking back, both Ulloa and Wood could claim to have played an important role in securing Play-Off spots for their respective sides. But just as important in the relegation scuffle was Barnsley's acquisition of **Jason Scotland**. The Trinidad and Tobagonian international netted on his first three run-outs in Barnsley colours, two of which were crucial late winners. He then popped up with a goal on the final day, helping Barnsley to a point that would ultimately keep them in the division at the expense of Peterborough. Not bad at all for a three month cameo.

STANDOUT PERFORMERS

The announcement of PFA 'Team of the Year' is always a controversial day in the footballing calendar, as fans of clubs critique the selections. Of course there were several stand-out figures during 2012/13, but while the likes of Hudson, Ince and Vydra have deservedly been the subjects of many column inches, there are plenty of non-selected players across the twenty-four Championship clubs worthy of recognition.

Alongside **David Marshall**, the name of **Jordan Rhodes** was perhaps the harshest/most baffling omission from the PFA's Championship Team of the Year. The former Huddersfield man netted just one fewer than the included thirty goal man **Glenn Murray** – both of whom beat the previous Championship scoring record of twenty-seven set by Rickie Lambert for Southampton last season. **Charlie Austin** of Burnley was not far behind either, bagging twenty-four goals overall including thirteen in seven early season matches. His latter season form and fitness let him down, you'd feel.

It's easy to forget that Austin is still only twenty-two, one of several young prospects to boost their reputations over the course of the campaign. While **Wilfried Zaha** did enough to secure a £15 million move to Manchester United, Peterborough's young forward **Dwight Gayle** is another who looks set to have a very bright future ahead of him. Whether he starts next season in League One remains to be seen.

Elsewhere, **Johnnie Jackson**, skipper of Charlton Athletic, excelled in the engine room for the Addicks during 2012/13,

GLENN MURRAY — ST

MATĚJ VYDRA — ST

WILFRIED ZAHA — ML

THOMAS INCE — CM

PETER WHITTINGHAM — CM

YANNICK BOLASIE — M

WAYNE BRIDGE — DL

WES MORGAN — DC

MARK HUDSON — DC

KIERAN TRIPPIER — DR

KASPER SCHMEICHEL — GK

hipping in with twelve goals and taking up a lofty position as the ourth best midfielder in the Championship Actim index. Jackson was ust ahead of Watford's classy playmaker **Almen Abdi** who stood out t Vicarage Road alongside Nathaniel Chalobah − scorer of a goal of he season contender in the Hornets' penultimate match at Leicester.

THE FINAL ACT

ome final day, a second automatic promotion place, Play-Off berth nd a number of safety spots were still up for grabs. All would be ecided over the course of ninety (and a few more at Vicarage Road) inutes of Championship football.

Vith twelve teams still having realistic targets to aim for, the early ick-offs on May 4th included several intriguing final day showdowns not least **Nottingham Forest's** East Midlands derby with **Leicester ity.** The fixture was given extra spice by the fact that a win for ither side would guarantee them a Play-Off spot at the other's xpense. After a pulsating game, an injury time strike from **Anthony nockaert** proved the decider, giving Leicester sixth place and their rst win at the City Ground since 1972.

nother crucial face-off was on the cards at the John Smith's Stadium as **Huddersfield Town** took on David Flitcroft's arnsley in a good old-fashioned relegation dogfight. But as it happened, both stayed up as an eighty-ninth minute 1ile Jedinak header for **Crystal Palace** against Peterborough United sent the Posh down instead. However, the hangeable scores over the afternoon had both the Tykes and the Terriers going down at different stages.

s a Cardiff City fan it was a novel and refreshing experience to be spared any such end of season nerves, yet still be > heavily involved in proceedings. As we paid a visit to Hull City on final day, the Tigers knew that they would return > the Premier League after a three year absence as long as **Watford** did not better their result.

The script written at KC Stadium had the lot − an old boy scoring against his former side, a sending off, a magnificently saved injury time spot-kick, and finally an even later one converted by a player returning from a lengthy injury layoff. Had Watford capitalised on Hull's 2-2 draw with us, their promotion would have been one of the most dramatic in recent memory. Unfortunately for them, their lot was decided by two ill-fated errors from young 'keeper Jack Bonham, drafted into the Hornets' side following injuries to both Manuel Almunia and young Welsh 'keeper Jonathan Bond.

Watford's slip-up meant that it would be **Hull** joining the Bluebirds in the Premier League, with Gianfranco Zola's side having to settle for a Play-Off spot. Meanwhile, at the other end, the desperately unfortunate **Peterborough** joined **Wolves** and **Bristol City** en route to League One.

The fact that a team with the resources and quality of Wolves struggled to such an extent during the course of the season is testament to the quality of this tantalising division. More so, it further highlights the fine achievement of the Championship winning **Cardiff City** side that, at times, made it look easy.

THE ANORAK

THE BACKBONE

2012/13

SHARP SHOOTERS

- (8) **GUNNARSSON** ::::
- (8) **HELGUSON** ::::
- (8) **WHITTINGHAM** ::::
- (7) **NOONE** ::::
- (7) **CAMPBELL** ::::
- (6) **MASON** ::
- (5) **CONNOLLY** ::
- (5) **GESTEDE** ::
- (4) **BELLAMY** ::
- (4) **HUDSON** ::

THE ENERGY BUNNY
Andrew Taylor
(43 outfield appearances)

THE GLADIATOR
Craig Conway
(70 fouls incurred)

15 IMPACT PLAYERS
(apps from the bench)
Rudy Gestede - 22
Joe Mason - 16
Heidar Helguson - 11
Aron Gunnarsson - 10
Don Cowie - 10

THE PLAYMAKERS
Craig Bellamy
(8 assists)
Craig Noone
(8 assists)
Peter Whittingham
(7 assists)
Heidar Helguson
(6 assists)
Andrew Taylor
(5 assists)

THE VETERAN
Heidar Helguson
(35 years young)

BLUEBIRDS

2012/13 RECORD	P	W	D	L	GLS SCORED	CONCEDED
LEAGUE	46	25	12	9	72	45
CUP	2	0	0	2	2	4
TOTAL	48	25	12	11	74	49

FORM

SEASON 2012/13

MONTH	FORM	POINTS GAINED	POINTS AVAILABLE
Aug	WDL	4	9
Sept	WWWLW	12	15
Oct	WWLWW	12	15
Nov	LLWWWD	10	18
Dec	WWLWWW	15	18
Jan	WDW	7	9
Feb	WDWLW	10	15
Mar	LDDWL	5	15
Apr	WDDWDDD	11	21
May	D	1	3
TOTAL		87	138

65% HOME WIN

43% AWAY WIN

54% COMBINED WIN

26% HOME DRAW

27% AWAY DRAW

26% COMBINED DRAW

9% HOME LOSS

30% AWAY LOSS

20% COMBINED LOSS

1.57 AVERAGE GOALS PER GAME

THE ANORAK

CITY BY NUMBERS

21

Number of goals scored from outside the box by Cardiff City

51 YEARS

The number of years Cardiff City have been absent from the top flight.

39%

Clean sheets kept by **David Marshall** who played in all 46 league games.

26,558

New record attendance attained against Nottingham Forest on the 13th April 2013

22,998

Average attendance from the Cardiff City faithful

18

Number of goals scored in the last fifteen minutes, more than any other segment

STAR MAN

GAMES
37

GOALS
8

ASSISTS
7

SHOTS
61

WHITTINGHAM

SOCIAL ISSUES

34,962 👍

FACEBOOK LIKES
as of 16/05/13

FOLLOWERS
41,030
@ CardiffCityFC

BIGGEST SCORES

BIGGEST HOME WIN - 27th October 2012: City 4-0 Burnley

BIGGEST AWAY WIN - 7th December 2012: Blackburn 1-4 City

HIGHEST SCORING GAME - 6th April 2012: Charlton 5-4 City

YEAR TIMELINE

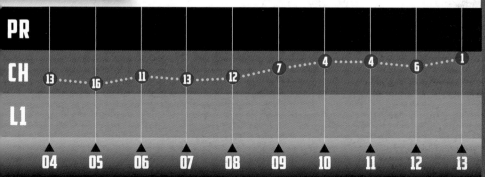

PR

CH   13 ···· 16 ···· 11 ···· 13 ···· 12 ···· 7 ···· 4 ···· 4 ···· 6 ···· 1

L1

04   05   06   07   08   09   10   11   12   13

Stats courtesy of Soccerbase, Football 365 and ESPN Soccernet, corresponding to fixtures in the 2012/13 Championship only.

CHAMPIONSHIP
CELEBRATIONS

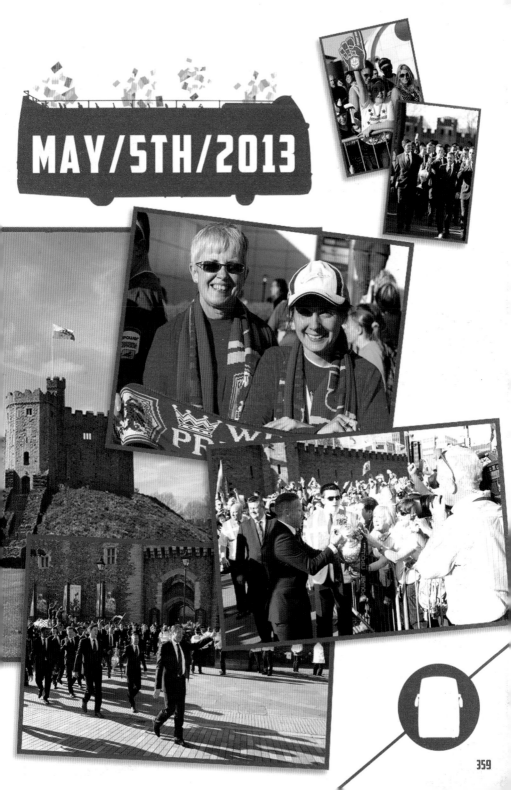

MAY/5TH/2013

FIRST TEAM STATS

CARDIFF CITY FC · EST 1899 · FIRE & PASSION

SEASON 2012-13

Player columns:
1 David MARSHALL · 2 Kevin McNAUGHTON · 3 Andrew TAYLOR · 4 Filip KISS · 5 Mark HUDSON · 6 Ben TURNER · 7 Peter WHITTINGHAM · 8 Don COWIE · 9 Etien VELIKONJA · 10 Robert …

Date	Opponent	H/A	Time	Att	(away)	R	F-A	Pts	Pos	Referee	1	2	3	4	5	6	7	8	9	10
AUGUST																				
Tue 14	Northampton Town	A	19.45	2,819	(388)	L	1-2	-	-	D. Phillips										
Fri 17	Huddersfield Town	H	19.45	21,127	(554)	W	1-0	3	-	R. East	•	•		•	(85)+	••	•	•	•(78)-	U	U
Tue 21	Brighton & H. Alb.	A	19.45	25,518	(825)	D	0-0	4	6	M. Halsey	•	•		U	•		•	•	(77)+	U	U
Sat 25	Bristol City	A	13.00	14,368	(1,862)	L	2-4	4	15	M. Jones	•	•		U	•		•	•	(75)+	U	U
SEPTEMBER																				
Sun 02	Wolves	H	14.00	22,020	(1,479)	W	3-1	7	8	A. D'Urso	•	•		•	•		•	••••	(74)+	U	
Sat 15	Leeds United	H	15.00	23,836	(1,777)	W	2-1	10	5	P. Tierney	•	•		•	•		•	••	(83)+		
Tue 18	Millwall	A	19.45	9,295	(469)	W	2-0	13	5	S. Hooper	•	•		•	•		•	••	U	U	
Sat 22	Crystal Palace	A	15.00	12,757	(1,135)	L	2-3	13	6	G. Ward	•	•		U	•	U	•	•(75)-	U	
Sat 29	Blackpool	H	15.00	21,216	(539)	W	3-0	16	2	C. Boyeson	•	•		U	U	U	•	••	(81)+	U	
OCTOBER																				
Tue 02	Birmingham City	H	19.45	20,278	(506)	W	2-1	19	1	K. Friend	•	•		U	U	••	•	(79)+	U	
Sat 06	Ipswich Town	A	17.20	16,434	(253)	W	2-1	22	1	E. Ilderton	•	•(90)-		U	U	(90)+	•	•	U	
Sat 20	Nottingham Forest	A	15.00	21,486	(1,859)	L	1-3	22	2	D. Drysdale	•	•(81)-		•	U	U	U		
Tue 23	Watford	H	19.45	20,077	(454)	W	2-1	25	2	M. Heywood	•	U		•	•(74)-	•	•		
Sat 27	Burnley	H	15.00	21,191	(477)	W	4-0	28	1	N. Miller	•	U		U	•	••	•		
NOVEMBER																				
Sat 03	Bolton Wanderers	A	17.20	17,304	(1,510)	L	1-2	28	1	A. Bates	•	U		U	•	•	•		
Tue 06	Charlton Athletic	A	19.45	15,764	(822)	L	4-5	28	3	K. Stroud	•	U		U	•	•	•(65)-		
Sat 10	Hull City	H	15.00	20,058	(432)	W	2-1	31	3	I. Williamson	•(19)-	•		(19)+(46)-	••	•	•		
Sat 17	Middlesbrough	H	15.00	21,578	(739)	W	1-0	34	2	O. Langford	•	•(26)-		•	•(14)-	•		
Sat 24	Barnsley	H	15.00	8,227	(669)	W	2-1	37	1	D. Whitestone	•	•		•	•	•		
Tue 27	Derby County	A	19.45	20,911	(727)	D	1-1	38	1	M. Brown	•	•		U	•	•		
DECEMBER																				
Sun 02	Sheffield Wed.	H	15.00	22,034	(1,006)	W	1-0	41	1	G. Scott	•	U		•	•	U		
Fri 07	Blackburn Rovers	A	19.45	12,460	(594)	W	4-1	44	1	S. Hooper	•	U		••	•	•		
Sat 15	Peterborough Utd.	H	15.00	26,073	(264)	L	1-2	44	1	D. Coote	•	•(51)-		•	•	•	•	•(53)-	
Sat 22	Leicester City	A	15.00	25,055	(2,127)	W	1-0	47	1	G. Salisbury	•	U		•	•	•	(55)+	
Wed 26	Crystal Palace	H	15.00	26,098	(1,190)	W	2-1	50	1	P. Gibbs	•	U		•	•	•	•	
Sat 29	Millwall	H	15.00	24,263	(435)	W	1-0	53	1	M. Halsey	•	•		•	•	(73)+	
JANUARY																				
Tue 01	Birmingham City	A	15.00	17,493	(2,270)	W	1-0	56	1	R. Madley	•	U		•	•	(51)+	
Sat 05	Macclesfield Town*	A	15.00	3,165	(641)	L	1-2	-	-	A. Madley	•	•(58)-		•(72)-		•
Sat 12	Ipswich Town	H	15.00	22,727	(525)	D	0-0	57	1	S. Mathieson	•	U		•	•	U	
Sat 19	Blackpool	A	17.20	13,998	(930)	W	2-1	60	1	M. Naylor	•	•		•(48)-	(76)+	
FEBRUARY																				
Sat 02	Leeds United	A	15.00	19,236	(446)	W	1-0	63	1	M. Dean	•	U		•	•	U	
Sat 09	Huddersfield Town	A	15.00	15,265	(1,727)	D	0-0	64	1	M. Brown	•	•(46)-		•	•	U	
Sat 16	Bristol City	H	13.00	25,586	(2,054)	W	2-1	67	1	E. Ilderton	•	U		•	(64)+	U	
Tue 19	Brighton & H. Alb.	H	15.00	23,782	(902)	L	0-2	67	1	K. Stroud	•	U		•	•	U	
Sun 24	Wolves	A	14.00	20,934	(2,500)	W	2-1	70	1	S. Attwell	•	(75)+		•(75)-	•(80)-	
MARCH																				
Sat 02	Middlesbrough	A	15.00	15,440	(611)	L	1-2	70	1	M. Haywood	•	•(46)-		•	U	
Tue 05	Derby County	H	19.45	21,544	(550)	D	1-1	71	1	D. Deadman	•	U		•	U	
Tue 12	Leicester City	H	19.45	23,231	(976)	D	1-1	72	1	N. Miller	•	(46)+		•(46)-	U	
Sat 16	Sheffield Wed.	A	15.00	24,191	(1,366)	W	2-0	75	1	J. Linington	•	U		•	••	
Sat 30	Peterborough Utd.	A	15.00	9,236	(2,174)	L	1-2	75	1	E. Iderton	•	U		•	•(68)-	
APRIL																				
Mon 01	Blackburn Rovers	H	15.00	24,327	(399)	W	3-0	78	1	C. Pawson	•	•		(81)+•	U	
Sat 06	Watford	A	17.20	15,550	(2,129)	D	0-0	79	1	M. Halsey	•	(10)+		•	U	U	
Tue 09	Barnsley	A	19.45	22,584	(243)	D	1-1	80	1	F. Graham	•	•		••	(68)+	
Sat 13	Nottingham Forest	H	15.00	26,588	(2,046)	W	3-0	83	1	A. Marriner	•	•		(87)+	
Tue 16	Charlton Athletic	A	19.45	26,338	(620)	D	0-0	84	1	S. Mathieson	•	•		•	U	U	
Sat 20	Burnley	A	12.45	13,264	(1,635)	D	1-1	85	1	S. Attwell	•	•		•	U	(74)+	
Sat 27	Bolton Wanderers	H	15.00	26,418	(1,635)	D	1-1	86	1	M. Naylor	•	•(83)-		•	U	U	
MAY																				
Sat 04	Hull City	A	12.45	23,812	(2,483)	D	2-2	87	1	K. Stroud	•	•	•	•■	•	U	•(46)-	

*Subs used v Macclesfield Town: Luke Coulson (58)+, Tommy O'Sullivan (64)+, Theo Wharton (72)+

13 Bo-Kyung KIM	14 Tommy SMITH	15 Rudy GESTEDE	16 Craig NOONE	17 Aron GUNNARSSON	18 Jordan MUTCH	19 Kadeem HARRIS	20 Joe MASON	21 Joe RALLS	22 Heidar HELGUSON	23 Nicky MAYNARD	24 Simon LAPPIN	25 Kerim FREI	125 Leon BARNETT	27 Fraizer CAMPBELL	31 Ben NUGENT	32 Joe LEWIS	33 Nat JARVIS	35 Adedeji OSHILAJA	36 Kevin SAINT-LUCE	37 Stephen MCPHAIL	39 Craig BELLAMY	42 Declan JOHN
					(51)+		●(51)-	●	●(61)-					●		●	(61)+	●	●	●(19)-		
		●(85)-	●				(78)+		●		●					U					●	
		(46)-	●		●(46)-		(46)+		●(77)-							U					●(73)-	
	●(75)-			●(46)-	●(80)-		(46)+	(80)+	●●						U	U						
U	●		●(74)-	(59)+	●(59)-		(68)+		●	●(68)-					U	U						
●(80)+	●		●(64)-	(76)+	●(76)-		U		(67)+	●(67)-					U	U					(64)+●	
88+	●(88)-		(75)+	●●			(82)+		●							U					●(82)-	
●72+	●(25)-		●	●			(25)+		●(81)-							U					●(72)-	
84+			●(84)-				●		●							U					●● (79)-	
U		(64)+	●(55)-	●			●(64)-		●●●							U						
U		(65)+	(62)+	●(65)-			(81)+	U	●●							U						
U	●(84)-	(74)+	●	●	(84)+●		(46)+		●							U					●(46)-	
●(78)-		(63)+	●●(83)-		(78)+●		●●		●(63)-		(83)+					U						
●(70)-		(63)+	●●	(70)+			●(83)-		●(63)-		(83)+					U						
●65+		(73)+	●●	(65)+●			●●		●●(73)-		●(65)-					U						
●		(66)+	●	●			●	(46)+	●●(66)-		U				-U	U						
●		(61)+		U	●(61)-		●	(26)+	●		U				(14)+	U					(61)+	
●		(61)+	●	●●	70)-	(70)+	●(75)-	U	●(61)-		●	■			●●	U					(75)+	U
●		U	● ■	●(73)-	(70)+		(79)+		●●(79)-						●	U					●(70)-	U
●(60)-		(70)+		(79)+	● 79)-		(60)-		●(70)-	U						U						
69)+●		(90)+	● (69)-	U			(80)+●		● (90)-	U						U					●(80)-	
U		(64)+●	●	(51)+	(53)+		U		●	U						U					●●	
●(55)-		(51)+	U	(76)+	●(76)-		U		●(51)-							U					●●	
U		(57)+	● ●(76)-	(46)+●	●(46)-		(76)+		●(57)-	U						U					●	
U		●●(77)-	●(73)-	(45)-	(45)+		U		(77)+							U					●	
●(67)-		(70)+	(67)+	●	●(51)-		●●(70)-	U	U		●					U					●	
						●(64)-		●									●	●	●●	●	●	
U	(68)+	●(46)-	●(68)-	●			(46)+		(86)+							U					●	
●(76)-	●●(65)-	U	U	●	U		●		(65)+					(48)+		U					●	
●(61)-	●		U	●			U		(79)+				(61)+●			U					●	
●(46)-	●(73)-		U	●			U		(46)+				(73)+	(46)+		U					●	
84)+	●(64)-		●(84)-	●	U		U		(72)+				●●(72)-	●		U					●	
U	●		●(53)-	●			U		(84)+				●(84)-			U					●	
80)+			U	●	U		U		(82)+				●●(82)-			U					●	
U	●(58)-		(74)+	●●			U		(58)+				●	(46)+		U					●(74)-	
U	● (72)-	●(84)+	(72)+●				(76)+		●(76)-				●	●		U						
U		(70)+●	●(46)-	●			U						●	●		U					(46)+	
U	(81)+	(87)+		●	U				● (87)-				●	●		U					● (81)-	
U	●	(58)+		●●	U		(77)+		●(77)-				●(58)-			U						
●		(88)+	U	●	●		(58)+●				U		●	●●(58)-		U					●(88)-	
●	(69)+	(56)+	●	●			●(56)-		U				●			U					●	
●(68)-	●(80)-	U	U	●	●		●(58)-		(58)+				●			U	U				●	
●	●(74)-	(46)+●●	(74)+	●	●(87)-		U		●●(46)-				●			U	U				●	
●	(71)+	●	●(71)-	●			U						●			U	U				●	
●			●(66)-	●	●(74)-		U				U		●		(83)+	U					(66)+	
●	(63)+	●	(59)+●	●	●(63)-		U						●			U					●	
(64)-	U	(64)+	●(84)-	●					(84)+●	U			●		(46)+●	●	U					

363

2012/13 STATISTICS

CARDIFF CITY DEVELOPMENT RESULTS 2012/13

DATE	TEAM	COMPETITION	H/A	SCORE	SCORERS
Aug 22	Brighton & Hove Albion	Pdl2 (South)	H	2-1	Darko (P), Hill
Sep 03	Queens Park Rangers	Pdl2 (South)	H	1-4	Keinan
Sep 07	Ipswich Town	Pdl2 (South)	A	0-6	
Sep 25	Charlton Athletic	Pdl2 (South)	H	2-0	Conway, John
Oct 01	Brentford	Pdl2 (South)	A	1-2	O'sullivan
Oct 30	Millwall	Pdl2 (South)	H	4-0	Velikonja (3), Jarvis
Nov 05	Brighton & Hove Albion	Pdl2 (South)	A	0-1	
Nov 13	Swansea City	Pdl2 (South)	H	2-1	Conway, Darko
Nov 20	Colchester United	Pdl2 (South)	H	4-0	Velikonja (2), Mutch, Kiss
Dec 03	Queens Park Rangers	Pdl2 (South)	A	1-2	Coulson
Jan 14	Barnet	Pdl2 (South)	H	2-0	Kiss, Velikonja
Jan 28	Brentford	Pdl2 (South)	H	2-1	Velikonja, Ralls
Feb 04	Bristol City	Pdl2 (South)	H	4-0	Velikonja (3), Mutch
Feb 18	Charlton Athletic	Pdl2 (South)	A	0-4	
Feb 26	Swansea City	Pdl2 (South)	A	2-1	Mutch, Gestede (P)
Mar 12	Millwall	Pdl2 (South)	A	2-1	Velikonja, Coulson
Mar 18	Colchester United	Pdl2 (South)	A	3-1	Healey (2), Kiss
Mar 25	Ipswich Town	Pdl2 (South)	H	3-1	Velikonja, Healey, Kiss
Apr 03	Bristol City	Pdl2 (South)	A	3-2	Healey, Kiss (P), John
Apr 10	Barnet	Pdl2 (South)	A	3-1	Healey, Harris, Velikonja
May 07	Leicester City:	Pdl2 semi-final	A	3-2	OG, Oshilaja (2)
May 11	Charlton Athletic	Pdl2 final	H	1-3 aet	Kiss

CARDIFF CITY U18 ACADEMY RESULTS 2012/13

DATE	TEAM	COMPETITION	H/A	SCORE	SCORERS
Aug 18	Brighton & Hove Albion	Pdl2 (South)	A	1-2	Hill (P)
Aug 25	Ipswich Town	Pdl2 (South)	H	1-4	Bowen
Sep 01	Queens Park Rangers	Pdl2 (South)	A	0-1	
Sep 15	Brentford	Pdl2 (South)	H	3-0	Patten, Roche, Hill
Sep 22	Charlton Athletic	Pdl2 (South)	A	1-1	J Watkins
Oct 06	Swansea City	Pdl2 (South)	A	2-3	Hill, O'sullivan
Oct 20	Bristol City	Pdl2 (South)	H	4-2	Bowen, O'sullivan (2), Southam
Oct 27	Millwall	Pdl2 (South)	H	2-1	C Watkins, Wharton
Nov 10	Brighton & Hove Albion	Pdl2 (South)	H	1-1	Southam
Nov 17	Colchester United	Pdl2 (South)	A	2-3	Bell, Hill
Dec 01	Queens Park Rangers	Pdl2 (South)	H	0-1	
Dec 12	Nottingham Forest	Fa Youth Cup R3	A	1-2	Hill
Jan 12	Barnet	Pdl2 (South)	A	5-1	Griffiths (2), Hill, O'sullivan, Tutonda
Jan 26	Brentford	Pdl2 (South)	A	0-1	
Feb 16	Charlton Athletic	Pdl2 (South)	H	1-2	Southam
Feb 22	Swansea City	Pdl2 (South)	H	6-1	O'sullivan, Yorwerth (2), Healey, Bell, Griffiths
Mar 02	Bristol City	Pdl2 (South)	A	1-1	Griffiths
Mar 16	Colchester United	Pdl2 (South)	H	1-3	Patten
Mar 23	Ipswich Town	Pdl2 (South)	A	2-4	O'sullivan (P), Bowen
Apr 03	Millwall	Pdl2 (South)	A	0-2	
Apr 13	Barnet	Pdl2 (South)	H	0-0	

CARDIFF CITY SENIOR WOMEN RESULTS 2012/13

DATE	TEAM	COMPETITION	H/A	SCORE	SCORERS
Sept 16	Port Talbot Town	Women's Welsh Premier League	H	6-0	Walsh (2), Bird (4)
Sept 30	Garden Village	FAW Women's Cup	A	7-1	Walsh (3), Bourne (2), Rowe, Price
Oct 07	Caernafon Town	Women's Welsh Premier League	H	5-1	Broadhurst, Bourne, Rowe (2), Price
Oct 28	Cardiff City Ladies	FAW Women's Cup	A	0-6	
Nov 04	Cardiff Metropolitan	Women's Welsh Premier League	H	1-0	Jones
Nov 11	Swansea City	Women's Welsh Premier League	A	3-0	Wathan, Walsh (2)
Dec 02	Llandudno Junction	Women's Welsh Premier League	H	11-1	Wathan, Walsh (3), Broadhurst (3), Jones, Powell (2), OG
Dec 09	Llandiloes	Women's Welsh Premier League	A	5-0	Wathan (3), Jones (2)
Dec 16	Newcastle Emlyn	Women's Welsh Premier League	H	3-0	Wathan, Broadhurst, Rowe
Jan 13	Northop Hall	Women's Welsh Premier League	A	7-0	Wathan (4), Powell (2), Guard
Jan 27	Port Talbot Town	Women's Welsh Premier League	A	3-2	Wathan (2), Rowe
Feb 17	Aberystwyth Town	Women's Welsh Premier League	A	1-0	Wathan
Feb 24	Aberystywth Town	Women's Welsh Premier League	H	3-2	Wathan, Broadhurst (2)
Mar 03	Cardiff Metropolitan	Women's Welsh Premier League	A	0-1	
Mar 10	Swansea City	Women's Welsh Premier League	H	4-0	Broadhurst, Rowe, Edwards
Mar 17	Northop Hall	Women's Welsh Premier League	H	3-1	Walsh, Bourne, Edwards
Mar 31	Llandudno Junction	Women's Welsh Premier League	A	7-1	Wathan, Walsh (2), Bourne (3), Jones
Apr 07	Llandiloes	Women's Welsh Premier League	H	3-1	Bourne, Rowe, Summers
Apr 14	Newcastle Emlyn	Women's Welsh Premier League	A	4-0	Wathan (2), Walsh, Jellings
Apr 28	Wrexham	Women's Welsh Premier League	A	2-0	Walsh (2)
May 12	Caernarfon Town	Women's Welsh Premier League	A	16-0	Broadhurst (4), Rowe (4), Wathan (4), Walsh (3), Summers
May 19	Wrexham	Women's Welsh Premier League	H	5-2	Broadhurst (2), Davies (2), Rowe

CARDIFF CITY DEVELOPMENT WOMEN RESULTS 2012/13

DATE	TEAM	COMPETITION	H/A	SCORE	SCORERS
Sept 02	Bridgend	South Wales Women's League	A	17-1	Murray (5), Bolas (4), McIlroy (3), Bailey (2), Underdown (2), McNamara
Sept 23	Newport County	South Wales Women's League	H	3-0	Murray, Bailey, OG.
Sept 30	Hafod	South Wales Women's League	A	4-1	Murray (2), Bolas, Salter
Oct 14	Cwmbran	South Wales Women's League	A	1-7	Underdown
Oct 21	Dinas Powys	South Wales Women's League	H	13-0	Murray (2), Davies (2), McIlroy, Bailey (2), Green (2), Turner (3), Chown
Oct 28	Cardiff University	South Wales Women's League	A	4-1	Murray (2), Davies (2)
Nov 11	Cyncoed	South Wales Women's League	A	2-3	Davies, Bolas
Nov 18	Garw	South Wales Women's League	A	14-0	Murray (5), Davies (4), Bolas, McIlroy, Bailey, Turner, Dyer
Dec 02	Dinas Powys	South Wales Women's League	A	9-0	Murray (4), Davies, Bolas, Underdown (2), Pugh
Feb 03	Hafod	South Wales Women's League	H	11-0	Murray (4), Davies (2), Bolas, McIlroy (3), Green
Feb 17	Cwmbran	South Wales Women's League	H	1-5	Chown
Feb 24	Cyncoed	South Wales Women's League Cup	H	1-1	Salter
Mar 10	Sully	South Wales Women's League	A	8-1	Murray, Davies (2), Bolas, Bailey, Green, Dyer, Pugh.
Apr 04	Pontypridd	South Wales Women's League	A	3-2	Murray (2), Davies
Apr 21	Pontypridd	South Wales Women's League	H	3-1	Murray (2), Davies
Apr 28	Cascade	South Wales Women's League	A	15-0	Murray (2), Davies (5), Bolas (2), Green (3), Underdown, Chown (2)
Apr 30	Cyncoed	South Wales Women's League Cup	A	4-3	Davies (2), Bolas, Pugh

CARDIFF CITY SENIOR FUTSAL RESULTS 2012/13

DATE	TEAM	COMPETITION	H/A	SCORE	SCORERS
Aug 08	FS Ilves Tampere	UEFA Futsal Cup	-	0-3	
Aug 09	FC Grand Pro Varna	UEFA Futsal Cup	-	1-4	Haralambous
Aug 11	FC Ibra Gothenborg	UEFA Futsal Cup	-	0-8	
Sep 16	Oxford City Lions	FA Futsal League	A	1-12	Mondo
Sep 23	Birmingham	FA Futsal League	A	4-1	Maynard, Nelson, Mills, Green
Oct 07	Birmingham Tigers	FA Futsal League	A	5-8	Austin, Hardin, Croft, Aved (2)
Oct 19	Team Bath	FA Futsal League	A	1-9	Mills
Nov 04	Gloucester Futsal Revolution	FA Futsal League	H	5-6	Croft, Harding, Dahir, Mills (2)
Nov 25	Loughborough	FA Futsal League	A	2-9	Green, Minetti
Dec 02	Loughborough	FA Futsal League	H	1-9	Harding
Dec 09	Oxford City Lions	FA Futsal League	H	2-7	Mills (2)
Jan 13	Birmingham	FA Futsal League	H	2-6	Webbe, Milton
Feb 03	Team Bath	FA Futsal League	H	1-5	Milton
Feb 15	Birmingham Tigers	FA Futsal League	H	4-2	Huxtable, Milton, Farthing, Webbe
Feb 17	Gloucester Futsal Revolution	FA Futsal League	A	4-7	Bourdin, Croft, Milton, Farthing
Feb 27	Hereford	FA Futsal League	A	4-9	Maynard (2), Bourdin, Harding
Mar 01	Hereford	FA Futsal League	H	0-0	
Mar 24	TNS	FAW Futsal Cup	-	2-2	Maynard, Mills
Mar 24	Ammanford	FAW Futsal Cup	-	9-3	Mills (3), Webbe (2), Farthing, Dyer, Maynard, Austin
Mar 24	Cardiff University	FAW Futsal Cup (S/F)	-	4-3	Webbe (3), Mills
Mar 24	Wrexham	FAW Futsal Cup (F)	-	-3-3*	Webbe, Mills, Austin

*0-0 AET, Wrexham win 4-2 on penalties

Cardiff City Football Club's #ClubGOTM (Club Goal of the Month) initiative received national recognition during 2013. Instigated by City's Audio-Visual Manager Jamie DeCruz, #ClubGOTM gathers nominations from each of Cardiff City's seven senior side/advanced age level coaches before collating footage of each goal and broadcasting for a monthly public text vote. Season statistics from six of our seven senior sides are published in this section (First-team, Development, Academy U18, Women, Futsal, Disability & Deaf). The seventh goal each month comes from Malaysia — specifically the Cardiff City coaches working with young players under the 1MCC umbrella. For more information, visit www.1mcc.my

Incidentally, at the Club's May 2013 Gala Dinner, **Thomas Waite** (pictured) of Cardiff City's DSActive side was awarded the #ClubGOTS (Club Goal of the Season) award, defeating the likes of Craig Conway and Joe Ralls in the process. To find out more about this initiative and to see this season's goals, visit the official Club website.

ARDIFF CITY BOYS FUTSAL RESULTS 2012/13

ATE	TEAM	COMPETITION	SCORE	SCORERS
:t 03	Northampton A	South Midlands Division League 1	9-1	Wilcox (2), De Jesus (3), Davies, Akeem Cullen (2), Roberts
:t 10	Cheltenham Town C	South Midlands Division League 3	2-1	Emanuel, D'Abusco
:t 10	Bristol City D	South Midlands Division League 4	12-1	Hawkins (3), Owen (2), Owen, Smith, Actie, Griffiths (3), Williams
:t 17	Bristol City B	South Midlands Division League 2	6-0	Allen (4), Roberts, Ellis
:t 17	Cheltenham Town A	South Midlands Division League 1	2-0	Wilcox, Dahir
ɔv 07	West Bromwich Albion C	South Midlands Division League 2	5-10	D'Abusco (4), Richards
ɔv 07	Cheltenham Town D	South Midlands Division League 4	5-5	Actie, Ashley (2), Stretton, Griffiths
ɔv 14	Northampton Town B	South Midlands Division League 2	7-1	Wigmore, Wilcox (2), Peachey (2), Mayers, Davies
ɔv 14	Bristol City A	South Midlands Division League 1	2-4	Allen, Dahir
ɔv 21	Derby County C	South Midlands Division League 3	2-2	D'Abusco, Actie
ɔv 28	Cheltenham Town B	South Midlands Division League 2	7-3	Roberts, Ellis (4), Saunders, Mayers
ɔv 28	Bristol Rovers A	South Midlands Division League 1	3-0	*Match Abandoned. Cardiff awarded 3-0 win*
ec 05	Bristol City C	South Midlands Division League 3	7-3	Humphreys, D'Abusco (4), Richards, Warman
ec 05	Derby County D	South Midlands Division League 4	7-4	Griffiths, Berry (3), Owen (2), Nolan
ec 12	Hereford United A	South Midlands Division League 1	5-3	Ellis (2), Allen (2), Dahir
ec 19	West Bromwich Albion D	South Midlands Division League 4	2-3	Griffiths, O.G
า 09	Northampton Town A	South Midlands Division League 1	1-2	Dahir
า 16	Cheltenham Town C	South Midlands Division League 3	3-2	Richards (2), Emanuel
า 16	Bristol City D	South Midlands Division League 4	5-0	Hawkins (2), Griffiths (2), Roach
า 30	West Bromwich Albion C	South Midlands Division League 3	1-7	D'Abusco
า 30	Cheltenham Town D	South Midlands Division League 4	6-3	Williams (2), Hawkins, Actie, Owen, Wallbank
b 06	Northampton Town B	South Midlands Division League 2	6-0	Wigmore (3), Roy, Mayers, Saunders
b 06	Bristol City A	South Midlands Division League 1	1-2	Ellis
b 20	Cheltenham Town A	South Midlands Division League 1	1-7	Richards
b 20	Bristol City B	South Midlands Division League 2	3-4	Humphreys, Owens, Berry
b 27	Derby County C	South Midlands Division League 3	5-1	D'Abusco, Berry, Searle, Jones, Emanuel
ar 06	Bristol Rovers A	South Midlands Division League 1	8-1	Williams (3), Roberts (2), Actie, Griffiths, Wallbank
ar 06	Cheltenham Town B	South Midlands Division League 2	7-0	Ellis (3), Searle, Davies (2), Wilcox
ar 13	Bristol City C	South Midlands Division League 3	7-1	Warman, Richards, Emanuel, Flynn, Ayed (2), Smith
ar 13	Derby County D	South Midlands Division League 4	5-1	Stretton, Owen, Berry, Ashley, O.G
ar 20	Bristol Rovers B	South Midlands Division League 2	3-3	Ellis (2), Roberts
ar 20	Hereford United A	South Midlands Division League 1	5-4	Dahir (3), Saunders, Wigmore
ɔr 10	Bristol Rovers B	South Midlands Division League 2	3-5	Allen (2), Roy
ɔr 10	Bristol Rovers C	South Midlands Division League 3	8-5	D'Abusco (5), Searle (2), Emanuel
ɔr 17	West Bromwich Albion D	South Midlands Division League 4	2-5	Wallbank (2)
ɔr 17	Bristol Rovers C	South Midlands Division League 3	12-1	D'Abusco (6), Smith (3), Richards (2), Warman
ɔr 24	Northampton Town A	South Midlands Division League 1	9-1	Akeem Cullen (4), Wilcox (2), Wigmore, Dahir, Roberts
ay 01	Bristol City D	South Midlands Division League 4	7-1	Cooper, Roach (2), Griffiths, Jones (2), O.G
ay 01	Cheltenham Town C	South Midlands Division League 3	6-4	Richards (2), Smith (2), Emanuel, Warman, Searle
ay 8	Cheltenham A	South Midlands Division League 1	3-5	Allen (3)
ay 8	Bristol City B	South Midlands Division League 2	3-6	Wigmore, Ellis, Roberts
ay 15	WBA C	South Midlands Division League 3	2-4	D'Abusco, Stretton
ay 15	Cheltenham D	South Midlands Division League 4	5-0	Hawkins (2), Jones (2), Ashley
ay 22	Northampton B	South Midlands Division League 2	3-3	Ellis (3)
ay 22	Bristol City A	South Midlands Division League 1	1-9	Cullen

CARDIFF CITY GIRLS FUTSAL RESULTS 2012/13

DATE	TEAM	COMPETITION	SCORE	SCORERS
Nov 08	Swindon Town Ladies A	Scholarship League	3-0	Murray (2), Underdown
Nov 08	Swindon Town Ladies B	Scholarship League	3-0	Walsh (2), Cuming
Nov 08	Swindon Town Ladies B	Scholarship League	5-0	Underdown (2), Murray (2), Dyer
Nov 08	Swindon Town Ladies A	Scholarship League	2-2	Walsh, Miles
Nov 08	Exeter City Ladies A	Scholarship League	4-1	Bailey (2), McIlroy, Murray
Nov 08	Cardiff City Ladies B	Scholarship League	3-1	Murray, Miles, Chown, Walsh
Nov 08	Exeter City Ladies A	Scholarship League	7-0	Bourne (3), Walsh, Chown, Cuming, Salter
Nov 15	Gower College	Friendly	18-2	Bourne (6), Price (2), Pugh, Miles, Kincaid, Walsh (2), Simkiss (2), Chown (2), Salter
Nov 22	Swindon Town Ladies A	Scholarship League	7-2	Davies (4), Miles (2), Pugh
Nov 22	Exeter City Ladies A	Scholarship League	6-4	Murray (3), McIlroy, Dyer, Bailey
Nov 22	Exeter City Ladies A	Scholarship League	8-1	Davies (3), Pugh (2), Chown (2), Cuming
Nov 22	Swindon Town Ladies A	Scholarship League	3-0	Walsh (2), Cuming
Nov 22	Cardiff City Ladies B	Scholarship League	4-3	Murray (2), Warman, Cuming (2), Davies (2)
Dec 06	Swindon Town Ladies A	Scholarship League	8-1	Kincaid (2), Chown (2), Bourne, Walsh, Miles, Pugh, Cuming
Dec 06	Exeter City Ladies A	Scholarship League	6-2	Underdown (4), Dyer, Warman
Dec 06	Exeter City Ladies A	Scholarship League	9-2	Davies (3), Walsh (2), Miles, Bourne, Kincaid, Pugh
Dec 06	Swindon Town Ladies A	Scholarship League	2-1	Murray, Underdown
Dec 06	Cardiff City Ladies B	Scholarship League	8-3	Miles (3), Kincaid (2), Bourne, Davies, Cuming
Jan 17	Swindon Town Ladies A	Scholarship League	3-1	Bolas, Pugh, Salter
Jan 17	Exeter City Ladies A	Scholarship League	6-1	Underdown, Warman, Bolas, Kincaid, Pugh, Salter
Jan 31	Exeter City Ladies A	Scholarship League	11-1	Pugh (4), Miles (3), Bourne (2), Cumin (2)
Jan 31	Swindon Town Ladies A	Scholarship League	0-3	
Jan 31	Cardiff City Ladies A	Scholarship League	5-1	Underdown, Miles, Pugh, Bourne, Cuming, Chown
Jan 31	Swindon Town Ladies A	Scholarship League	4-0	Pugh (2), Miles, Bourne
Jan 31	Exeter City Ladies A	Scholarship League	8-2	Murray (4), McIlroy (2), Bailey, Underdown
Feb 16	Nottingham College	British Championships	1-1	Bolas
Feb 16	Runshaw College	British Championships	0-5	
Feb 16	Kilmarnock College	British Championships	8-1	McGlynn, Murray (3), Underdown (2), Miles, Bailey
Feb 16	Grimsby Institute	British Championships	4-1	Bolas (2), Dyer, McIlroy
Feb 16	Worthing College	British Championships	1-1	Bailey
Feb 16	Truro & Penwith College	British Championships	0-1	
Feb 16	Newcastle Under Lyme	British Championships	2-2	Murray, Underdown
Feb 17	Barnet & Southgate College	British Championships	0-1	
Feb 17	Tyne Met College	British Championships	5-0	Underdown, Bailey, Miles, Dyer, McIlroy
Feb 17	Easton & Oatley College	British Championships	4-2	Miles, McIlroy (2), Murray
Feb 28	Exeter City Ladies A	Scholarship League	2-0	Davies, Walsh
Feb 28	Swindon Town Ladies A	Scholarship League	0-2	
Feb 28	Swindon Town Ladies A	Scholarship League	6-4	Walsh (3), Davies (2), Miles
Feb 28	Exeter City Ladies A	Scholarship League	3-0	Warman, Bailey, Bolas
Feb 28	Cardiff City Ladies A	Scholarship League	2-2	Warman, Bailey, Chown, Kincaid
Mar 07	Gloucester University	Friendly	8-4	Walsh (4), Kelly Bourne (2), Miles, Pugh
Mar 14	Swindon Town Ladies A	Scholarship League	4-1	Davies (2), Walsh (2)
Mar 14	Exeter City Ladies A	Scholarship League	9-0	Murray (4), Dyer (2), Bailey, Underdown, McIlroy
Apr 18	Swindon Town Ladies A	Scholarship League	3-8	Bailey (2), Cuming
Apr 18	Exeter City Ladies A	Scholarship League	7-0	Davies (3), Walsh (2), Bourne (2)
Apr 26	Bath University	Friendly	13-1	Walsh (6), Chown (3), Miles (2), Davies, Cuming
May 2	Cardiff City Ladies B	Scholarship	6-2	Bourne (2), Walsh, Miles, Davies, Cuming, Bolas, Bailey
May 16	Exeter City A	Scholarship	2-1	Bailey, Kincaid
May 16	Swindon Town A	Scholarship	8-1	Walsh (3),

CARDIFF CITY DISABILITY & DEAF RESULTS 2012/13

DATE	TEAM	COMPETITION	H/A	SCORE	SCORERS
UNDER 16 LEARNING DISABILITY					
Oct 12	Race Rovers	South Wales PAN league	-	0-1	
Oct 12	Dinas	South Wales PAN league	-	0-1	
Oct 12	RCT Tigers	South Wales PAN league	-	0-1	
Oct 12	Newport Dragons	South Wales PAN league	-	0-1	
Nov 12	Race Rovers	South Wales PAN league	-	5-4	Deacy, Perry, Young
Nov 12	Dinas Powys	South Wales PAN league	-	0-5	
Dec 12	RCT Tigers	South Wales PAN league	-	1-2	Perry
Dec 12	Newport Dragons	South Wales PAN league	-	1-3	Young
Dec 12	Dinas Powys	South Wales PAN league	-	0-1	
Dec 12	Race Rovers	South Wales PAN league	-	1-2	Patel
3 Mar	Vale Reds	South Wales PAN league	-	4-2	Gee, Davies
3 Mar	Pont	South Wales PAN league	-	5-3	Perry, Deacy, Young
SENIOR DEAF					
Oct 12	Black County DFC	Deaf Cup	H	1-8	Evans
Feb 03	Manchester United DFC	Deaf Cup	H	0-15	
Feb 17	Nottingham DFC	Deaf Cup	A	4-3	Price (2), Watkins (2)
Mar 24	Everton DFC	Deaf Cup	A	1-7	Griffiths
U18 DEAF					
Mar 13	Belfast DFC	Deaf Cup	-	3-5	Price, Abdo, Mohammed
Mar 13	Everton FC	Deaf Cup	-	7-0	Price (4), Abdo (2), Mohammed
Mar 13	Everton FC	Deaf Cup	-	5-3	Abdo (3), Price (2)
Mar 13	Belfast DFC	Deaf Cup	-	4-1	Abdo (2), Price (2)
Mar 13	Belfast DFC	Deaf Cup	-	2-6	Price (2)
U16 DEAF					
Mar 13	Braidwood School	Deaf Cup	-	1-8	Olding
Mar 13	Derby	Deaf Cup	-	1-5	Coleman
Mar 13	Sunderland	Deaf Cup	-	6-1	Coleman, Iqbal, Olding, Munir
Mar 13	Bradford City	Deaf Cup	-	14-4	Coleman (6), Olding (2), Munir (4), Iqbal (2)
Mar 13	Castell Ford	Deaf Cup	-	5-1	Coleman (4), Olding
Mar 13	Sunderland	Deaf Cup	-	3-5	Olding, Munir, Coleman
U12 DEAF					
Mar 13	Morecambe	Deaf Cup	-	2-2	M.Thomas, Pearce
Mar 13	Bolton	Deaf Cup	-	1-2	W.Thomas
Mar 13	Robin Hood AS	Deaf Cup	-	3-0	Jayne, Williams, M.Thomas
Mar 13	Everton	Deaf Cup	-	5-3	Carter, M.Thomas (2), W.Thomas (2)
Mar 13	Bolton	Deaf Cup	-	3-1	M.Thomas, Jayne
Mar 13	Morecambe	Deaf Cup	-	1-8	Pearce
Mar 13	Derby	Deaf Cup	-	1-4	Williams
Mar 13	Derby	Deaf Cup	-	3-4	M.Thomas, W.Thomas, Powell
DS ACTIVE					
Mar 17	Ipswich Town	DSActive Cup	-	9-0	Waite (4), Rohan (2), Baker, John, Hollingworth
Mar 17	Charlton Upbeats	DSActive Cup	-	2-0	Waite, Baker
Mar 17	Newcastle United	DSActive Cup	-	8-0	Waite (3), Baker (2), Wiseman, Rohan (2)
Mar 17	QPR	DSActive Cup	-	4-4	Waite (2), Baker, John
CEREBRAL PALSY					
Feb 17	Yorkshire CP	CP Sport Tournament	-	4-4	Carrol, Hegarty, Staffurth, Rix
Feb 17	Northern CP	CP Sport Tournament	-	3-3	Carrol, Blake, Jenkins

Men of Harlech (Stop Your Dreaming)

Men of Harlech, stop your dreaming.
Can't you see their spear points gleaming?
See their warrior's pendants streaming
To this battlefield.

Men of Harlech, stand ye steady.
It cannot be ever said ye
For the battle were not ready.
Stand and never yield.

Through the hills surrounding
Let this war cry sounding
Summon all to Cambria's call,
The mighty force surrounding.

Men of Harlech, on to glory!
This shall ever be your story.
Keep these fighting words before ye:
Cambria (Welshmen never) will not yield.